MAR-A-LAGO

ALSO BY LAURENCE LEAMER

The Paper Revolutionaries: The Rise of the Underground Press (1972)

Playing for Keeps in Washington (1977)

Assignment (1979)

Ascent: The Spiritual and Physical Quest of Willi Unsoeld (1982)

Make-Believe: The Story of Nancy and Ronald Reagan (1983)

As Time Goes By: The Life of Ingrid Bergman (1986)

King of the Night: The Life of Johnny Carson (1989)

The Kennedy Women: The Saga of an American Family (1994)

Three Chords and the Truth: Hope, Heartbreak, and Changing Fortunes in Nashville (1997)

The Kennedy Men: 1901–1963: The Laws of the Father (2001)

Sons of Camelot: The Fate of an American Dynasty (2004)

Fantastic: The Life of Arnold Schwarzenegger (2005)

Madness Under the Royal Palms: Love and Death Behind the Gates of Palm Beach (2009)

The Price of Justice: A True Story of Greed and Corruption (2013)

The Lynching: The Epic Courtroom Battle That Brought Down the Klan (2016)

The President's Butler (2016)

MAR-A-LAGO

Inside the Gates of Power at
Donald Trump's Presidential Palace

LAURENCE LEAMER

FLATIRON
BOOKS
NEW YORK

MAR-A-LAGO. Copyright © 2019 by Laurence Leamer. All rights reserved. Printed in the United States of America. For information, address Flatiron Books, 175 Fifth Avenue, New York, N.Y. 10010.

www.flatironbooks.com

Designed by Kathryn Parise

The Library of Congress Cataloging-in-Publication Data is available upon request.

ISBN 978-1-250-17751-3 (hardcover)
ISBN 978-1-250-17752-0 (ebook)

Our books may be purchased in bulk for promotional, educational, or business use. Please contact your local bookseller or the Macmillan Corporate and Premium Sales Department at 1-800-221-7945, extension 5442, or by email at MacmillanSpecialMarkets@macmillan.com.

First Edition: January 2019

10 9 8 7 6 5 4 3 2 1

In memoriam
Ambassador Faith Whittlesey
(1939–2018)

Contents

Author's Note

My wife and I purchased our home in Palm Beach in 1994, the same year that Donald Trump turned his Mar-a-Lago estate into a club. I am not a member but have several friends who are. A number of times each season they invite me for lunch or dinner or to play tennis on the red clay courts. For most of those years, on the weekends Trump was omnipresent, dining with family and friends, strutting around the mansion greeting members, and until he gave up the sport, an exuberant presence on the tennis courts.

When I was researching my 2009 book about Palm Beach, titled *Madness Under the Royal Palms,* I intended to make Trump a major character. But my editor put the kibosh on that.

He said that Trump was overexposed, a tedious bore whom no one wanted to hear about any longer. Soon afterward, I attended an event at Mar-a-Lago and told him the exchange I'd had with my editor. "Overexposed?" he replied. "You've got to be fucking kidding. I'm Donald Trump."

Palm Beach is a very closed and private world. Residents think that if they are written about at all it should be in celebratory tones, and my book was definitely not written that way. It was greeted with outrage. People didn't dare to read it in public in Palm Beach. At an editorial meeting of the *Palm Beach Daily News,* the editor said my name was never again to be mentioned in its pages, a ban that continues to this day. When I was driving around town with a French television crew filming a documentary, the car was driven off the road by an SUV. A few days later, at a charity event, police chief Michael Reiter suggested I should hire security, as my life might be in danger. When local NBC Channel 5 was filming a segment about the book, a passerby ran into the camera shot and started screaming at me.

I have the same friends I have always had and I like where I live. I asked myself long and hard, Did I want to risk going through that all over again? My answer is this book. I am convinced that Donald Trump's life in Palm Beach is an absolutely essential way to understand his character. All that he learned there contributed greatly to his successful run for president and to his becoming the kind of leader he is.

My research began by going back to the interviews about Trump I recorded for my earlier book but for the most part didn't use. At that time, many people I talked to spoke about Trump with an openness that would be rare today in Palm Beach.

When I started doing new interviews for this book, few members of Mar-a-Lago were willing to have their names attached to whatever they said. Several of them told the story of the member who came into the buffet one day, where, set among the platters of food, was a silver bowl of caviar with a tiny spoon next to it. The man grabbed a soup spoon and dished out enough to make the caviar his main course. When Trump learned this, he threw the man out of the club. I could not verify the story, but people at the club believe it. If Trump would heave a member out for eating too much caviar, what would he do to members who spoke to me if he didn't like my book?

It was amazing how nervous people were. One member had been my friend since I arrived in Palm Beach. When I called her and left a message saying I wanted to interview her, she didn't return my phone call, and despite other calls, she never spoke to me again. But in the end, I did find a number of people to talk openly and I have peppered these on-the-record sources through the book, mixed with anonymous interviews.

I have also been an eyewitness to events in these pages. At one such evening at the Trump International Golf Club in West Palm Beach, I asked President Trump for an interview. "Let's make it happen," he said.

My subsequent requests went unanswered, but many other people spoke to me, and the result is this book. While much in these pages might seem unbelievable, I assure you it is true.

Laurence Leamer
Palm Beach, Florida
September 14, 2018

MAR-A-LAGO

1

Trump's Palm Beach

The forty or so billionaires who winter in Palm Beach want everything done their way in their time. When they play golf, they insist on teeing off as soon as they arrive at their golf course. When they go out to dinner in the exclusive Florida resort community, they expect to be shown immediately to a table, and not just any table, but one of the best in the house. When they drive in their Bentleys and Rolls-Royces, they take it for granted they will be able to glide around the barrier island without interruption. And when they fly into Palm Beach International Airport in their private planes, they consider it their right to land immediately and to be driven to the island without delay. The fact that the drawbridge might be up is a terrible imposition.

But on the first Friday of February 2017, these billionaires who waited for no one had no choice but to wait for one of their kind. President Donald J. Trump was coming to town. For most of his three decades in Palm Beach, he had railed against the planes that flew over Mar-a-Lago interrupting the tranquility and fouling his estate. That was no longer a worry. In advance of Trump's arrival, everything airborne had been shut down. No planes would fly anywhere near Mar-a-Lago until he headed back to Washington.

After Air Force One landed at Palm Beach International Airport just after 4:30 P.M., the president walked down the ramp, where he kissed his wife, Melania, who had arrived on an air force Gulfstream from New York City. Melania was continuing to live in New York until their son, Barron, finished his school year, and for the most part, she saw her husband only on weekends.

A welcoming crowd of about fifty supporters, donning the trademark red Make America Great Again hats, had come to the West Palm Beach airport to welcome and cheer the seventy-year-old leader. A parade of thirty-one vehicles sat on the tarmac ready to take Trump's party to Mar-a-Lago. This was his first presidential trip out of Washington, and an extraordinary number of advisers and staff had accompanied the president aboard Air Force One.

Chief of Staff Reince Priebus and chief strategist Steve Bannon were by Trump's side, constantly jockeying for position to be nearest. They represented two poles of power in the White House, and each man tried to keep as close to the president as he could. Each had his own aides and other staffers, and they all wanted to be present and not to miss anything.

Southern Boulevard had been emptied so the presidential cavalcade could speed eastward from the airport without slowing. Although the vehicles only briefly traversed I-95 over a bridge, traffic on the state's crucial north-south highway had been stopped. Even trains traveling through West Palm Beach had been halted. The drawbridge onto the island of Palm Beach stayed down for Trump, backing up a number of boats as he zoomed right through in his armored black Chevy SUV.

South Ocean Boulevard had been shut down for half a mile north of the estate, effectively blocking north-south traffic on the island. It would stay this way until the president flew back to Washington. Secret Service agents positioned themselves around the buildings, grounds, and surrounding areas. A patrol boat sailed slowly back and forth past Mar-a-Lago on the Intracoastal Waterway and a coast guard ship sat offshore on the Atlantic Ocean, ever vigilant on the far horizon.

Stores, restaurants, and gas stations along Southern Boulevard and Dixie Highway were empty because customers couldn't get to them. Business owners who voted for Trump saw this as a minor price to pay to have their stalwart in the White House. Those who opposed him were outraged that he was adversely affecting their businesses.

This was Trump's first visit to Palm Beach, Florida, since he was sworn in as president only two weeks earlier. His Mar-a-Lago estate was so important to his sense of well-being that he was not willing to wait any longer to spend time there.

Trump has owned the estate for more than thirty years, and he spends most of his cold-weather weekends there. The long presidential campaign had caused him to give up those visits a lot more often than he'd liked. But after his victory in November, he was determined to get back to this routine.

Mar-a-Lago is Trump's spiritual home, the place where he can be himself. Many presidents have had winter retreats, a number of them in Florida. Richard Nixon flew down to his waterfront home in Key Biscayne. John F. Kennedy took over the family estate in the north end of Palm Beach as his winter White House. Harry S. Truman turned a house in Key West into his Little White House. But these were private residences, and Mar-a-Lago is a club where people flow in and out by the hundreds.

It's hard to imagine any of these other presidents wanting to be inundated at their Florida retreats with all kinds of people whose only commonality is that they have paid the money to be there. But Mar-a-Lago energizes the president, with its wealthy members who these days pay two hundred thousand dollars for the privilege to dine at the club's upscale restaurant, lounge by its pools and beach during the day, play tennis on the red clay courts, and, if they cough up a couple of hundred thousand more dollars for a second membership, play a round of golf at the nearby Trump International Golf Club.

Right after his election, Trump let the Secret Service know he intended to visit Mar-a-Lago regularly, and with all the people who would be running in and out of the club, they quickly recognized the immense challenges his request would create. Trump didn't seem to care what problems he presented to the Secret Service. He was used to getting whatever he wanted, and now, as president, he had near-limitless power to ensure things were precisely as he wanted them.

The new president was unconcerned about the costs or disruptions of his visits. *The Washington Post* estimated that if Trump flew down to Mar-a-Lago most cold-weather weekends over his first term as president, the costs to the U.S. government for his trips would run around $130 million.

As the presidential SUV drove through the gates of Mar-a-Lago, Trump was back where he belonged. The estate is the most grandiose statement of his success, the symbol of his life and its myriad challenges. He had almost lost Mar-a-Lago once and had saved it only by turning it into a club. Mar-a-Lago means so much to him that he fought an unyielding battle against the Palm Beach elite, who had at best always been suspicious of the flashy real estate tycoon and at worst despised him.

In so many ways, the island was Trump's training ground, a place where he learned techniques that he used in his race for the White House. The relentless, combative style he perfected in this enclave of billionaires would ultimately be part of his appeal to the common man and a key to how he won the highest office in the land. It was at Mar-a-Lago that he served his apprenticeship for the most unlikely victory in presidential history.

Not only did Trump beat the Palm Beach establishment the way no one ever had, but he marginalized them, pushing them back and making room for the ascendency of a new moneyed class of which he is the acknowledged leader. "I'm the king of Palm Beach," Trump boasted to author Timothy L. O'Brien. "They all come over, they all eat, they all love me, they all kiss my ass. And then they all leave and say: 'Isn't he horrible.' But I'm the king."

Even within the protected confines of Mar-a-Lago, some members of the club abhorred him. Trump didn't care. Love. Hate. They were just words. What mattered was that people paid attention to him. All was right with the world when controversy swirled around him, just as long as he stood in the eye of the hurricane.

Trump had hardly been in the White House long enough to know where all the rooms were, and already the critics were describing his administration as drowning in chaos. A mark of this disorder was Trump's executive order halting visitors to the United States from seven largely Muslim nations. The document was so ineptly written and legally flawed that as Trump was flying to Palm Beach, a federal judge in Seattle ordered the government to stop enforcing the ban.

His first full day in Palm Beach, Trump sent out a barrage of tweets attacking the judge's decision. Then he went over to the Trump International Golf Club in West Palm Beach for a round of golf before returning to have a phone call with President Petro O. Poroshenko of Ukraine late that afternoon. In between that and getting ready for dinner, the president found time to talk to any number of Mar-a-Lago members, bathing in their tributes to his greatness and also putting them in the unique position of advising the president on whom he should appoint to positions within his administration.

That evening Trump was slated to attend the sixtieth annual International Red Cross Ball, long regarded as the most prestigious charity event in Palm Beach. The event was to be held in the Donald J. Trump Ballroom on the estate grounds. The massive hall is Trump's personal creation. The exterior looks like a perfect adjunct to Mar-a-Lago's Moorish exterior, but the interior has what he calls "the feel and look of Louis XIV, and that's my favorite style."

Trump spent forty million dollars on the ballroom—four times what he paid for Mar-a-Lago and all its possessions—building the twenty-thousand-square-foot structure in 2004. His model was the magnificent Hall of Mirrors at Versailles. The whole thing was about showing the money, laying out what he had in all its glorious excess. He spent seven million dollars alone on twenty-four-karat gold sheets that shimmered from the ceiling, which was also adorned with seventeen crystal chandeliers. Even the bathrooms were mini palaces with golden basins, and everywhere one looked the gilded palace screamed out its affluence. Gold. Gold, and more gold.

That night, the president stood at the entrance to the ballroom in black formal dress beside Melania in a long, red sleeveless gown, perfectly rendered for the regal scene set out before them. When Trump looked out on the vast ballroom, he saw a splendid assemblage. The ladies wore gowns of every description, and the gentlemen were impeccably garbed in tuxedos.

The waiters wore powdered wigs and satinlike knee breeches, while the waitresses dressed in period dresses. No peasants tried to storm the barricades outside the ballroom, but roughly three hundred protesters marched along the road to Mar-a-Lago, their shouts fitting into the royal theme.

Trump's aides may have flown down with the president, but that did not mean they joined him at the ball. This evening Trump was alone with his Palm Beach world, and for a few hours, he appeared to want nothing to do with the problematic world of Washington.

The social elite of Palm Beach had regarded Trump as a vulgar interloper when he first came to the island. The Red Cross Ball was *their* event, and they didn't like having him play much of a role. But things were different now. The old establishment had lost its hold on things, overwhelmed by new money, and it was these new-money people who filled the ballroom this evening. As for Trump, he had gone from being barely tolerated at the event to becoming its central figure.

In Palm Beach, there is no higher social honor than chairing the Red Cross Ball, and this year's chairman, Janet Cafaro, was emblematic of how much the island had changed since the days it was run by a WASP elite. Her husband, John "J. J." Cafaro, is a convicted felon who in 2001 pled guilty to conspiracy to bribe a U.S. congressman. In 2010, he again pled guilty to siphoning illegal campaign contributions to his daughter's race for the Ohio legislature.

The old Palm Beach would not have been so accepting of the Cafaros, but after the Ohio mall developer contributed $50,000 to the Trump Foundation in 2016, Trump said that Cafaro was a "fantastic man." The president appeared to view these crimes as no worse than a couple of speeding tickets. As long as the Cafaros had enough money to make a substantial contribution to the Red Cross, what was wrong with Janet Cafaro speaking for a few minutes before the president of the United States while her felon husband looked on proudly?

In Trump's world, money spoke. It spoke louder than truth, louder than culture, louder than class, louder than manners. It simply overwhelmed.

Seated next to Trump at his table was fellow Palm Beach winter resident Wilbur Ross, whom the president had made his choice for secretary of commerce in part because Ross claimed he was a billionaire. One of the speakers this evening was another of Trump's wealthy Palm Beach friends, the ball's honorary chairman, Patrick Park. Trump planned to make Park his ambassador to Austria.

Finally, Trump got up to speak at a dais, which had affixed to it the presidential seal. "I don't think I've ever seen the room looking more beautiful—perhaps at our wedding—right, Melania?" he said, looking over at his wife. "We're very proud of Mar-a-Lago and all the money we've raised in this room and in this wonderful house."

The Red Cross spent $436,125 putting on the event, a substantial portion of that going to Mar-a-Lago. Like every other charitable event at the estate, it was a profitable venture for Trump. There was no reason why this couldn't continue during his presidency. Trump did make his own donations at charity events, but close inspection usually revealed he had done so with someone else's money.

The president stayed late that evening, appearing to savor each moment. The Secret Service was omnipresent, warding off any unwanted well-wishers, but Trump accepted accolades from scores of the attendees at the ball. This was his golden ballroom and his golden night. He and Melania danced to "Old Time Rock and Roll," in what truly was now, undisputedly, Donald Trump's Palm Beach. The president was home.

2

Fantasy Island

Freezing temperatures were gripping New York City in early 1982—so much so that Donald and Ivana Trump decided to fly south for a few days in the Florida sun. They didn't know much about Palm Beach, but they had been to Miami many times and were looking for someplace new. Wherever they traveled, they stayed in the best hotels. In Palm Beach that meant the Breakers.

It sounded like a great plan, but as soon as the Trumps arrived at the Breakers, it began to pour rain. Trump was not the kind of man to relieve his boredom by putting in an hour on an exercise bike in the gym. Instead, he called down to the concierge and ordered up a limousine for a tour of the island.

When the driver took the Trumps around the resort town, he was showing them not only one of the wealthiest towns in the world, but a community that was the creation of one man. In the late nineteenth century, Henry Morrison Flagler had the grandiose idea to turn the largely unpopulated island on the east coast of Florida into a winter paradise for the American elite. Thirty-five-year-old Trump believed that society advanced itself by singular men doing singular things, and the more he heard about Flagler, the more he admired the founder of Palm Beach.

Flagler, in partnership with John D. Rockefeller, had built Standard Oil into the country's largest corporation. Reviled by many of their fellow citizens as robber barons, these immensely wealthy men were among the emblematic characters of the Gilded Age. Rockefeller used his philanthropy to sweeten that malevolent image, and in his last years, many Americans came to revere him as a kindly gentleman who passed out dimes to children.

Flagler didn't share Rockefeller's concerns over image, and he took no pleasure in handing out money. His first step in fulfilling his dream was to build a railroad down the eastern coast of the state. Florida had been part of the union since 1845, but it was largely as wild and unpopulated as the remote regions of the West, and building the Florida East Coast Railway, as it would be named, was a major engineering feat.

When the rails reached most of the way south, Flagler constructed a hotel in the jungles of Palm Beach. Flagler was not one for modesty, and his new hotel would not be humble. In order to get people to take an overnight train down from the North, the oil tycoon built, in less than a year, a massive hotel facing Lake Worth, later part of the Intracoastal Waterway that separates Palm Beach from the mainland. Flagler named it the Royal Poinciana Hotel, after a tree that blooms fire-red flowers, and opened it in January 1894.

People came in such numbers that two years later Flagler constructed an imposing all-wooden hotel, the Palm Beach Inn, a half mile eastward on the oceanfront. When guests started asking for rooms "down by the breakers," Flagler changed the hotel's name to the Breakers. He brought in a railway link to carry passengers right up to the door of their hotel, but motorized vehicles were not allowed on the island. Guests either walked between the two hotels along the palm-tree-bordered pathway, boarded a trolley car pulled by a mule, or took one of the scores of "Afromobiles," wicker chairs set on bicycles pedaled by young black men wearing white knickerbockers.

Both hotels were hugely successful, and in 1901 Flagler built an addition onto the Royal Poinciana, turning the eighteen-hundred-foot-long structure into the largest hotel in the world. The Royal Poinciana had so many dining rooms that all seventeen hundred guests could sit down to dinner at the same time, including the maids and valets, who had their own separate dining room. If one walked into the lobby and looked at the expanse of the place, the impression was of an enormous greenhouse, with palms, ferns, and all kinds of plants in the rotunda and halls blending into the moss-green carpeting and the pale-green tint of the walls, set off by white and gold furniture.

Elaborate breakfasts were served, and there were afternoon teas and evening dances, leading guests to change their outfits three or four times a day. The rich and famous came in droves. You could be walking along the beach path, and there would be Mark Twain strolling with a cigar in his mouth. Or at dinner you might spy the celebrated novelist Henry James, who was enthralled by the hotel: "To stand off and see it rear its incoherent crest above its gardens was to remember—and quite with relief—nothing but the processional outline of Windsor Castle that could appear to march with it."

Flagler had opened the Royal Poinciana with only seventeen guests, but it seemed that almost overnight he turned Palm Beach into the most celebrated winter resort in America. If you were wealthy and privileged, it was the place to be. The establishments were filled not just with celebrities, millionaires, and their entourages but with people who paid good dollars to rub shoulders with their social betters.

One of those staying at the hotel in February 1911 was John "Honey Fitz" Fitzgerald, the mayor of Boston, who had arrived from the Northeast with his daughter Rose, who would one day become the mother of President John F. Kennedy. Fitzgerald was a boisterous, irascible politician who had won election attacking the very upper-class Americans who patronized the hotel. Yet this didn't stop him from wanting to hobnob with them.

"This was the greatest ball I ever saw," Fitzgerald said after a dance in the hotel ballroom. "Just think of the millions and millions of dollars represented on that floor tonight, not alone in the jewels and dresses, but in the capitalists who stand for so much. All you have to do is put out your finger, and you are pointing out a millionaire."

Flagler's overwhelming success with his hotels didn't help him much with the problems he faced in his personal life. When his first wife died of tuberculosis, he married her nursemaid, Ida Alice Shourds. His bride went slowly mad, a condition possibly exacerbated by her husband's many affairs.

Most husbands of that era would have felt they were stuck with a sick wife. Not Henry Flagler. After institutionalizing Ida Alice, he went to the Florida legislature and got the politicians to pass a special law so he could divorce his spouse. Like many Palm Beach denizens to come, Flagler seemed to feel that having a sick spouse was a reminder of his own mortality, while a young thing gave him his own personal fountain of youth. The mogul waited only ten days after the divorce became final to marry his longtime mistress Mary Lily Kenan.

Wealthy Americans like Flagler were obsessed with royalty. Although the American Constitution forbade citizens from receiving noble titles, the moneyed could at least live in palaces fit for kings and queens. With that in mind, Flagler built a seventy-thousand-square-foot winter residence next door to the Royal Poinciana that the *New York Herald* described as "more wonderful than any palace in Europe, grander and more magnificent than any other private dwelling in the world."

Flagler named the immense structure Whitehall and gave it to his third wife as a wedding gift. And, of course, the whole point of having a young bride and a glorious home with rooms fit for public occasions was to have grand dinner parties and private balls to show your peers that they were not your peers. No one had more splendid evenings than the Flaglers. But as large as Whitehall was, it did not contain anything like the grand ballroom at the Royal Poinciana, and the Flaglers frequented major evenings there, too, receiving accolades and deference as the reigning couple of Palm Beach.

When eighty-three-year-old Flagler tumbled down the marble staircase at Whitehall in 1913 and died, the third Mrs. Flagler didn't wear her widow's weeds for very long. She reconnected with a beau from her youth who was four and a half years younger than she; women, too, in Palm Beach were not immune from seeking the fountain of youth in a younger partner.

During Donald and Ivana's tour of the island, they saw only a few signs of Palm Beach's early years. The Breakers, where the couple was staying, rose high above the Atlantic beach, but this was not the original structure. When the wooden Breakers burned down in 1925, concrete was used to rebuild the massive hotel. The Royal Poinciana could not compete with the Breakers' up-to-date facilities, and in 1935, the hotel was torn down. Flagler's Whitehall mansion still stood, but in 1960 it became the Flagler Museum, memorializing an extravagant way of life that, by the time Trump arrived there, seemed gone forever.

Trump did see, in a number of places, the legacy of architect Addison Mizner, the other most important figure in the island's early history. Many of Mizner's childhood years were spent in Central America, where his father was an ambassador, and the future architect's young mind was deeply influenced by the medieval Spanish style he saw. Mizner abhorred the boxlike structures of Flagler's two hotels. He believed that might have been perfect for the north, but in a climate that is warm most of the year, the closed-up buildings were often mercilessly hot. Even when there weren't suffocating conditions, Mizner said that hotel guests lived an "artificial life," spending their days changing from one confining outfit to the next.

No tour of Palm Beach was complete without a drive down Worth Avenue. At the end of one of the most celebrated luxury shopping streets in the world stood Mizner's first commission and most important building, the Everglades Club. The giant structure was built in 1918 and was financed by Mizner's partner in the project, Paris Singer, a son of the sewing machine dynast. The two friends originally planned a hospital for wounded officers, but with World War I over, there was no need, and it was changed to a private club.

Mizner was a fantasist of the highest order, and he said he was creating "a nunnery, with a chapel built into the lake." The building was like a medieval palace, akin to the Alhambra in Andalusia. The walls were thick and the ceilings high, fostering a coolness even on the hottest day.

To complete his dream, Mizner oversaw everything from the top of the Moorish tower to the smallest footstool in the corner of the remotest room. He had the whimsical daring to use twenty-two wildly different window treatments on the north facade. From his studio in West Palm Beach, he created furniture and tiles that his workers made to appear centuries old. These weren't so much fake antiques as spirited re-creations of an invented past.

Patrons of Palm Beach with real money soon vacated the hotels, leaving them to the tourists, and commissioned Mizner to build them their own winter residences. He designed scores of Palm Beach homes. In 1923 alone, he oversaw eighteen major projects. He did not work from plans, and the rooms seemed to meander in unexpected ways. What they all had was an aura that elevated and broadened the make-believe of Palm Beach.

As the Everglades Club grew in popularity, it became the social center of the island. Membership had to be renewed each season, and Singer filled the palacelike building with people who entertained him. "To him what was ugly or boring was bad, and what was beautiful or amusing was good," recalled a friend, Alice DeLamar. "He felt hostility to bores alone."

In Palm Beach society, the highest calling was to amuse and to be amusing. Everyone had money, but money was not what mattered. Palm Beach was full of all kinds of gloriously unique characters. Wit sparkled, and there was a genuine frivolity.

In the late twenties, the heiress Marjorie Merriweather Post built a new club, the Bath and Tennis (B&T), across from her Mar-a-Lago estate, another place for the anointed to frolic. In those years, the socially prominent included a number of German American Jews. They played an integral part in the town's social life in the years after World War I, often listed in the *Social Register* and invited everywhere.

At the opening of the B&T in February 1929, one of the original two hundred club members, the Jewish banker Henry Seligman, hosted eighteen guests. His fellow club member, the banker and philanthropist Julius Bache, was also present that evening, as were the celebrated financier Bernard Baruch and his wife. When the Everglades Club got in severe financial trouble in 1937, one of the twenty-two members to help bail the club out was the Jewish banker Louis G. Kaufman.

In the years after World War II, with a large influx of Eastern European Jews to the island, the two leading clubs, the Everglades and the Bath and Tennis, closed their doors to anyone Jewish. That loss, coupled with the often staid, uninteresting people who were joining, caused the clubs to become far less cosmopolitan than they had been in their early years.

Mizner, who died at the age of sixty in 1933, likely would have been distressed at what happened to his island in the half century after his demise. Most of his houses were still there, but in many cases, renovations had been done in such arrogantly foolish ways that his magic was gone. He had aspired to live in a community of radical individuality where people could be what they wanted to be and say what they wanted to say, and that was gone, too.

In the Reagan years, conduct that Mizner would have deemed provocative and amusing was considered in bad taste. On Worth Avenue, even on the sunniest days, only a few shoppers ambled along. People dressed up to walk down the famous shopping street and would not have abided someone like the disheveled Mizner. Considering all his social sins, his dress being the least of it, he would doubtlessly have been blackballed from the club that had been built and founded as an expression of his own brilliant creativity.

Membership in either the Everglades Club or the Bath and Tennis Club, or both, was crucial to belonging to the elevated Palm Beach world. You couldn't simply apply. You had to be invited by a member and then go through a rigorous vetting process. By the time Donald Trump rode in his limo on his tour of the town, blandness was essential for admittance. If an applicant had even a taint of scandal or display of tackiness, he was bound to be rejected. Those turned down often sold their homes and left the island. The elite Jewish Palm Beachers had their club, too, the Palm Beach Country Club. For the most part, it copied the customs and mores of the WASP clubs and was every bit as snobbish, its members looking down especially on other Jews who didn't make the cut.

Three drawbridges linked the island to the mainland. They could be raised in a couple of minutes; Palm Beach was arguably the first gated community in America. It was a tiny enclave from which winter residents rarely ventured. Across the waterway, West Palm Beach was a déclassé place where service people and minorities including African Americans lived. It was here that cars were repaired, dangerous chemicals stored, sick people hospitalized, and the dead buried. The Valley of Ashes to Palm Beach's East Egg.

Donald Trump was a Miami Beach kind of guy. Even if you were a member of some group disdained in Palm Beach, you felt welcome in one of the art deco hotels along Miami Beach's Collins Avenue. If you wanted to sunbathe topless on the beach, nobody was going to stop you; if you were gay, go to it; and if you wanted to practice your Orthodox Jewish faith, that was fine, too. Everything went in Miami Beach.

When he was a boy, Trump's father took him on vacations to the flashy resort town, where the family stayed on Collins Avenue in the gloriously gaudy Fontainebleau, with its humongous seventeen-thousand-square-foot lobby and its celebrated Boom Boom Room and Poodle Lounge. Morris Lapidus designed the hotel to be a dramatic scene. The Fontainebleau defined Miami Beach in the public imagination, and for an impressionable boy like young Donald, it was a splendid place.

Donald's father, Frederick Christ Trump, was impressed, too. The German American businessman had made his fortune constructing middle- and working-class housing in New York's outer boroughs, and his visits to the Fontainebleau influenced him to add a touch of the hotel to the Coney Island condos he was marketing. The builder figured people would pay a premium for fancy lobbies, and he persuaded a reluctant Lapidus to work on a number of his projects. When his son got into the business, he seemed to bring a little Fontainebleau to everything he did.

The more Trump saw of Palm Beach, the more different it was from the Miami Beach he had long known. Everything was in your face in Miami Beach. Here in Palm Beach, everything was hidden. The island was known for its great estates, but as he drove around that weekend, he could see almost nothing, because almost everything was secreted behind high hedges. In the North End was the Mizner-designed mansion where the Kennedys had come since the twenties. The home of the thirty-fifth president was a place tourists to the island wanted to visit. But no matter how slowly one drove by, all there was to see was a long wall and a door.

Trump may have been on vacation, but his mind was always working and playing around with one deal or another. There was always something out there, if you knew what to ask and where to go, even in a place like Palm Beach that hid itself away from outsiders.

"What's for sale here?" Trump asked. The purpose of the trip hadn't been to buy a place. Checking out real estate was just something he did almost any-place he went.

"Well, the best thing by far is Mar-a-Lago, but I guess you wouldn't be talk-ing about that," the driver said, figuring this young man and his wife were unlikely to be interested in one of the most expensive estates in America.

"What's Mar-a-Lago?" Trump asked.

Most members of the eastern elite would likely have heard of Mar-a-Lago, considering how embedded it was in the history of Palm Beach. But Trump was an outsider to that world, and he knew nothing about one of America's most splendid homes.

Marjorie Merriweather Post built the seventeen-acre estate from 1923 to 1926, employing as many as six hundred laborers. The cereal heiress lived in it for six decades during the winter season. Mrs. Post employed a thirty-nine-member household staff supplemented by waiters and others hired for the eve-ning. It took around thirty groundskeepers to make sure the lawns were impeccable. An American palace.

Mrs. Post had been in residence when President John F. Kennedy made the family's Palm Beach home his winter retreat. In her last years, Mrs. Post envi-sioned her own Mar-a-Lago as America's permanent winter White House. It would be the vacation home not for one president but for all of them, and Mar-a-Lago would live forever as part of the nation's heritage.

When Mrs. Post died in 1973, her will deeded the Palm Beach property to the National Park Service. It seemed like an immensely generous thing to do until one noticed the enormous tax write-off it gave her three daughters, who were her primary heirs. Beyond that, they each received between forty and fifty million dollars in the will and had no reason to complain about their mother's bequest to the government.

In her will, Mrs. Post did something else to try to make sure things went on as before. Worried that the Bath and Tennis Club, on the beach just south of Mar-a-Lago, might not have enough oceanfront property to prosper and grow, she authorized the executors to sell Mar-a-Lago's beach to the club, "providing a reasonable sale price can be obtained." That way the B&T would have a wide swath of beach in perpetuity.

Mrs. Post assumed everyone within her vision was wealthy, but many of the B&T members in this bastion of the old Protestant world were living on the fumes of their inheritances. Their one creative act was to pretend they had money that was long gone. They weren't about to vote for a stiff assessment to buy nothing but a little more beach. The club decided to purchase only the fifty-three feet directly affixed to the B&T. Jack Massey, the neighbor to the north, bought the other 403 feet of the 456-foot parcel for $348,321. The Nashville businessman purchased the land so he could sell the property to someone he would want as a next-door neighbor.

In the ensuing years, the beachfront land remained vacant and no president chose to make use of the estate. In 1981 Congress gave Mar-a-Lago back to the Post Foundation. The skeletal crew overseeing the estate spent their days in darkened rooms, the furniture covered in cloth. The ocean air was merciless, and much of the art and fixtures slowly deteriorated.

Trump arranged to see the estate. He did not ask a local Realtor to show him the property but instead went directly to the Post Foundation (that way, if he purchased Mar-a-Lago, the foundation would not have to pay a commission and he could likely make the purchase at a lower selling price).

Mrs. Post had named the estate Mar-a-Lago, Spanish for "sea to lake." To the east, the villa faced across South Ocean Boulevard to the Atlantic Ocean; to the west, to the Intracoastal Waterway, a riverlike body of water that separated the island from the mainland. As Trump's limousine drove south along South Ocean Boulevard, he saw on the west side of the road the tower of Mar-a-Lago rising seventy-five feet high into the South Florida sky.

From the road, Trump could see only a little of the seventy-five-thousand-square-foot main house, larger than some shopping centers. Mrs. Post had not wanted the estate to look too large or for passersby to view much of the humongous mansion, and she had put up high hedges. To the east of the road stood more hedges, hiding a swimming pool and the private beach. Mar-a-Lago included a citrus grove, a pitch-and-putt golf course, servants' quarters, two bomb shelters, and a tunnel under South Ocean Boulevard allowing guests to reach the beach-side swimming pool and ocean without having to cross the road.

The Moorish-style mansion had pink walls that stood out brilliantly underneath the orange-tiled roof. Although Princeton-educated architect Marion Sims Wyeth worked for a time on the project, the vision was largely that of Joseph Urban, an Austrian American scenic designer who crafted the interior as well. Urban had designed sets for the Metropolitan Opera as well as the Ziegfeld Follies. The 250-pound designer brought that same extravagant artistic imagination to Palm Beach, taking Mizner's classical sensibility and revving it up into a magnificent stage setting.

The Trumps' chauffeur drove Donald and Ivana onto the estate through an ornate pinkish-brown Spanish-tile gateway guarded by two pageboy statues atop pink columns. The sentinels held lamps that were meant to welcome visitors into Mar-a-Lago, but years had gone by and their gilding had corroded away. One of the statues was cracked and had been propped up with a board. Looking up to the roof, along the drainpipes one saw an array of monkeys, parrots, and rams' heads, an exotic bestiary that hinted of more wonders inside the great building.

The Trumps immediately encountered the estate's three-hundred-pound main doors, made of latticelike iron and glass, which were a work of art by themselves. The walls of the entrance hall were decorated with fourteenth- and fifteenth-century Spanish tiles, which also adorned the rest of the 114-room mansion. The black-and-red-painted wooden beams maintained the Iberian motif. Eight ancient Spanish lanterns hung on chains from the ceiling. Dresden urns were set within recessed niches. Lions and griffins—a mythological beast that was part lion, part eagle—looked down from panels near the ceiling.

Along the top of the walls were set ten coats of arms celebrating the Merriweather and Post families. Double doors leading into the main part of the house had thirty-four recessed panels, each one containing a cherub. The entrance hall's disparate decorations could have been a hopeless mishmash, but like everything else in the mansion, they held together as part of a clear, compelling vision.

When Trump moved into the living room, he stood in the arena where

Urban had given his artistic sensibilities their fullest rein. The living room ceiling reached up thirty-four feet with such brilliant gold, it was like an artistic rendering of the sun brought inside to shine down on those below. The walls were festooned with a treasure of gold leaf and an aviary of bird motifs. But the frescoes of Medici princes and their entourage had begun to fade over the decades, giving them the look of having been painted in the fifteenth century.

The seven silk tapestries that hung in the room were not replicas and came from a Venetian palazzo. Across the room and up five marble steps protected by two Romanesque lions was a fourteen-foot-wide plate-glass window looking out toward the Atlantic Ocean. That was the only indication that the room was in Florida and not rising out of the plains of Andalusia or the mists of Xanadu. No wonder Trump was so taken by what he saw. Mar-a-Lago was sui generis, one of a kind, and so, Trump believed, was he.

The dining room off the living room was designed as a splendid venue for entertaining. Italian artisans had been flown to Florida to paint the room with mosaics based on those in the Chigi Palace in Rome. In Florence, fifteen artisans had spent more than a year creating the four-thousand-pound marble table inlaid with semiprecious stones.

Mrs. Post's dinner parties had been the most desired invitations on the island. A footman stood behind each of the thirty-six chairs at the long dinner table. They removed the covers from the dishes at precisely the same moment and set the plates before the guests.

The crystal and silverware were equally exquisite, with enough different forks to test whether one knew which ones to use, thus determining if one truly belonged at Mrs. Post's table.

On the other side of the dining room was the library. The imported walnut paneling was chosen to resemble a study in an English country house. A portrait of Mrs. Post occupied the center of the small room, but by the time of Trump's visit, mold had grown around it.

To ensure some measure of privacy, Mar-a-Lago faced west, turning its back to the ocean-skirting road. The living room doors opened onto a verandah looking out toward Lake Worth. Many of Mrs. Post's parties took place at tables set on this massive terrace.

Marble stairs led to the lily pond adorned with stone parrots or the court-yard and the entrance to the "Owner's House," whose rooms announced in every way that this was a lady's private quarters. The bedroom suite was deco-rated in the ornate, elaborate style of Louis XV.

It was not a place to sprawl or to live casually. This was the home of a grande dame, proudly feminine, and meticulous in its arrangement. The rooms were not enormous, and that was fine for a woman of decorum and careful ritual. The high-backed chairs and the animal figurines in the living room bespoke formality, as did the elaborate bed in the bedroom. The walls of the dressing room and bathroom were of pink Siena marble.

Downstairs, Mrs. Post's daughter Dina Merrill, the actress, had lived as a child in what was called the "Baby's House." The rooms were a mini town house, containing a vestibule, bedroom, nurse's bedroom, sitting room, play-room, bathroom, and sleeping porch. There was a golden canopy bed fit for a princess, a rug interwoven with fairy-tale characters from "Sleeping Beauty," door handles shaped like squirrels with long tails, and so many pink roses on the fire screen that it looked like a garden in bloom. After the kidnapping and murder of the Lindbergh baby in 1932, Mrs. Post insisted that metal grating be applied on the windows. Urban minimized the foreboding nature of this by cre-ating ornate iron window covers with the themes of nursery rhymes.

The five guest suites were upstairs, each one in a different style. Colonial-style furniture set the motif for the Adam suite. The Portuguese suite had dark furnishings. The Dutch suite was graced with Delft tiles and a white fireplace. The Spanish suite had ancient crests in the beams and a superb round fireplace in one corner. The Venetian suite earned its name with its crystal chandeliers.

A winding stairway up into the tower led to an art deco sitting room. Above that, on the fourth floor, a sleek bedroom was adorned with silver wallpaper. At the highest level of the tower was an outside deck with a panoramic view around the island.

Downstairs there was a large room with creamy white walls named the Teahouse that was large enough to sit fifty people. Beyond that was an even larger room for major events, the Pavilion, built in the early sixties. Although the room was decorated in Moorish style with a mural of an Arab horse and rider at one end, in comparison to the rest of Mar-a-Lago, it was almost austere, a setting Mrs. Post created primarily for her weekly square dances as well as showings of the latest Hollywood movies.

A social impresario like no other, Mrs. Post needed one other element to complete her vision. That was her own club, which she constructed on the oceanfront just south of the estate. She could sashay through the tunnel and enter the Bath and Tennis Club in five minutes, where she could lunch or have drinks with her friends. The B&T had several hundred members, but everyone knew it was Mrs. Post's club.

The British novelist William Thackeray famously said that it took three generations to make a gentleman. That may have been the way things worked in Great Britain, but in America, ladies and gentlemen were sometimes churned out in a generation.

Mrs. Post's father had begun life as a peddler and had made his fortune in the cereal business. His only child was accepted as an aristocrat. The four-time-married heiress played the role with great aplomb. For a time, Mrs. Post was the richest woman in America. She used that wealth to create *her* world around her. What was it for her to hire Ringling Bros. and Barnum & Bailey Circus to put on three performances for her friends and then invite children living in the county home and Girl Scouts for another show? Wasn't it a hoot to bring down a Broadway show and have them singing and dancing at Mar-a-Lago? And when she wanted to throw a scavenger hunt, how about hiding diamonds in the ice cream and giving the guests gold picks to find the treasure in their desserts?

In the days when everyone was doing the fox-trot and the waltz, Mrs. Post wasn't shy about her passion for square dancing. No one in Palm Beach society could have imagined contorting themselves in anything so déclassé as a square dance. But Mrs. Post loved the dance, and everyone flocked to her weekly square dances.

The mistress of Mar-a-Lago staged these Thursday evening events with the aplomb and precision with which she did everything. Cocktails were at 7:30 P.M.

The guests arrived on time, dressed in what the invitations specified as "Daytime Dress." As a Christian Scientist, Mrs. Post did not imbibe. She had drinks for her guests, but the short cocktail hour was for a purpose. A half hour later everyone sat down for dinner at long tables on the verandah.

Mrs. Post's guest lists included everyone from Rose Kennedy to General Omar Bradley, the Aga Khan to the Japanese ambassador. At 9:00 P.M. the invitees moved into the ballroom for the square dancing. Several professional dancers guided the uninitiated in the steps. At precisely 11:00 P.M. Mrs. Post signaled that the evening was over by having the guests join hands and sing, "May the Good Lord Bless and Keep You . . . Till We Meet Again."

Mrs. Post was known for inviting people who amused her. As her hearing failed, she sat next to those with the loudest voices. In her last, declining years, she often didn't even come to the dinners but stayed on the second floor looking down on her guests through a peephole.

As the years went by, Palm Beach increasingly became a matriarchy, driven by the wives or widows of fabulously wealthy men. These were not bold feminists overturning the social order, but sober matrons overseeing the traditional social life of the island. Their husbands were bankers, industrialists, and attorneys who came down to Florida to play golf and tennis. They let their wives plan where and with whom they dined. These men very often married younger women, many of them second or third wives. While that often gave them a few years of amusing diversion, it also created a good number of wealthy widows with both time and money. Mrs. Post was just one of a number of socially formidable grandes dames, including Eva Stotesbury, a financier's wife; Mary Sanford, a carpet manufacturer's wife; and Sue Whitmore, a Listerine heiress.

Trump knew nothing about these Palm Beach matrons and their wealthy but circumscribed lives. His model for life was his father. Frederick Christ Trump was a man of New York's outer boroughs. He had done well for himself building where he belonged and thought better than entering the brutally competitive Manhattan real estate world. His son had a different vision of success, and

Donald Trump had already made his way constructing upscale properties in the city. Still in his early thirties, Trump began rebuilding the moribund Commodore Hotel on Forty-second Street with a construction loan guaranteed by his father, and in the process played a role in revitalizing the area of midtown Manhattan around Grand Central Terminal. From there he went on to construct Trump Tower, a fifty-eight-story skyscraper at Fifty-sixth Street and Fifth Avenue.

Everything Trump did was to be in his image, and both these buildings shouted, "Look at me!" Trump always went for flash, having inherited his father's admiration of the Fontainebleau Hotel style, and when he believed the occasion deserved it, he was prone to full-blown, sparkling, over-the-top glitz.

Visitors to the six-story atrium at Trump Tower entered past guards dressed in a Disney-like fantasy of English grenadiers in scarlet coats and enormous, fur-adorned hats. They walked through a giant lobby decked out in what architectural critic Ada Louise Huxtable described as "posh ladies' powder-room décor," where they were serenaded by "Student Prince tea music, exhumed from some extinct resort-hotel circuit, a marvelously funny touch at the bottom of that pink marble maelstrom." Trump dismissed the critics and bragged that thousands of tourists made their pilgrimage to Trump Tower a mandatory stop on their visits to the city.

Trump owned a triplex in his building on Fifth Avenue and a mansion in Greenwich, Connecticut, but when he saw Mar-a-Lago, he knew they did not compare. To him, Mar-a-Lago was "maybe the greatest place in the world." The Palm Beach estate was a monument to a woman's sensibility and her love of ornate, precious décor. Trump considered it a "museum," and certainly not a place for someone like him. But he also knew that owning the estate would bring him a certain cachet in a world of which he was not a part. He coveted the place even though he doubted he would enjoy living there. "I never thought it was going to be a particularly comfortable place, but I thought it was so incredible as a statement that it would be wonderful to own," he later said. He just had to have it.

The estate was priced at twenty million dollars, at that time by far the highest price ever for a private home in America. That did not dissuade Trump. Mar-a-Lago had been sitting on the market for less than a year, but Trump could already smell blood in the water. What was twenty million dollars but an asking price? There was always a deal to be made, and he believed nobody made deals better than Donald J. Trump.

3

Estate Sale

S oon after Trump flew back to New York from Palm Beach, he made an offer for Mar-a-Lago. He told others about the magnificent splendor of the
historic estate, but he wasn't about to offer anything like the twenty-million-
dollar asking price. He offered less than half of what the estate wanted.

His nine-million-dollar bid also came with strings attached. Not only did
he want to get Mar-a-Lago for less than half the asking price, but he planned
on building fourteen homes on the property and immediately turning a profit.
Not surprisingly, the Post Foundation rejected that offer.

Trump didn't have the means to live in such a magnificent estate. Tax returns
and other documents Trump provided to the New Jersey Casino Control Commission in 1981, when he was applying for a casino license, showed him with an
annual income of around one hundred thousand dollars. He had a one-million-
dollar trust fund given to him by his father, around four hundred thousand dollars
in checking accounts, a 1977 Mercedes 450SL, a series of apartments in which
his equity was worth around two million dollars, and $22.5 million in real estate
debts on leveraged property, for a net worth of around five million dollars.

Trump told many fibs in his life, but nothing so crucial to his image as the tale that he had made it on his own. That was the American dream. After all, this was a country where a young man could raise himself up by his boot-straps by relying on initiative, daring, and grit. Of course, it helped if behind you stood someone grabbing your britches and lifting you up in a way nobody could see.

Trump averred that all he had ever taken from his wealthy father was a one million dollar loan that he returned as he built a multibillion-dollar empire. In its extensive reporting, *The New York Times* found no evidence that he had ever paid that money back. The falsehood of Trump's claim is evident even in the financial statement he gave the casino commission. Those apartments he owned were gifts from his father, and that was only the beginning of Fred Trump's largesse. At this point, he had already given his son millions of dollars, allowing him to gallivant around the nightspots of Manhattan playing the self-made millionaire with aplomb.

The young heir surely knew that if the deal for Mar-a-Lago had gone through, he would have had to get a mortgage, likely cosigned by his father, and sell those fourteen plots of land immediately and probably the diminished estate. But his father was always there ready to bail him out, and Trump might have been able to hold onto the estate.

Later in 1982 *Forbes* published its first list of the richest Americans. Trump should not even have been a candidate, but he knew that it was crucial to his business success to be there. America was changing from a country run by cor-porate CEOs to a nation of mega-entrepreneurs who were strutting across the economic horizon, and the Forbes 400 proved to be one of the seminal social documents of the era. Bankers read *Forbes*, and if you got on that list, you could borrow almost limitless amounts of money and you were invited into deals with the other biggest players.

As Trump saw it, getting named wasn't about financial statements and facts. It was about cutting a deal and beginning way higher than where he hoped to close. He didn't leave this to some smarmy PR type who would try to finesse his client's way onto the list. Trump called twenty-five-year-old *Forbes* reporter Jonathan Greenberg himself, not once but many times. Trump began by assuming much of his father's fortune. Then he flattered the kid. He cajoled him. He threatened him. And sometimes Trump called pretending he was someone else deputized to speak about the incredible financial acumen of the brilliant Trump. And to sock the reporter with the knockout punch, he had his killer lawyer Roy Cohn call to tell him the intimate secrets of Trump's incredible wealth. That's how Trump ended up in the magazine as the 286th richest man in America, worth one hundred million dollars, roughly twenty times what he was truly worth.

It bothered Trump not at all that his offer for Mar-a-Lago was in some ways insulting. He was acting as a bottom-feeder, swooping in when desperation was in the air, and he knew his time might still come. Although Trump walked away without making another offer, he kept close watch on the myriad attempts to sell the estate.

Doyle Rogers, the Palm Beach lawyer handling the sale for the Mar-a-Lago Foundation, was waiting for a deal that would prove he had been a worthy steward of the estate. Mar-a-Lago had been on the market since the U.S. government returned ownership to the Post Foundation in 1981, and it was turning out to be a hard sale. Not only was the price a stretch for all but a few Americans, but restoring the home to a level worthy of its past would take another fortune. Maintaining the house and the grounds was costing up to a million dollars a year, including taxes, legal fees, and other expenses, and the estate required a large staff to keep it running. Beyond that, many contemporary multimillionaires craved privacy and couldn't stand the idea of omnipresent employees twenty-four hours a day.

None of the Post heirs wanted anything to do with the sale. They had taken their tax write-offs when the U.S. government took possession of the property, and the sale would add nothing to their coffers. If they had cared about being good stewards of the Post legacy and the family fortunes at their most exalted, they might have paid a certain attention, but they had the lassitude of inheritors and had no interest.

It fell upon a non-blood relative, Rodion Cantacuzene, to represent the family as the Post Foundation secretary. Cantacuzene was married to Post's granddaughter Melissa. He was President Ulysses S. Grant's great-grandson, and though he had been brought up in a middle-class household, his father was a Russian prince who had lost everything in the revolution. Prince Michael taught his son that wealth and class often had little to do with each other.

Cantacuzene and his wife shared this attitude about money. The Cantacuzenes had an unpretentious farmhouse in Virginia horse country where they raised racehorses. The couple could have turned the home into a showplace, but they didn't care. Dogs and cats ran through the living room. A cat played with a pink Fabergé diadem sitting on a coffee table.

Early on in 1981, Cantacuzene had been contacted by the Marriott Corporation, which was willing to pay twenty million dollars for the property, but Marriott wanted to build a cottage community where people could come on their vacations. Town officials made it clear to Marriott that Palm Beach would likely never approve such a plan, and the company walked away.

Three years later—and after having turned down Donald Trump's nine-million-dollar offer—Cantacuzene was again closely involved on behalf of the foundation when Houston developer Cerf Ross signed a contract to purchase the estate for fourteen million dollars. Ross planned to put the home back on the market right away with only 4.1 acres of land, while breaking away the rest of the property and dividing it up into eight different parcels where luxury homes would be built. It was the kind of blatantly commercial venture that would have appalled the town council a few years earlier, but by this time, no one had lived in Mar-a-Lago for eleven years and one deal after another had fallen through.

Cantacuzene appeared before the town council seeking approval for the subdivision. "We have tried—God knows we have tried [to sell Mar-a-Lago]," he said. "We have entertained dozens of offers—some of them off-the-wall offers." He went on to declare Ross's proposal "good for Mar-a-Lago. It is what Post would have wanted to do."

Cantacuzene spoke with the imprimatur of the Post family, and he made a forceful presentation. His pitch was convincing enough that the elected officials gave Ross's plan tentative approval. But then Ross, uncertain that he could make this all work out, backed away from the deal, leaving behind a substantial deposit that was added to the Post Foundation coffers.

This was a devastating setback to Cantacuzene, who thought he finally had sold Mar-a-Lago. Cantacuzene, desperate to sell, remembered Donald Trump.

It was December, and Cantacuzene heard that the Trumps would be in Aspen for the Christmas holidays. So he called his brother's wife there and asked if she would give a dinner party for the New York couple. During the evening, she could gently nudge Trump toward buying Mar-a-Lago.

Trump arrived in a ribbed turtleneck, Ivana in a Bogner ski suit. His wife had become a prime asset, a glamorous woman who enlivened any gathering she attended. Cantacuzene's sister-in-law managed to mention Mar-a-Lago once or twice, but Trump appeared uninterested.

In the summer of 1985, yet another buyer made his way to Palm Beach, O. W. Smith, the president of a gold refinery. He was willing to pay fourteen million. But the Scotsman had one serious stipulation. The deal must include the oceanfront land in front of the mansion that the Post estate had sold to Jack Massey.

The Post Foundation's attorney Rogers could have told Smith to buy the beachfront himself. Instead, the foundation attorney signed a contract to purchase Massey's land for the astounding price of two million dollars and added it to the deal. With this, Smith had everything he wanted and more, but like his predecessors, when he looked at the total financial picture, at the last minute he gave it up, losing by his reckoning a million dollars in the process. That meant the Post Foundation still had Mar-a-Lago, but it also now had a two-million-dollar contract for the beachfront.

That was the moment in the fall of 1985 when Trump swept in with a deal that only a year before the foundation would not have even considered. "Sometimes you play dirty in life, so I snatched it," Trump was to say sixteen years later.

At this point, Trump owned two casinos in Atlantic City, the Trump Plaza and the Trump Castle, spewing out millions of dollars in cash, and he could deal in a real way. Trump's career in business had taught him to be a quick study of human character. He was not wise, but he was shrewd. He read people, not in any deep psychological sense, but what they wanted and how he could use them to get what he wanted, and he read Cantacuzene perfectly.

Trump could tell he wasn't dealing with a man who cared about the money. He craved the burden off his back. The other Post relatives didn't care, either.

They just wanted the whole business done with, so they could go on with their privileged lives without this unseemly business going on forever.

Trump also understood Rogers, and that was even more important to the deal. The lawyer was a model Palm Beach gentleman. He and his wife, Nicola, were members of the Bath and Tennis and the Everglades. Rogers was the president of the Palm Beach Civic Association and on the board of any number of nonprofits, while Nicola was a prominent real estate agent.

They were an admired couple. There were rules against doing business at their clubs, and that was just fine with the Rogerses. They could cut their deals elsewhere, with other gentlemen and ladies like themselves. No one pushed for rude advantage. No one sought unseemly bargains. Everything was aboveboard.

Life was going fine for Rogers until he so foolishly signed a two-million-dollar contract for Massey's strip of beachfront, double the appraised valuation. His wife was the Realtor for the property, a bit of synergy that in many places would have been considered unethical.

Rogers was left having to follow through with the wildly overpriced purchase or renege on it and lose the foundation's deposit, in either case a disgraceful bit of mismanagement. No one would have been so gauche as to confront him at the Everglades, but behind his back they surely would have talked, and it would not have been good for his business or his wife's.

Rogers shunned other possible buyers, who would likely have jumped at a mildly lowered price, and quickly sold to Trump for far less than any other potential offer. Trump purchased the mansion and its seventeen acres for five million dollars. Trump also paid three million dollars for the furnishings, which were estimated to be worth between three and five million dollars and in the end proved to be worth more than the highest estimate. In addition, he purchased the beachfront land for two million dollars, getting Rogers out of the trouble he'd gotten into earlier.

Palm Beach Realtors were distraught that the property had been sold without their having any inkling of the extraordinary drop in price. "I was surprised, very surprised," reflected Rodney Dillard of Sotheby International. "It's hard to believe. I would have thought the trustees would have consulted with certain real estate agents in Palm Beach who had been working with potential buyers." Dillard said his company had several interested buyers who could well have paid as much as double what Trump paid.

When the sale went through, Nicola Rogers's company got a commission of up to $120,000 as the broker for the narrow strip of beachfront property. Both Doyle and Nicola Rogers scored big windfalls from the sale. The attorney billed the Post Foundation thousands of dollars for his work, while his Realtor wife got an enormous commission. After the sale closed, Trump invited Doyle and Nicola Rogers to one of his first dinner parties at Mar-a-Lago and hired Doyle as his Palm Beach attorney. Trump may simply have come to regard Rogers enough to want to work with him, but to the skeptical observer it had all the appearances of a payoff for services rendered.

Trump worked the deal to his own advantage in other ways as well. He knew that in Palm Beach, he would be living with some of the biggest players in America. To most of them, having a home mortgage signaled that you weren't really one of them. So Trump paid cash, writing the multimillion-dollar check without flinching.

Trump could do that because he had gotten a secret $8.5 million loan from the Chase Manhattan Bank. Trump used eight million dollars of that to buy Mar-a-Lago and its furnishings. The remaining five hundred thousand dollars became a down payment for the oceanfront strip, with the owner giving him a $1.5 million mortgage to complete the deal. Trump put up $2,812 to pay for recording fees and such. Today, Mar-a-Lago is worth as much as half a billion dollars, making Trump's initial purchase one of the greatest residential real estate deals in American history. And he did it with less than three thousand dollars of his own money.

Most of Trump's new Palm Beach neighbors were older and had the glories of their careers largely in the past, but thirty-nine-year-old Trump was a phenomenon of the moment. A man of unbridled ambition, he owned casinos in Atlantic City and a football team in the fledgling United States Football League, and on the West Side of Manhattan, he was planning to construct the tallest building in the world (a project that never came to fruition).

The way Trump saw the world, you had to get bigger and bigger and higher and higher or you were headed down to the abyss. From his first appearance on the *Forbes* list in 1982—credited wrongly with one hundred million dollars—he kept pushing and pushing until in 1985 *Forbes* gave Trump a worth of six hundred million dollars, a figure far beyond reality. That six hundred million dollars became his signature, his crucial identity as he arrived in Palm Beach.

Two weeks after Trump signed the contract for Mar-a-Lago, a front-page story in the *Palm Beach Daily News* listed "Who's Who in Palm Beach." The newspaper was must reading for most people on the island. The daily had gotten its nickname the "Shiny Sheet" because it was printed on paper whose ink did not rub off on readers' hands.

Although Trump had yet to spend a night at Mar-a-Lago, he was the only person the Shiny Sheet placed in the three major categories. The six hundred million dollars credited to Trump by *Forbes* tied him for the fourth-richest person on the island, in a group of "Super Rich," all of whom were decades older than he was. Money talked loud and clear. Palm Beachers pretended that what mattered in their seasonal paradise was a person's class and culture, but they looked with laser intensity at the new arrival, figuring where he stood in the hierarchy of wealth and how warmly he should be greeted.

The paper also named Trump one of the island's "Celebrities," and he was deemed one of the "Socialites," a title that would have astounded the Park Avenue set in Manhattan, who wanted nothing to do with him. In New York, Donald didn't do the things a wealthy person is supposed to do to be socially accepted. He rarely attended charity events and his name was not on the list of generous donors to institutions like the opera or the Metropolitan Museum, where one could rub shoulders and dollars with what was left of the old elite.

Trump didn't like to be around people he deemed inferior, and that was his judgment of almost all of humanity. "For the most part, you can't respect people because most people aren't worthy of respect," Trump reflected to *The New York Times* in 2016. He looked out on a world that he thought full of the mediocre. Society types—his new Palm Beach neighbors—were among his least favorite members of the human species. "I generally find them to be extremely unattractive people, among the most unattractive I've ever met," Trump told *New York* in 1990. "I find women that try to make themselves more attractive by putting on $25,000 dresses, and then they walk into the ballroom and nobody notices them anyway."

Many on the island saw Trump as both a trip to the future and a ride into the past. "Will Trump, the parvenu, the man who once wore maroon suits, be considered too *outré* for the inner circle of island society?" asked the *Palm Beach Post*. "Donald Trump has a lot of qualities Palm Beachers admire—money, youth and a flair for the grand entrance," wrote Clarke Ash, a columnist for the *Post*. "People there are hoping the colorful Trump might restore the kind of verve that has characterized Palm Beach social life through the ages."

Crucial to how Palm Beach accepted the real estate magnate was Ivana, his wife and the mother of their three children. When Trump was starting out in real estate, he hadn't wanted to get sucked into a dynastic marriage that was more a coupling of fortunes than of a woman and a man, and he avoided shepherding around the daughters of wealth in Manhattan.

Trump had met Ivana Zelnicek, a Czech model and expert skier living in Montreal, at Maxwell's Plum, a New York art deco watering hole where the models were thin and the drinks stiff. Trump liked tall women, and the first thing he noticed about Ivana was that she was a spectacular six feet tall. Born in Gottwaldov, Czechoslovakia, to a Czech father and Austrian mother, Ivana escaped the gray world of Communist Czechoslovakia by marrying an Austrian businessman. When she and Trump met, she was no longer married but was dating a Czech skier, George Syrovatka, with whom she had been living in Canada.

Ivana spoke with a thick accent accompanied by garbled syntax. Although Ivana claimed she had been an Olympic skier, nobody had any record of it. She boasted that she had been a top model, but the closest she had come to that was walking the runways in Montreal department stores. After meeting Trump, Ivana quickly dumped the skier and started a relationship with the real estate developer. They were married in April 1977.

With Mar-a-Lago theirs, the Trumps set their sights on gaining membership to the most elite social circles Palm Beach had to offer. Their guest list for their first dinner party, for thirty-two people, at Mar-a-Lago included two of the most powerful political and social figures in Palm Beach, town council president Paul Ilyinsky and former mayor Earl E. T. Smith. Both men were old enough to have known Marjorie Merriweather Post and to have experienced some of the social life of her era.

Every time the two elderly gentlemen came to the mansion, they thought of life at Mar-a-Lago in Mrs. Post's days. "It was mind-boggling, a sort of fairyland, a Sigmund Romberg fantasy set," Ilyinsky said, referring to the composer of such operettas as *The Student Prince*.

The Trumps cut bold, youthful figures on the island quite unlike anyone else. The eternally blond Ivana wore one stunning designer dress after another. The charismatic Trump had small blue eyes that often darted back and forth with the nervous energy of a squirrel.

In their first months in Palm Beach, Donald and Ivana did all the expected things one should do to gain entree to Palm Beach society. They went to several charity balls, and Trump signed on to be the honorary chairman of the 1986 Heart Ball. Attending the galas reminded Trump how much he disliked these events. In the first place, he had long since considered these massive gatherings machines for passing on disease. When somebody thrust his hand out to him and expected him to grasp it, he practically saw and felt the germs crawling up his arm.

His late brother, Fred Jr., had been an alcoholic, and Trump didn't drink. In a large gathering, he liked to sip his drink though a straw rather than risk getting sick from a contaminated glass. Beyond that, Trump liked simple food, meat loaf or a hamburger, and these charity galas generally had the most extravagant menus.

Although Trump had created an image of himself as a flamboyant extrovert, he was more a cured introvert, a loner whose life was a theatrical display. In events like these Palm Beach galas, he was just another guest in black tie, and he largely receded into the background.

Because Trump was so self-absorbed, it was hard to realize what insight he had into his own psyche and the social world around him. For the most part, he considered these balls little more than gatherings of "The Lucky Sperm Club," a room "full of phonies and unattractive people who often have done nothing smarter than inherit somebody else's wealth." They talked enthusiastically about little but the last gathering of the club.

In their most significant social gesture, the Trumps agreed to host the annual Preservation Foundation of Palm Beach Ball at Mar-a-Lago. The foundation was generally considered the most prestigious organization on the island. Its goal was "preserving our architectural and cultural heritage and the unique scenic quality of Palm Beach." The Preservation Foundation had been holding its annual ball at the shuttered Mar-a-Lago, the one event still held at the estate. The affair had taken on a haunted quality as many of the guests wondered if the estate would join all the others and be torn down.

Its members looked up and down the Florida coast and across the Intracoastal Waterway to West Palm Beach and saw the growing array of high-rise condominiums, and they vowed to fight to maintain the villagelike essence of Palm Beach. The era when the megawealthy aspired to live in monumental estates appeared to be over, and one by one the largest mansions, emblematic of the old Palm Beach world, had been torn down. One of the few left and the greatest of them all was Mar-a-Lago, the de facto symbol of their movement.

There was great excitement leading up to the evening at the newly reopened Mar-a-Lago for the March 1986 event, when guests would get a chance to see what the new owners had done with the place. All of the 450 tickets sold, at five hundred dollars apiece, as soon as the evening was announced. That's when Ivana decided she wasn't going to have her exquisite estate overrun by lookie-loos, and she announced that only 350 guests could attend. The organizers had to disappoint one hundred would-be attendees and pay back fifty thousand dollars, most of which would have gone to further the foundation's work.

The more Ivana thought about it, the more she realized she couldn't tolerate these people invading her precious realm. The Trumps told the committee that the gala could not take place inside the mansion and that the Preservation Foundation would have to rent a tent for the property. The Trumps didn't seem to grasp that these were the crème de la crème, who were not about to stain the ornate sofas with greasy hands.

The dinner-dance guests were allowed to enter through the house in their finery on the way out to the tent. Ivana's new butler, forty-eight-year-old E. James Illenye, stood at the entrance with a ramrod posture. He called Ivana "Madame," while the lesser butlers referred to her as "Mrs. Trump." Illenye had previously worked for Saudi Arabia's King Faisal and Jordan's King Hussein and treated the Trumps like royalty. (A few months later, Illenye's teenage male lover murdered him in "a fit of rage and anger" in the home they shared.)

Trump invited Robin Leach, the host of the syndicated television show *Lifestyles of the Rich and Famous*, along with his camera crew to cover the ball. "There were some frowns of disapproval from other members of the media as we were the only press allowed inside," Leach recalled. It wasn't just the media frowning. The other guests were used to the *Palm Beach Daily News* photographer taking flattering pictures of those entering in their formal wear, but for most of the island's history, it had been unthinkable to have a reporter inside sitting down to dinner.

As far as many of the guests were concerned, Leach and his colleagues didn't belong on the island at all. Although inviting him to Mar-a-Lago for the event went against the rules of the old Palm Beach, Trump wasn't going to let his purchase of the historic estate go unnoticed. He had ordered the hedges trimmed way down so everyone passing by could see what he owned. *CBS Sunday Morning* had already shot a segment, but that show was for an older audience watching TV on Sunday mornings. *Lifestyles* went out to a far broader audience of gawkers. In many ways, the show was a forerunner of the kind of reality TV programming that would propel Trump to greater levels of fame in the future.

Trump had appeared on the first episode of Leach's show in 1984. At that point, the real estate developer was far less famous than any of the other subjects, including Princess Diana, Cher, and Burt Reynolds, but Leach felt that even if Trump didn't represent the "fame," he certainly had the "rich" part of his show's title, although even that was not as true as Leach thought it was. The two men also trafficked in endless hyperbole. "Rome wasn't built in a day, but it might have been—and at a handsome profit—if this man lived there: Donald J. Trump," the narrator bubbled in the segment. "Even his peers, few that there are, hold him in awe. He puts deals together like other people play Monopoly."

Lifestyles linked wealth and celebrity in ways they rarely had been and perfectly articulated Trump's own beliefs and what was beginning to happen in America. He usually hated evenings like the Preservation Foundation Ball, but he somehow instinctively knew this was the beginning of his making the old Palm Beach part of *his* movie.

By forcing the ball into a tent and inviting a guest who did not belong in such company, Trump had sent a clear message that he didn't intend to be an old-school gentleman of the Palm Beach form. Some of the guests thought Trump was such a lowlife that he hadn't even grasped what he had done. But a few understood the other alternative, that he didn't care what they thought. He was going to do just what he wanted to do.

When the Trumps flew down to Palm Beach most weekends, they often brought prominent New Yorkers with them and gave dinner parties mainly for outsiders. One of their first dinners was for Trump's longtime lawyer and mentor Roy Cohn. As Trump had known for years, Cohn was a closeted homosexual. The lawyer was dying of AIDS. He continued to maintain that he was straight and that he had liver cancer, while also pretending to be a patriot, even though he was on the verge of disbarment and the U.S. government said he owed almost seven million dollars in unpaid taxes.

As a young lawyer, still in his early twenties, Cohn had helped lead Julius and Ethel Rosenberg to the electric chair and later sat beside Senator Joseph McCarthy in his demagogic hearings ferreting out supposed Communists. Cohn seemed to know everyone in New York and to have negative information about most of them.

Cohn was the city's ultimate fixer. A brilliant if disorganized lawyer, he had so few scruples that he was at times under indictment himself. In his legal practice in New York City, Cohn traveled from the heights of society to the depths among mobsters and criminals. He knew how to get things done.

Trump met Cohn for the first time one evening at Le Club, a private nightclub frequented by a certain class of prominent New Yorkers, and the two men hit it off. They shared similar attitudes on life and approaches to business. Trump might sing rhapsodies about the glories of the free enterprise system, but in the world of commercial real estate, tax abatements and other governmental perks often determined whether or not real money was made. If you didn't get those advantages—and get them big-time—you were finished before you began. Trump reached out to Cohn as the man who could get him what he needed from city government.

Cohn enjoyed nothing more than sinking his incisors into an enemy. Trump quickly learned from Cohn the workings of power and politics and why it often came down to knowing a person well enough to know what he wanted and figuring out how to give it to him. Trump took Cohn's lessons to heart. He didn't care about Cohn's sexual proclivities or that he was widely reviled. Cohn was loyal to Trump, and that's all that mattered.

In March 1986, Trump gave a dinner party in Cohn's honor at Mar-a-Lago. Ivana was obsessed with the spread of AIDS. Her housekeeper said that if Ivana suspected a guest might have the disease, she ordered the silverware washed in a Clorox solution so strong that it ruined the heirloom settings.

For a man like Trump, who feared contagion from a water glass, Cohn was a plague. Yet Trump had invited him here to honor him this evening, in the end remaining loyal to his friend. Cohn looked haunted. He had lost so much weight that his famous hooded eyes had turned in on themselves and appeared embedded deep in his skull. His partner that evening was Jay Taylor, who had been Cohn's companion over the years. Palm Beach had been frequented by homosexuals since the earliest years. They were prominent among decorators and art dealers and were widely accepted, but Taylor was not the kind of gay man welcomed in the estates of Palm Beach.

Everyone at the party knew this was the last time they would celebrate Cohn's life. Trump was a stellar host, moving from guest to guest and asking them to give their tributes to Cohn. The guests included Chrysler CEO Lee Iacocca, Manhattan borough president Andrew J. Stein, and his father Democratic power broker Jerry Finkelstein. And then it was over, and Cohn left Mar-a-Lago. He died that August.

❦

For the Trumps' next dinner party, Trump brought together those from the highest ranks of Palm Beach society, including his new attorney Doyle Rogers and his Realtor wife, Nicola; the Cuban Americans Alfonso and Tina Fanjul; Prince Michel de Bourbon-Parme and Princess Maria Pia di Savoia; and Sue Whitmore, one of the social queens of the island.

After dinner, when the waiters were serving coffee, Trump stood up at the head of the table. "I'd like to go around the table," he said, sweeping the room with his hand, "and have everyone get up and say a little about themselves, where they are from and what they do."

Some of these guests had attended Mrs. Post's Sunday evening square dances. To win her favor, they had moved to the commands to "allemande left" and "do-si-do," but that was one thing and this was altogether another.

One of the grandes dames rose slowly and stood quietly as she looked across the table. "I live in Palm Beach," she said finally. "And I do nothing."

With that she sat down while the other guests contemplated her words. Another of the ladies, copying the first speaker's words, rose and said, "I live in Palm Beach. And I do nothing."

Trump had merely been trying to enliven the island's tired social rituals, but he discovered that most of these people did little. That was the point. They didn't have to do anything. They stayed among their kind. They never went places where someone would ask anything so impertinent and expect one to stand up and answer.

Another of the dinner guests, Richard Cowell, observed these proceedings with astonishment. Born in 1927, Cowell had lived in one of the first fifty houses on the island and gone to the Palm Beach Day School. To him, Mar-a-Lago was not a legendary estate but the landed expanse that he and Dina Merrill, the actress and Mrs. Post's daughter, had roamed as children. Cowell was the second generation of his family to belong to the Everglades and the Bath and Tennis, and he saw himself as the keeper of certain aristocratic traditions.

Cowell watched that evening at Mar-a-Lago with bemused fascination as Trump belly-flopped in front of the social arbiters of the island. "All of the top people were there, the peak of the Bath and Tennis and the Everglades," Cowell said three decades later, his memory vivid. "Everybody was laughing at him.

That was his first major blunder with that group." The guests left right after coffee, and by the next morning the story of Trump's behavior was all over the island.

Trump paid no attention to the naysayers. He would rise to the heights of Palm Beach life, and Mar-a-Lago would be the splendid device that would take him there. Trump knew when he purchased Mar-a-Lago that it would take several million dollars to restore the estate to pristine condition. He had no problem with that. His directive was to return the historic home to what it had been, not to do what could be done within a certain budget. He liked to do things quickly, but he understood that this was a project that could take years.

One weekend, Trump drove up to Mar-a-Lago in a limousine. His three young children, Donald Jr., Eric, and Ivanka, jumped out of the vehicle and started running up and down the drive. As Trump corralled his kids, he saw a worker on a scaffold up near the top of the tower. Trump stood beneath, looking up, and shouted, "You're doing a great job!" He had no idea what the man was doing or how well he was doing it, but it was a strong gesture of encouragement. The worker, Richard Haynes, could barely hear what Trump was saying and climbed down the ladder to meet his boss.

Haynes told Trump that his father, Wiley T. Haynes, had been the chief gilder when Mrs. Post built Mar-a-Lago. Gilding is the craft of applying gold leaf to surfaces, originally practiced in Europe. The elder Haynes had taught himself how to do the complicated job. His son told Trump that his father was the reason the tower and much that was inside Mar-a-Lago glowed with a brilliant sheen from the meticulously applied gold leaf. So much gold leaf had been used in the project that for a while almost none was left elsewhere in America.

Even after the initial work was finished, Wiley Haynes continued working for Mrs. Post, and his son recalled visiting the estate as a boy. Wiley taught his son the gilding process, and when he encountered Trump that day, Richard was revitalizing the work his father had first done more than half a century before.

The Haynes men were of a sort common in Europe but almost extinct in America. Proud artisans comfortable with their place in their world, they sought nothing else because they had everything they felt worth seeking. Richard's father was still alive, and occasionally he dropped by, walking with a cane, to observe his son's handiwork.

The gold leaf came in three-inch-square sheets that were thinner than tissue. An untrained hand risked dissolving the squares into powder. Only after the surface to be gilded was sanded, smoothed, painted a gold finish, and prepared with liquid sizing would Haynes take out a gold leaf square and set it down with precision. He slowly and meticulously reapplied the twenty-three-karat gold leafing, working at his own pace in his own way.

"If you need more gold, we'll get it," Trump said. In restoring Mar-a-Lago, Trump was developing a fixation with gold that would make James Bond's nemesis Goldfinger seem a piker.

Trump named Haynes artist in residence, and that he truly was. He did much more than apply gold leaf. He went around to the faded murals and restored them so that the images were once again vividly alive, even though they still looked centuries old.

Mrs. Post had lived in the mansion for only two months each winter, from Christmas to Washington's Birthday, yet it was stunning how much she accumulated. One day workers opened up the safe and found a collection of gold-plated settings and silverware. "There was such beautiful stuff in there," Haynes recalled, "but Mr. Trump really didn't care about most of it. He would say, 'I don't want that.'" Most of the unwanted items were ferreted away to be sold later.

Trump even wanted to get rid of the meticulously decorated 1927 Steinway baby grand piano in the living room and replace it with a new one. It took all Haynes's persuasion to convince Trump that the piano should stay and that Haynes could restore it.

When Haynes took a break, he often wandered the mansion, discovering all kinds of marvelous and strange things in the attic. Once, on the second floor, he found the peephole Mrs. Post used to spy down on her guests and pointed it out to Trump. "Before the days of tape recorders, she used to sit up there and listen to people as they came in," Trump later said. "If they said anything she didn't like, they'd never be invited to another party. They'd be banned, and they never knew why."

Trump's young daughter Ivanka discovered the peephole, too. When her parents were having their dinner parties, she sat up there with her friends observing the goings-on below.

Trump also knew that most of Mar-a-Lago's original furnishings needed to be reconditioned, and even before he closed on the property, he hired an interior decorator who specialized in restoration, a field that in South Florida was almost nonexistent.

Buffy Donlon had grown up in the small southern town of Selma, Alabama. Her mother taught her to treasure the possessions of the past. "I'm a product of my upbringing, and china, crystal, and linens are the epitome of everything," Donlon said. These objects were passed on from generation to generation as a proud part of one's heritage.

During Donlon's first visit to Mar-a-Lago, she walked into the butler's pantry, where she discovered nineteen sets of china, each with a service for thirty-six. It was all of the finest quality, impeccably maintained, and the sheer magnitude was overwhelming. There were also two hundred silverware place settings.

Then Donlon went into the dining room and on the table found stacks of linens rising toward the ceiling. Ivana was with her when they came upon the linens. Donlon recalled: "[She] made this call and said to her friend she just couldn't believe that she was going to be the mistress of this house and that it had such fabulous linens and china."

Donlon continued through the fifty-eight bedrooms and twenty-seven servants' rooms, which would be her domain for many months. The house contained fifty-three thousand movable items, and she had to deal with each one in some manner.

The bedrooms had only one thing in common: on each dresser was a cheap ice bucket emblazoned with the words TRUMP CASTLE. Donlon cringed as she saw those. This was precisely what the gatekeepers of Palm Beach were looking to find—some unconscious vulgarity that would mark the new owners as unworthy of inhabiting Mar-a-Lago.

Donlon wasn't the only one put off by the plastic ice buckets from Trump's Atlantic City casino. "Well, you just don't do those things," said Reidun Torrie, a Mar-a-Lago maid who was so aghast at the Trumps' behavior that after working at the estate for the five previous years, she quit three months after the Trumps arrived. "They have no class," Torrie said.

Part of the problem Trump had with the estate's staff members—and which left them disgruntled—was that he did not believe his Palm Beach employees should be tipped. Weekend guests were used to leaving a few dollars in their bedroom for the housekeeper, or slipping a ten-dollar bill to someone who had been especially helpful, but Trump made it clear that was inappropriate. "They wouldn't let us accept gratuities," one of the employees told the *Palm Beach Post*.

Then there were the meals. It was tradition in Palm Beach that anyone who worked in a home got free lunch. It may not have been filet mignon, but it was something decent. Like tipping, Trump considered that an excessive perk.

Torrie didn't say it outright, but she felt she appreciated and respected Mar-a-Lago more than her employers did. Not only did Ivana have bad taste, but she had "steel rods up her nose—and a hot temper." As for the master of the house, Trump watched television in bed while eating fried chicken on top of a precious lace bedspread.

Others found that same conduct unpretentious and charming. The columnist Liz Smith, a frequent weekend guest, recalled, "He liked to get in bed at night and watch sports events on television, and eat a hamburger. That was his idea of heaven."

Many on the island felt there was just something about the Trumps that was a little off, and it wasn't just about tawdry ice buckets. Ivana was on the cover of *Town & Country*, a magazine read by many in Palm Beach, photographed in a number of elegant ball gowns at Mar-a-Lago. But then she would be seen driving down Worth Avenue in her flashy Mercedes with its IVANA license plate. The other wealthy people drove fancy cars, but in more subtle blacks and blues, without advertising who they were and why they had money. Ivana was just a little too showy, and she had a mouth so foul that she would have made a sailor blush.

Interior decorator Donlon thought it wrong, even cruel, the way so many on the island looked down on the Trumps. Particularly glaring from the beginning was that Donald and Ivana were not invited to join the Bath and Tennis Club. This was especially significant because the club was almost directly adjacent to Mar-a-Lago and connected to the grounds by a tunnel Mrs. Post had built for her guests to get to the club.

Trump considered it "utter bullshit" that they hadn't been asked to join. "Do you think if I wanted to be a member, they would have turned me down?" he told *Vanity Fair* in 1990. "I wouldn't join that club, because they don't take blacks and Jews."

In fact, soon after the Trumps arrived in Palm Beach, Ivana had discussed joining with James Oelsner, the B&T president. Oelsner liked the Trumps, but he understood the dynamics of his club, and Trump was such a controversial figure that other members were sure to blackball the couple if they tried to join. The club president knew it would not be good to turn down their powerful next-door neighbor, and Oelsner did his best to convince Ivana to forget about the B&T. "I thought it would be good for everyone if they didn't apply," Oelsner said. "It would save a lot of embarrassment." Others gave Ivana's husband the same advice, and the couple decided not to apply. It would have been the same story at the Everglades Club.

So instead of making a likely futile attempt to join the restricted clubs, Trump continued to work on the restoration of his home. For the most part he stayed out of the specifics of the restoration except for a few places that were important to him. Mrs. Post had hung a small portrait of herself in the library that fit in impeccably with the European art hanging on the mansion's walls. The new owner of Mar-a-Lago wanted *his* portrait on the wall, and he gave the assignment to Palm Beach artist Ralph Wolfe Cowan. The portraitist was known for flattering his affluent subjects in what was little more than visual sycophancy.

This time Cowan outdid himself. His twenty-four-thousand-dollar portrait of the master of Mar-a-Lago, titled *The Visionary,* was far larger than Mrs. Post's and was blazingly bright. Here was the youthful Donald in a white sweater and pants, the sinewy, strong form of a young Adonis with a face that looked like a movie star's. The portrait was hung in place of Mrs. Post's, replacing the old with the decidedly new.

4

Tabloid Prince

Trump flew down to Palm Beach almost every weekend during the winter season. One day early in 1986, Trump was driving alone in West Palm Beach when he saw twin spires rising thirty-two stories. In Manhattan, the structure would have been in the shadow of scores of buildings, but here it dominated the horizon, the tallest structure in West Palm Beach, looking down on Palm Beach across the Intracoastal Waterway.

Trump believed that some people had good timing and good luck, and when he learned about the building, he felt once again he had both. The twin towers were called "The Plaza." The structure had been built as upscale condominiums, but the builder was about to be foreclosed in a ninety-one-million-dollar judgment. The Plaza was only weeks away from being sold at auction on the county courthouse steps.

If Trump had talked to those who knew about South Florida real estate, they would have told him there are good neighborhoods in West Palm Beach, but that the area around the Plaza was not one of them and it had been a mistake to build a massive upscale condominium in such a place. Trump operated from his gut, not from expensive research, which he felt was full of ands, ifs, and buts created by hand-wringers. He believed that most people were hapless losers, without the gumption to take real chances. It took people like him to make things happen.

Trump had begun his career as a builder, but he was becoming more a real estate investor, putting his name on properties that often had been built by others. He cut deals and then moved on. The world had only a few great deal-makers, and Trump saw himself as one of them.

That was the Donald Trump who in July won the auction for the Plaza in West Palm Beach at a net bid of forty-one million dollars. The Bank of New York, which had originally financed the project, was the big loser. As for the big winner, Trump named himself. How could he not win buying this new building for less than half what it cost to construct? To pay for the Plaza, Trump took out a sixty-million-dollar loan from the Marine Midland Bank, which gave him nineteen million dollars to finish the building in style.

To manage the project, Trump brought down Richard Maloney, one of his casino executives. Maloney wasn't just selling condominiums in the twin-towered building. He was selling Donald Trump. "He's the biggest thing to hit Palm Beach since John Kennedy," Maloney said. "They both have the same charisma."

While Realtors in the county shook their heads at the idea that Trump could sell scores of condos in West Palm Beach at above-market prices from $272,000 to $1.5 million per unit, Maloney tried to paint a picture of Palm Beachers running across the bridge to get into the action. "It was unbelievable," Maloney said as he tried to hype things up. "People came with their checks in hand. They were just waiting."

Trump didn't leave the promoting to Maloney. He went to work selling the condos with a flick of his silver tongue. Want to know who my partner is? Trump boastfully asked. Lee Iacocca, the chairman of Chrysler and the most admired businessman in America. He asked how buyers could go wrong with the team of Trump/Iacocca.

Iacocca had purchased three apartments in the condominium that he quickly resold, but Iacocca was not Trump's partner. Iacocca didn't publicly challenge Trump, but this taught him enough about Trump to keep his distance.

Trump named his newest purchase "Trump Plaza of the Palm Beaches." He believed that people wanted to get near him and have his money rub off on them. What better way than living in a building with TRUMP in bold letters on a one-ton brass-and-granite marquee at the top of the twin towers?

Trump believed that the building's success depended on convincing buyers that owning a piece of Trump Plaza carried with it the full cachet of Palm Beach. He did this not just by putting his name on the building, but by locating it in an imaginary community he called the Palm Beaches. He wanted buyers to pay the same price for a condo in West Palm Beach as they would for one on the ocean in Palm Beach. "I expect a great many residents from Palm Beach to move up to the 'Trump Plaza of the Palm Beaches' in the next year," Trump said.

"Looking down at Palm Beach" was the early advertising slogan for the building. That may have simply been referring to the splendid views from the higher floors, but many in Palm Beach saw it as an arrogant dismissal of the island. It was just another reason for Palm Beach society to want nothing to do with Trump.

Trump was right that if you looked east from the upper windows of Trump Plaza, the view of the Palm Beach skyline was far more interesting than merely seeing ocean looking out from the island. "I wish I could transform these views over to Mar-a-Lago, because there's nobody over in Palm Beach that has anything even closely comparable to that," Trump said.

Unfortunately, if you looked directly down from the building, you saw a strip of concrete running along the Intracoastal Waterway, which was decidedly not for swimming. To the west was a Haitian community, and beyond that were slums as bad as those on the South Side of Chicago. "Two blocks away they are practicing voodoo," one real estate agent told *The Wall Street Journal*, hardly a reassuring statement to skittish potential buyers.

The advertising copywriters knew better than to look in the wrong direction. Their newspaper ads for Trump Plaza were, by Trumpian standards, understated and elegant. One that ran at Christmastime 1986 in the *Palm Beach Post* had the words TRUMP PLAZA OF THE PALM BEACHES above a picture of two polo players and their pony. The caption read: "Donald has such a knack for picking the right neighborhood."

But Trump hadn't picked the right neighborhood, and potential purchasers realized it. The hype and exaggerations had not worked, and the condominiums were not selling in anything like the numbers Trump and Maloney said they were. The executive had been doing what Trump told him to do, but only four months after Maloney arrived in South Florida, Trump told him to pack up his bags and fly back north to be reassigned to another executive position.

It wasn't only Maloney who had to go. Trump decided he hated the images of polo players in the ads when they should be showing the condos. So Trump fired the Miami advertising agency. He also got rid of his interior designers (including Buffy Donlon, though he let her finish up her restoration of Mar-a-Lago).

These actions created a public relations problem for Trump. Firing his entire team after only a few months sent a message that the condos weren't selling and the whole thing might collapse. Ever the master of spin, Trump had a simple explanation. His initial group had been only "temporary" to hold things down before the "permanent" team arrived. He claimed that the original employees had done "unbelievably well" and the units were selling better than great.

Trump was also developing a reputation for paying slowly or sometimes arbitrarily paying less than the amount he owed, yet he continued to hire all kinds of small businesses to work at Trump Plaza and Mar-a-Lago. He couldn't treat major corporations that way without facing the wrath of their lawyers, but the small businesses that fixed the plumbing, the electricity, or the landscaping didn't have the resources to fight back. And for them, it took only a few customers not paying their bills to move their business into financial disaster.

Scott Lewis had a small landscaping and gardening company that had worked at Mar-a-Lago during the years the estate was for sale. Scott's Garden Center wasn't large enough to handle the massive property, but the Post Foundation called in Lewis to help with the landscaping. When Trump purchased Mar-a-

Lago, Lewis continued to work on the property, and Trump hired him to do work at Trump Plaza.

That went well, too. Around Christmas 1986, Lewis received a check for 85 percent of the approximately fifteen thousand dollars Trump owed him. When Lewis called a Trump associate to ask for the rest of the money, the executive praised the landscaper and said he should go ahead with the second part of the job. "I will as soon as I get my money," Lewis said. "I'm small, and I can't afford this." The executive stonewalled Lewis and said he should continue with the work.

When Trump continued stiffing him, Lewis pondered what he should do. He knew if he fought back, Trump would no longer hire him. Beyond that, the multimillionaire could make life tough for the small West Palm Beach businessman. He was out a little less than two thousand dollars—not that much money for one person—but if Trump did this to enough people in enough ways, it became real money. Lewis decided that what Trump did was wrong. He didn't know much about the law, but he filed a small-claims suit against Trump.

Trump was known for bringing legal fire and wrath upon anyone who dared to sue him. In this instance, he used a top Florida law firm, Boose, Casey, Ciklin. On the October trial day, Lewis arrived with several witnesses including his wife, who worked as his bookkeeper, and even some Trump employees who were distressed at the way their boss had treated the landscaper.

Lewis sensed that Trump's attorney, Cory Ciklin, was ashamed and embarrassed to be representing Trump in this matter. Ciklin asked for a continuance, saying his witnesses had been "unavoidably unavailable for trial." On the new trial date, in July 1987, the lawyer did not show up, and the judge ruled in Lewis's favor. Trump had to pay the amount he owed to the landscaper. Lewis never worked for Trump again.

Trump didn't concern himself much with his endless legal squabbles. That was just part of business, as far as he was concerned, and when he was in Florida, he had a social life in Palm Beach that demanded his attention. For the second year in a row, the Trumps agreed to host the Preservation Ball at Mar-a-Lago as long as the guest list was limited to 350 and the event again took place outside in a tent.

Each social season, several storms fall upon Palm Beach, but the one that hit on this March 1987 evening was rare in its fierceness. As the guests got out of their cars and walked the few feet to the main entrance, the wind did such damage to the elaborate coiffures of the women that most of them went quickly to the ladies' room for repairs. After that, their escorts walked them to the receiving line, where the event chairman and his wife stood next to the Trumps. Donald was in black tie and Ivana in a floor-length white gown. As much as Trump abhorred stilted formalities, he was gracious at moments like this, exchanging a few words with everyone who arrived.

The Trumps had invited the television interviewer Barbara Walters and the opera star Beverly Sills for the weekend. After drinks, they and the other guests moved outside, braving the winds once again to enter the large white tent. The wind was so strong that some people worried the tent might collapse. The guests pretended that everything was right with the evening, but most of them left early, once again hurrying through the wind and the rain.

Many of those at the ball felt contempt for Trump, not only because of his refusal to allow the event to take place inside Mar-a-Lago itself, but because they believed he represented the battering ram of the vulgar new. Others looked at those same qualities and considered Trump the savior of a community that didn't realize it was slowly dying, suffocating in outdated customs and rituals.

A new generation had begun moving to Palm Beach. They were far younger than those who used to make the island their home. For the most part, they were less interested in the clubs and charity balls and the ceaseless social life. These wealthy new arrivals included forty-five-year-old designer Calvin Klein, forty-nine-year old retailing billionaire Leslie Wexner, and forty-six-year-old industrialist Nelson Peltz. In the Palm Beach world, they were positively pubescent. Not every new arrival was a billionaire, and there were so many younger people that charities such as the Norton Gallery decided to have junior committees with lower ticket prices for their galas.

"Donald Trump started the trend for self-made millionaires to appreciate the Palm Beach lifestyle," Ben Johnson, the president of Previews Realty, told the *Palm Beach Post* in 1988. "That's usually the way these things work—one person moves to a place and others follow him." Trump was loud about everything, and his actions in the area publicized the island in places and ways that once would have been unthinkable. Many Americans who had not known about Palm Beach before knew about it now because of Trump. "A lot of young people are following us to Palm Beach," Ivana told the *Palm Beach Post*.

The aristocratic old-timers, many of whom were regular attendees at the Preservation Ball, didn't want the nouveaux riches invading their island, and they thought Trump's conduct shameful. They had been brought up believing that a lady's name appeared in the paper only when she was born, married, and died, and perhaps beneath a few dignified photos in the *Palm Beach Daily News* at the Red Cross Ball or similar events. And a gentleman's name appeared hardly more often. For Trump, a day without publicity was a day without sunshine, and he was always finding ways to keep the sun shining.

Trump's obsession with publicity may have offended some in Palm Beach, but it didn't appear to bother the heir to the British crown. When Prince Charles flew into Palm Beach International Airport in March 1988 for a polo match in Wellington, he called from the plane shortly before arrival, asking if he could drop in to Mar-a-Lago to say hello.

Trump was out on the golf course, but he hurried home to greet the Prince of Wales as if he had been preparing for his arrival for days. Events like the prince's visit gave Trump reason to believe he was part of a natural aristocracy of celebrity, power, royalty, and wealth that far transcended the insular world of Palm Beach.

In his first book, *Trump: The Art of the Deal,* Trump wrote about the day in 1953 when Prince Charles's mother was crowned Queen Elizabeth in Westminster Abbey. For the first time, the ceremony was shown on television all around the world, and Trump's Scottish American mother sat in front of the TV set in her Queens living room for hours mesmerized by the royal drama.

His father kept entering and pacing around the room, appalled that his wife was squandering her day on this. "For Christ's sake, Mary," Fred Trump said. "Enough is enough, turn it off. They're all a bunch of con artists."

Donald Trump loved the splendor of the royal drama almost as much as his mother did, but his father was not wrong. It was a meticulously constructed fantasy that got the yokels to doff their hats and swoon. Trump saw both things at once and understood intuitively how useful the royal mythology might be even in a nation in which there was no nobility.

Trump had met Prince Charles and Princess Diana at the United World College Benefit at the Breakers hotel in November 1985, when he was closing on Mar-a-Lago. The royal couple had flown to the United States to be at the event the *Palm Beach Daily News* called "the biggest, most celebrated bash ever in Palm Beach."

The air of excitement that filled the ballroom had little to do with Prince Charles. When the Prince of Wales had last visited, in 1981, there had been only a few reporters covering the occasion. This time five hundred scribes from around the world scrambled for every scrap of information about Princess Diana.

This evening taught Trump what lengths supposedly democratic Americans would go to get close to royalty. The organizers of the event were charging fifty thousand dollars for a photograph with the royal couple. And people lined up like kids getting photographed with Santa Claus.

Much of this event may have enervated Trump, but it was most likely on this evening that his obsession with Princess Diana began, along with the idea that they might one day come together in a romance for the ages. She was only twenty-four years old, with a fresh-faced beauty that shone out across this room beyond any of the diamonds and other jewels. The princess wore a long-sleeved, floor-length pink velvet gown that in the context of this evening looked almost sedate and set off her radiant complexion. What a confluence of royalty, celebrity, wealth, and power, Donald Trump and Princess Diana, together. But alas, it was never to be.

To impress on the world that you were true royalty, you needed a golden palace that rose above all others, and Trump surely had that. You also needed a jet, not some measly puddle-jumper of a plane that soybean executives might use to fly for a meeting in Omaha, but a mammoth jet that could seat a couple of hundred people if you were so foolish as to configure it that way, a jet that could travel the world, a jet big enough to put the letters TRUMP in massive letters on the side. In 1987, Trump found a used 727 that he said he picked up for a mere eight million dollars, his best deal since buying Mar-a-Lago.

But that wasn't enough. You also needed a ship, not some piddly boat that could dock almost anywhere but a grand vessel that announced its presence wherever it went. Queen Elizabeth sailed the seas on the 412-foot-long royal yacht *Britannia*. Now that was a ship, and Trump yearned to have his own quasi-royal yacht, too.

When Trump learned that billionaire Adnan Khashoggi had fallen on such hard times that he had to sell *Nabila*, his eighty-million-dollar yacht named after his daughter, Trump saw an opportunity. The ship had eight staterooms and was the sixth-largest yacht in the world. At this point, Trump could borrow pretty much whatever he wanted, and he ended up buying the 286-foot yacht for twenty-nine million dollars and then put in another ten million dollars in renovations.

During the negotiations, Khashoggi asked that the ship's name be changed so he would not be haunted by his daughter's name sailing the seas, reminding him of all that had been. Trump got Khashoggi to agree to cut a million dollars off the price in return for Trump doing something he was going to do anyway. The first thing he did was to pry the name *Nabila* off the ship and replace it with, what else, his own: *Trump Princess*.

Yachts are known as pleasure ships, but Donald Trump was not about pleasure as it was commonly defined. Nor was his ship. His spokesman said the *Trump Princess* was "the floating trademark of the Trump Organization." Like everything Donald touched, the ship became a movable billboard advertising Trump. Every salon or public room on the yacht had silver-framed pictures of Ivana in a ball gown, Trump in black tie, and some of the many magazine covers that featured the Trumps. The ship had a disco, and that might have seemed like a place for a respite from the ubiquitous Trump photos, but if one looked up, flashing on the ceiling was a series of pictures of the Trumps and their homes.

The *Trump Princess* may not have been the foolishly extravagant bauble it appeared, because Trump made use of it to advance his business interests. One of the few women to head a bank in the 1980s watched as her male colleagues marched up the gangplank for mind-blowing bashes. "I wasn't invited on the yacht, and we said no when Trump came to us for a loan," says the woman banker, who prefers to remain nameless. "The old boys who run our industry were invited, and when they got off, they loaned him billions of dollars, figuring he had to be good for it."

Trump liked to lure the New York media and show off what he called "the ultimate toy" when it was docked in New York Harbor or sailed to Atlantic City and the casino high rollers came aboard. Then the ship headed down the coast to Fort Lauderdale, where wealthy friends and big players clambered on for catered meals and cocktails.

Super Bowl XXIII, in January 1989, was being played in Miami, and that afternoon the Trumps sailed there from Fort Lauderdale accompanied by Don Johnson, the star of the television show *Miami Vice*, and his movie actress wife, Melanie Griffith.

The two couples flew off the yacht's helipad on Trump's helicopter, adorned with his name and copiloted by Johnson, landing on the helipad at Joe Robbie Stadium. The prime seats were full of celebrities and many of America's leading business executives, but no one arrived with such dramatic panache as the man Ivana called "the Donald."

Trump had spent a few hours on the *Trump Princess* that day, but that was unusual. Sailing was not for him. The yacht was costing him five million dollars a year for maintenance and the thirty-one-person crew, and he hadn't gone on a single cruise himself, but the *Trump Princess* was "the ultimate toy" no longer. He wanted more: more ship, more exposure, more publicity. It wasn't because he wanted to sail the seas. It was that he was the biggest and the best, and he had to have a ship to match.

In June 1989, Trump announced that he was seeking bids to build a new ship "something in excess of 400 feet long, closer to 500 feet." It would be the most expensive yacht in the history of the world.

At the same time, Trump became convinced that his Mar-a-Lago annual taxes of $208,341 were $81,525 too high. The Palm Beach County tax appraiser based Trump's tax bill on what they thought the property would sell for in the current market. Trump felt that he should be charged based on what he had paid for Mar-a-Lago. Trump sued and won in the lower courts, but the tax appraiser appealed the case.

Trump had bragged in his 1987 number-one bestselling book *The Art of the Deal* that he had initially offered fifteen million dollars for Mar-a-Lago, when the true figure was nine million. The larger sum was grand enough to show that the entrepreneur had been willing to pay a princely amount for the estate. It also made his eventual purchase of the estate for five million dollars seem to be an even more fantastic deal than it actually was.

But now that Trump had to pay taxes, he was arguing that the Post Foundation was fortunate he had taken the unwanted relic off their hands. Reporters described an incredibly wealthy man ordering his fancy lawyers to fight over an amount of money that would run the *Trump Princess* for less than a week.

Rodion Cantacuzene had been there in 1982 when Trump initially bid nine million dollars, and he called Trump out on his untruth. "If he had offered $15 million at that time, I believe at the bottom of my heart that we would have accepted it very, very quickly," the secretary of the Post Foundation testified.

Cantacuzene was one of many witnesses in proceedings that were widely chronicled in the media. "Send him a bill for all the publicity you're giving his book in this case," Palm Beach County Circuit Judge Richard Burk told property appraiser's attorney Gaylord Wood Jr. Most public figures would have cringed at such bad publicity. Trump saw it differently. What mattered to him was that people were talking about him. The more they talked about him, the bigger he was. After a five-year struggle, he lost the appeal and had to pay the full amount of the taxes.

While the appeal was going on in June 1989, the *Palm Beach Post* published a front-page story by Frank Cerabino, a young reporter writing about Trump for the first time. Cerabino took the two pages in *The Art of the Deal* that were about the purchase of Mar-a-Lago and had the *Post* print them side by side. The journalist annotated the pages, calling out the number of things in Trump's book that had been proven untrue through testimony in the tax case. Sixteen items on those two pages were either wildly embellished or false.

Over time, the tales Trump told about the purchase would get bigger and bigger. By 2015, in an interview with *The Washington Post*, the amount he initially offered for Mar-a-Lago had become a whopping twenty-eight million dollars, an offer that would have had the guardians of the estate waltzing through the living room in ecstasy. And he had a new twist on the story. Trump told *The Washington Post* that when his offer was rejected, he went ahead and bought the beachfront and threatened to build a house so large that it would block Mar-a-Lago's ocean view. "That was my first wall," Trump said. "That drove everybody nuts. They couldn't sell the big house because I owned the beach, so the price kept going down and down."

The 1989 *Palm Beach Post* article exposed how differently Trump and journalists saw the world. Reporters gathered those often dreary, pedestrian things called facts. But look how beautiful facts looked when blown up like hot air balloons and painted in bold colors. That way a smart fellow could turn black into white, brass into gold, and the mediocre into the extraordinary.

At about the same time as the *Palm Beach Post* story ran, Trump spoke on the record during a phone call from Wayne Grover, a journalist working for the *National Enquirer*. Few public figures would have accepted a call from a reporter working for the tabloid. In doing so, Trump began what became arguably the most consequential media relationship of his life.

In 1952, Generoso Pope Jr. purchased the largely moribund weekly, in part, allegedly, with a loan from mob boss Frank Costello. In 1971, Pope brought the publication from New York to its new nondescript, utilitarian headquarters in Lantana, ten miles and a universe away from Palm Beach. The MIT graduate had a brilliant understanding of what the American masses wanted to read, and he built the regular circulation as high as five million, making it by far the largest-selling weekly in America. The core audience was working-class Americans—largely ignored by the establishment media and political establishment—who got much of their news from a tabloid they picked up at their local supermarket.

The *National Enquirer* succeeded because it maintained a consistent world-view and a few major themes that never varied. In the coming decades, scores of stories about Trump in the weekly would highlight most of those themes. One was unlikely ways to make big bucks, and you can do it, too.

The first story about Trump, resulting from his interview with Wayne Grover and published in November 1988, was headlined: HE GETS $10 MILLION ESTATE AND $2 MILLION—FOR JUST $2,812. The two million dollars came when Trump refinanced the ten-million-dollar purchase with a new twelve-million-dollar mortgage.

The story began, "You've heard real estate tycoon Donald Trump is a genius—and boy, did he just prove it!" The piece went on to quote Trump as saying, "When you are trusted, and have a reputation for honest dealing, near miracles can be worked."

After that first story, Wayne Grover wrote to Trump's assistant, Norma I. Foederer, letting her know he wanted to write about Trump's teenage years. Foederer replied in a letter three days later and complimented him on his first story. She gave Grover a quote from Trump and the name and phone number of Jeffrey Walker, a top executive in the Trump organization. She also told Grover about Trump's life as a teenager at the New York Military Academy.

Foederer's letter said her boss had been an excellent student and a superb athlete. He wrestled at 180 pounds, played football, and was the best baseball player on the team. He was so good that "professional baseball teams asked him to try out, including the Chicago White Sox, but he had other interests."

The letter said nothing about the emotional realities of Trump's childhood and why he ended up at the military academy. His parents raised him in the disengaged manner common among the American upper class (though seen less in families that achieved riches for the first time).

"The most important influence on me, growing up, was my father, Fred Trump," Trump wrote in *The Art of the Deal*. "I learned about toughness in a very tough business." It was not just toughness in real estate, but to have a mercilessly tough attitude toward life. There were winners and losers, and in their ascent, the winners miss nothing, small or large. Blood relationships mattered beyond all else. To fail was to bring disgrace not only on oneself but on the Trump name.

Foederer's letter to Grover did not mention what a belligerent child Trump had been. "In the second grade I actually gave a teacher a black eye," Trump wrote in *The Art of the Deal*. "I punched my music teacher because I didn't think he knew anything about music, and I almost got expelled." The teacher, Charles Dodsley Walker, was the organist at the Church of the Heavenly Rest in Manhattan and presumably knew more about music than his unruly student.

That story is not an example of Trump's hyperbole, but is remembered by fellow students. In most schools, Donnie's misconduct would have gotten him thrown out, but his father was a generous donor, and that likely had something to do with why Trump stayed in school.

"I loved to fight," Trump reflected years later. "I always loved to fight." That sentiment did not make its way into the tabloid account, nor did the fact that the Trumps sent their son upstate to the New York Military Academy because he was so troubled. The *National Enquirer* story was a sanitized, romanticized account of Trump's complicated, often difficult childhood. The headline described the story perfectly: DONALD TRUMP WAS AN AMAZING SUCCESS— EVEN AS A TEEN: HONOR STUDENT, STAR ATHLETE, CLASSY DANCER & LADIES' MAN.

This *National Enquirer* story was but one example of how well Trump had learned to use the media. When he wanted something to happen, usually the first thing he did was to manage press accounts to his advantage. That's what he did when he became fixated on the planes that flew out of Palm Beach International Airport over Mar-a-Lago. It wasn't just the noise that rankled him; he also believed the planes were spilling fuel that was slowly destroying his precious estate.

There was a problem with the overflying planes, but when something troubled Trump, he wildly exaggerated his woes, and the planes were hardly dumping fuel. Moreover, he was not innocent. One of the noisiest of the planes was Trump's vintage Boeing 727, but at least he didn't have to hear that one.

Trump was so concerned with the planes that in February 1988, he called a press conference and talked to forty reporters at Trump Plaza. "Palm Beach should riot over what's happening with this airport," he said. It was hard to imagine the lords and ladies of the island smashing windows along Worth Avenue, but Trump made it clear they were not the only people he was addressing. "I'm talking about all of Palm Beach," he said.

It was not part of Trump's persona to spin chamber of commerce homilies saying that everyone should work together. Instead, he attacked. The airport was "too close to too many homes" and "shouldn't be allowed to be there."

In seeking the biggest, boldest headline, Trump shouted that the answer was to move what he called "the worst-managed airport" he had ever seen south to Lantana. The small community was already a dumping place for things nobody of consequence wanted around them, including three prisons.

Trump received a lot of media coverage that day, but the attention he called to himself distracted from the very real issue of the noise and what might be done to lessen it. Trump had not taken the time to learn what people in West Palm Beach felt. After decades of being considered nothing more than a low-scale service center for Palm Beach, the city was finally coming into its own. Its citizens took pride in Palm Beach International Airport, which had just undergone a sixty-million-dollar renovation. Residents may have agreed that the planes were too loud, but few people wanted to get rid of the airport.

The Good Neighbor Council for Control of Airport Noise had other supporters, but voters associated the issue with Trump and his outrageous demands. The group endorsed the two leading candidates for Palm Beach County Commission, James Quigley and Robert Wexler. But on Election Day, they lost to obscure opponents who were pushed to victory by the voters' visceral dislike of Trump. "The problem was the Donald Trump thing," Quigley said. "Voters perceived me as being involved in something bad because Donald Trump is involved."

Reporters were delighted to watch the well-heeled sitting upset by their heated pools as the planes soared above their heads. "Whenever I hear Palm Beachers complain about airport noise, I'm overcome with *schadenfreude*," wrote Dexter Filkins, a *Miami Herald* columnist.

"If Trump got his wish, which he has so clumsily tried to buy, the airport would be moved 10 miles to the south," Filkins wrote. "The idea that the County Commission would actually sell the 1,500-acre airport could only be advocated by someone as spoiled as Trump."

Trump believed that turning the other cheek was for poets and priests. He was so upset with the *Miami Herald* that a week after the column appeared, he had his ad agency cancel $150,000 in advertising for Trump Plaza.

Trump walked through life with a public smirk on his famous face, but beneath that he was full of inchoate anger. He would lash out like a Florida summer storm arising out of a sunny sky, and then just as suddenly return to his seemingly placid self. He knew he was smarter than anyone else. That his purchase of Trump Plaza was proving to be a disaster couldn't be his fault, but he was having a hard time finding who else to blame. He had been right that the miserable West Palm Beach Airport should be moved to the dumps of Lantana, but the foolish people of Palm Beach County turned against *him* and voted in commissioners who didn't understand.

It wasn't easy being Trump and being right so often when others were wrong. But he was not a man who gave up. He would find a way to get precisely what he wanted. It might take longer than he wanted, but he would get there or his name wasn't Donald J. Trump.

5

"Is That All There Is?"

Palm Beach was an island ruled mainly by women, and at Mar-a-Lago, Ivana Trump reigned supreme. Every weekend she invited a number of notable friends from New York to come down to Palm Beach. Among them were the New York *Daily News* columnist Liz Smith and the *New York Post*'s Aileen Mehle, aka Suzy, who repaid her generosity by celebrating the Trumps regularly in their syndicated columns. "What was to dislike about the Trumps?" recalled Smith shortly before her death in 2017. "They were very generous and genial. They seemed innocent and on the make, like everybody else in New York."

The Trumps' marriage would go down one day in a blaze of publicity devoured by millions, but the relationship truly ended on these long weekends at Mar-a-Lago when the couple confronted the reality that there was little left between them. Each saw what the other had become and neither one liked the picture.

Ivana had done everything—the executive jobs, the effort to stay thin, the work on her face—largely to hold on to her husband, but none of it mattered. Trump needed to come strutting into a room with a woman on his arm whom every man desired, not meandering in latched to a woman approaching middle age with the body of a mother who had thrice given birth and the droning voice of a bossy businesswoman.

Ivana filled her guests' days with activities, from massages and tennis to walks on the beach and kibitzing at the pool. She treated them with a schedule and activities worthy of a resort hotel. Her husband had little interest in this and considered most of her guests either silly socialites or women who made their living reporting on the inanities of this social world. He spent much of his time in his austere bedroom, watching sports on television, zapping around the channels like he was playing a slot machine, and doing anything but spending time with his wife.

In the evenings, Ivana had dinner parties where her guests mixed with Shiny Sheet notables. Trump was civil enough to his wife's guests, though he rarely turned on the burners the way he did if he wanted to impress someone, and he usually tried to get away as early as he could. He thought he was being polite, but Mehle and Smith were not stupid, and they could see he wanted little to do with his wife or her friends.

Trump didn't appear to be happy. Then again, he didn't know anybody great who was happy. And that's what he sought—greatness—not some blissful state. One of his favorite songs was the lament sung by Peggy Lee, "Is That All There Is?"

> *Is that all there is?*
> *Is that all there is?*
> *If that's all there is, my friends, then let's keep dancing*
> *Let's break out the booze and have a ball*
> *If that's all there is*

Whatever he did, however much he accomplished, it didn't give him the satisfaction he thought it would. He wanted more—more money, sex, power, deals, attention, and celebrity. Just more. He had only one subject that profoundly interested him. That was Donald J. Trump.

Trump had made Ivana president of the Trump Castle Hotel and Casino in

Atlantic City. She may have taken the job largely to please her husband, but she took her position seriously. The Trumps sometimes passed each other in the air, as she flew in a helicopter back to Manhattan from Atlantic City to spend the evenings with their children, and he flew to the gambling capital to oversee his casinos there.

Ivana was almost as good as her husband at generating publicity. The papers contained no end of stories about this devoted mother who was also brilliantly running the casino. None of the stories reported that the bottom line was deteriorating, Ivana's often abrasive management style wasn't helping, and Ivana's work was creating tensions in their marriage.

"Instead of having a wife, I had a businessperson, and that was not so good," Trump reflected to Howard Stern in 1997, not mentioning that it had been his idea. "And all of a sudden, I'd come home, and she'd say, 'Here's what we'll do tomorrow.'"

Things were so troubled in Atlantic City that in 1988 Trump removed his wife, but to prevent public relations problems, he announced that Ivana would become the president and CEO of his newest acquisition, the legendary Plaza Hotel on Fifth Avenue and Central Park South.

Trump appeared to be irritated by almost everything Ivana did. When they first married, she had been quiet. Now, according to him, she had become a loudmouthed know-it-all. He had loved her accent when he met her. "It was so cute, and then one day I woke up that it was terrible," he told Howard Stern in 1999. "I couldn't stand it."

When the top editors at the *National Enquirer* heard a rumor that Trump was having an affair, they called Wayne Grover, their resident Trump expert. Illicit affairs were to the *National Enquirer* what football was to *Sports Illustrated*, the category more than any other that put the weekly in millions of shopping carts across America. After all, what could be more pleasurable than learning that the rich and famous had lives of moral disgrace? Grover liked Trump as far as it went and had written many positive stories about him, but Trump would have to understand that business is business.

The *National Enquirer* flew Grover up to Manhattan so he could begin sniffing for an assignation. He got a room at one of Trump's hotels, the St. Moritz, where he had heard rumors Trump had secreted his mistress. The gossip was true. Trump's lover, a twenty-six-year-old actress and model from Alabama named Marla Maples, was ensconced at the Manhattan hotel.

Trump had an unerring instinct to choose women who were the object of other men's lust. Maples had what Trump called "a beautiful structure." For three years, Trump had dallied with Maples, hiding her in innumerable places, from a stateroom on the *Trump Princess* to a suite at the Trump Plaza Casino, always just out of Ivana's eyesight.

In Trump's life, there was no such thing as being offstage, where he could act without fear of scrutiny. He had to assume he was always being observed, and he was filming the latest scene in what he considered the greatest show on earth: the drama of Donald J. Trump.

What Trump didn't realize was that Grover was onto him. Thanks to his paid sources, Grover even knew the color of the silk bathrobe Trump wore for his assignations, and one day when no one was in suite 414, a hotel employee let him in to photograph the rumpled sheets.

Relationships that begin in duplicity usually end the same way. Trump believed he could trust no one, especially not Maples. "You really have to think of yourself as a one-man show," Trump reflected. "There are so many examples of men and women who go out and get taken advantage of by their own people. So, don't expect anyone to be on your side."

That was the lesson Trump learned from the passing of his big brother, Fred Trump Jr., in 1981. Growing up, Fred had been an exuberant, gentle spirit, a wonderful guide and model to his younger brother. He was a good man who acted the way preachers and teachers said a person should act.

Fred Jr. went into the family business, but he soon saw he was too generous and trusting to succeed in his father's world. Instead, he became a commercial pilot. In most families, that would have been an honored choice, but Fred Trump Sr. mocked his namesake as nothing more than a bus driver in the sky. Fred Jr. stopped flying and started drinking. Whatever they put on his death certificate, it was slow suicide.

"I saw people taking advantage of Fred, and the lesson I learned was always to keep up my guard one hundred percent," Trump said. "He didn't feel there was really reason for that, which is a fatal mistake in life. People are too trusting. I'm a very untrusting guy. I study people all the time, automatically; it's my way of life, for better or worse."

Trump wasn't going to let the world hurt him the way it hurt his brother. He trusted nobody fully, not even his wife, his mistress, or his closest associates. His actions suggest a man who felt that everyone would betray you one way or another if you let them. He would honor his brother's memory by living a life that was the opposite.

After Wayne Grover gathered enough information, he called Trump and told him he knew about Maples and would be writing a story. He didn't say when, and the way the tabloid worked, it might not appear for a month or two. But one day Trump and Maples's picture would be on the *National Enquirer* cover, and everyone would be talking about Trump's mistress and his doomed marriage. Trump did not rant and rave. Nor did he deny the story or implore Grover not to publish. He said almost nothing. And despite what Grover had told him, he continued his relationship with the *National Enquirer*, seeking to shape the stories the tabloid would surely be writing.

When Trump flew out to Aspen, Colorado, with his wife and children at Christmas 1989, the story of the divorce had not yet appeared in print, and he could have had one last loving vacation with his intact family. But Trump was not about to squander his holiday on family alone, and he flew Maples out in another plane and set her up in another hotel. Aspen is a small resort town, and people have a way of running into each other, especially when they are skiing on the same slopes at the same time. The inevitable happened when Ivana and Maples confronted each other outside Bonnie's, a popular restaurant halfway up Aspen Mountain.

When Maples looked back on that day, she was most troubled by the idea that Trump may have staged the whole event. She asked herself why there had been so many witnesses at Bonnie's. Had they all shown up just by chance or had they been forewarned that something might happen? Was it possible that Donald had so little regard for the emotional lives of the two most important women in his life that he had set them up to fight in public for the publicity effect?

In 1990, the media did not count time in nanoseconds and there was—believe it or not—a certain civility, even deference, among gossip columnists. In the Trumps' first weeks back, no stories appeared in the press about Trump's affair or the confrontation at Bonnie's. It was like the phony war at the start of World War II, with the enemies massing against each other but with almost no shells being fired.

After several weeks of frigid détente, Trump walked out of his twelve-year marriage. That was the signal in early February that Ivana needed. She had seen her estranged husband's mastery of the media and how he got ahead of stories, and now she did the same thing to him. Ivana called an overwhelmingly sympathetic Liz Smith and gave the columnist the gossip story of a lifetime. Ivana had cultivated Liz Smith during those long weekends at Mar-a-Lago, and the columnist felt it was her duty to chronicle the whole saga from the perspective of the betrayed wife and mother.

Later that month, the *National Enquirer* weighed in with the first of its cover stories on the broken marriage ("TRUMP'S MISTRESS: HE HID HER FOR 3 YEARS— THEN WIFE IVANA FOUND OUT!"). Any red-blooded American man could identify with the stud Trump running around with his sexy mistress, and he scored just fine in the tabloid cover story. The idea of two gorgeous women fighting in the snows of Aspen over his body would appeal to any real man, too, but Trump had not envisioned that women writers might be telling this tale and they would not be so amused.

People quoted one witness who heard Ivana shouting at Maples, "You bitch, leave my husband alone!" Like most of the media, the weekly was not going to let Trump look like anything but a weasel. They portrayed the villainous adulterer strapping on his skis to get away from the bickering women, but he was no match for Ivana. One observer swore "they saw her whip in front of Donald and then ski backwards down the slopes, wagging her finger in his face." How was that for the aggrieved wife sticking it to her cheating husband?

Trump wasn't going to sit back and let things stand like this. In the next episode of one of the greatest tabloid sagas of the decade, Trump told Grover his version of what supposedly happened when the family left Aspen and returned to New York. *National Enquirer* readers liked nothing more than stories of a good man gone bad who redeems himself, and Trump gave that to them in spades.

"'Marla, it's over—we're breaking too many hearts!'" the cover story began. "With those brief words, Donald Trump dumped his mistress of three years Marla Maples like a deal gone sour—after realizing the terrible suffering their affair had inflicted on his estranged wife Ivana, their three children . . . and his own father."

Who needed soap operas when the Trumps were available? "The Mighty Trump was reduced to tears," the *National Enquirer* wrote, capitalizing "Mighty" so one would doubt that Trump was Powerful. "Donald slumped into his chair as if he had been shot through the heart," the story went on. "He buried his head in his hands for what seemed like an eternity. When he finally lifted his head, tears were glistening in his eyes, and he whispered, 'Oh, my God, what have I done?'"

It was heart-wrenching stuff, but when Trump read it in the *Enquirer*'s March 6 issue, he called Glover and raged at the reporter. The story was totally false. He hadn't gone back to Ivana. That's not what troubled him. He was livid because the tabloid had him crying when he told Glover he never cried. The reporter was not so foolish as to defend himself by saying he had only written what Trump told him. Instead, he apologized for his mistake, and their collaboration continued stronger than ever.

Trump believed he deserved endless publicity, but even he was astounded at the overwhelming coverage. Americans could not get enough of this steamy tale of adultery and betrayal among the rich and celebrated. His leaving Ivana was what Trump called "the biggest thing that ever happened . . . bigger than [the divorce of] Richard Burton and Elizabeth Taylor." And that was big. It may have been a high price, but the scandal lifted Donald Trump to an upper room in the pantheon of celebrity.

Most of the media cast Trump as the villain and included a long checklist of the other women with whom he had supposedly slept. It didn't make for pleasant reading, but Trump had learned one of the crucial lessons of his life, and it had nothing to do with divorce or women. He loved publicity beyond life itself, and he realized it didn't matter if it was valentines or Bronx cheers, it was the same stuff. It made you famous. Who else in America was as well known as Donald J. Trump? He wasn't angry at Grover and the *National Enquirer*. They were playing the same game on the same team. People read this stuff and they hardly remembered whether it was good or bad. They just remembered your name and that you were this fabulous personality.

The *National Enquirer* was key to establishing Trump's populist image. To keep it building, all Trump had to do was to continue feeding stories to Wayne Grover. This cost nothing to Trump in terms of the people with whom he lived and socialized. Almost none of those in Trump's world read the supermarket tabloids, and most people he knew had no idea of the extent that Trump was collaborating with the downscale weekly.

What upset Trump was not the bad publicity but the threat of a large divorce settlement. He had long been anticipating the possibility of this moment and had Ivana sign four different prenuptial agreements. The latest, penned in 1987, was by far the most generous, but it granted Ivana only $25 million, a small portion of Trump's fortune, and was written to be legally impregnable. But now she was challenging that and demanding a bigger divorce settlement.

Trump's affair with Marla Maples was a betrayal of his marital vows, but in his view of the world, that mattered little when compared to Ivana's betrayal over money. His estranged wife saw it differently. Ivana argued that she had brought so much to her husband's business that she deserved far more than she had agreed upon in the latest prenuptial. To fight his wife's demands, Trump attempted to strip Ivana of anything of consequence she thought she had done. Trump's minions were quoted in the press that she was a clueless woman who could not even run herself, and certainly not a casino or a top hotel.

A week after his surrogates began attacking Ivana, and while he was continuing to see Maples, Trump added a scenario for the millions out there who

still believed in happy endings when he said, "There's always a chance for reconciliation." And what better time for this than on Ivana's forty-first birthday
on February 20, 1990.

Ivana and the three children flew down to Mar-a-Lago to celebrate, and
Trump joined them two days later, pulling through gates guarded by a contin-
gent of cops in squad cars and motorcycles, and an eighteen-person security
force. Also arriving at the estate were a truckload of flowers and a cake big
enough for a major wedding.

The birthday party beside the pool featured two strolling violinists and eight-
year-old Ivanka singing "Edelweiss," the sentimental anthem from *The Sound
of Music*. As the Trumps' only daughter performed for the twenty-five guests,
the occasion appeared to be a celebration not only of a birthday but of a happy
family. But when Trump flew back to New York, whatever talk of reconciliation there had been drifted away, and the public bickering resumed.

Ivana stayed in Palm Beach with her three children until the end of March.
To avoid the media, she did not venture beyond the gates of Mar-a-Lago. The
estate had all the amenities of a resort hotel, and though Donald Jr., Eric, and
Ivanka had plenty to do, they were the ultimate victims of the divorce and felt
profoundly the disappearance of their father.

The Trumps' neighbors in Palm Beach watched the endless drama with hor-
rified fascination. Divorces are part of the normal cycle of life in Palm Beach:
discard the old, hook up with the young, and go on forever. But Donald and
Ivana Trump introduced paparazzi photographers running up and down South
Ocean Boulevard and reporters writing stories so unseemly that the Shiny Sheet
had to use nuance to tell the sordid tales, if they even mentioned them at all.

A friend of Ivana's, heiress Marylou Whitney, was a Palm Beach winter resident, and she was nothing if not philosophical when it came to marriage. "I
always figure every man's going to have a flirtation or two," she said, Palm
Beach speech for an affair. But, she continued, "it should be done with discre-
tion and not flaunted."

Jesse Newman, the president of the Palm Beach Chamber of Commerce,
was so upset with the wildly public nature of Trump's affair with Marla being
played out in the press as well as Trump and Ivana sniping back and forth at

each other that he could no longer be silent. "Mr. Trump has a home here, but he's no Palm Beacher," Newman said. That was the meanest thing he could say about a person.

It wasn't just Ivana harping endlessly about all the money she deserved that troubled Trump. It was Marla. Trump continued to confide in Wayne Grover at the *National Enquirer,* telling him that he wasn't in love with Marla, even while she kept hanging on. He was no good at firing his mistress, and he needed a way out.

Grover reported that Trump was leaving Marla to save his marriage to Ivana, but even this didn't seem to persuade Marla that the relationship wasn't good for her. Three months later, Grover filed another story based on talking to Trump, claiming that Marla would have to go to save her lover's financial life. "Donald Trump's bankers have ordered him to dump Marla Maples—or else his entire financial empire may collapse!" the cover story began.

None of this happened to be so, a matter of no consequence to Trump. To him, truth was an invention. You said whatever you wanted to say and it was true. Then you said something entirely different, and that was true, too. To the readers of the *National Enquirer,* Trump had become one of the great entertainments of their lives. They read the latest story with awestruck anticipation. Having forgotten the details almost as soon as they finished reading, they were ready for an entirely different Trump story the next week when they picked up the tabloid at the supermarket.

Trump had strutted across the American landscape, boastful, flamboyant, the Liberace of real estate. He was so overleveraged that when one piece after another of his holdings did not perform at a high enough level for him to pay back his massive loans, the whole jerry-built empire began to totter and fall. He had no choice but to declare one business bankruptcy after another. Many entrepreneurs at some time in a long career are forced into bankruptcy, to restructure and rebuild. But this was on a whole different level.

Trump attempted to pin anything to his advantage—even financial disaster. He boasted that he never declared *personal* bankruptcy, only business bankruptcy, and described the latter as a smart tool that allowed him to unburden himself from his obligations and move on fresh and renewed. The device was so marvelous, he used it four times in succession, walking away from a mountain of debt. Never did he bow his head and mumble mea culpas when his businesses failed, and he made no apologies to casino workers who had lost their jobs or to investors who were out of millions of dollars due to Trump's missteps.

Trump was a marketing man selling his name, a moniker he considered one of the greatest luxury brands in America. Why would he sully that name with tales of failure? He simply moved on and boasted of how clever he was at squeezing out of his obligations and surviving on the diminished stipend of $450,000 a month agreed upon by his creditors and lawyers, cutting his expenses by about one hundred thousand dollars.

Trump fancied himself a much-admired figure, but now that he seemed to be going down, the average American looked on with undisguised pleasure. In a Gallup poll, almost two-thirds of the respondents figured he was getting just what he deserved.

For Trump, Palm Beach was a diversion from the stress of his business life in New York, but by 1990 the town had become another place where he was forced to confront his financial failures. Mar-a-Lago's proud owner was two years behind on paying the real estate taxes on the massive estate, whose maintenance, he said, was costing him $2.5 million annually plus $100,625 in monthly interest on the mortgage he now wasn't paying.

Across the Intracoastal Waterway, he had affixed his name to Trump Plaza, but the building had become an outsize monument to hubris. Trump was spending $413,000 a month on mortgage payments, maintenance, and marketing while taking in only $30,000 in income.

Trump demonstrated over and over that he was skilled at turning away from anything unpleasant and pretending it wasn't happening or had nothing to do with him. In that way, he showed no concern for the people who had listened to his endless hype and purchased units at Trump Plaza that were deteriorating in value. During the first five months of 1990, no one purchased an apartment in the twin towers. Many of those who lived in the ghostlike structure with more than 60 percent of the apartments empty felt duped by the grandiloquent Trump.

Mickey Miyagi, a Miami broker who sold three units to Japanese investors, said Trump's people tried to cut him out of his commission. And when the broker rented one of the three units before his client signed the lease, Miyagi claimed Trump's people jumped in and rented another empty apartment to the man. That led to a lawsuit in Palm Beach County Circuit Court.

Trump had borrowed sixty million dollars from the Marine Midland Bank to finance the purchase of the twin towers, and he had also agreed to be personally obligated for fourteen million dollars of that amount. That meant that unless he declared personal bankruptcy, he could not avoid repaying the bank. A few years back, he could have written that check with a smile, but not any longer. At this point, with all that he owed, his net worth was likely less than zero. If he could have declared another business bankruptcy and stiffed his creditors, he would have done so instantly, but personal bankruptcy hurt. That would affect his lifestyle. That was serious.

Trump's optimism might have been a tonic in good times, but in the depressed South Florida real estate market of the early 1990s, it was an illusion that almost everyone saw through. The brokers selling the condos would have had an easier time if the units had been in prime condition, but despite Trump's promise to complete the project, many of the apartments had concrete walls and pipes sticking out of the floors. The smartest move might have been to sell the remaining units at an absolute auction, but Trump wasn't into public humiliation. He decided to sell only forty-five units in a faux auction in which buyers had to pay a minimum price.

Trump loved free advertising, and he hoisted giant banners on the sides of the two towers: CONDO AUCTION. The signs were about as classy as the GOING OUT OF BUSINESS placards that dotted storefronts in Times Square. What's more, the banners weren't even legal, and when word got around that the city had told Trump he had to take the signs down, the whole fiasco generated enough negative publicity to risk turning people off from buying the apartments.

If Trump Plaza truly was the extension of Palm Beach Trump said it was, the auction could have been held in the building's giant lobby. But Trump chose to have the event at the Breakers hotel, apparently hoping that some of the patina of the fashionable establishment would extend into the frenzy of the auction, causing buyers to forget where the units were actually located.

Trump paid five hundred thousand dollars to LFC Real Estate Marketing Services to advertise as far as Asia for the December 1990 auction. The company also stood to earn commissions on auction sales. The thirty-member team arrived wearing impeccably tailored navy-blue suits. They brought in sixteen cheerleaders from Forest Hill High School in West Palm Beach, whose cheers and cartwheels would have been more effective at stimulating football players than they were with condo bidders.

At the last moment, Trump took ten apartments out of the auction, proclaiming that he was confident he could get a better price on his own. Trump may have been trying to avoid the embarrassment of leaving a slew of unsold apartments. Only 137 people preregistered to bid, far fewer than the massive marketing campaign should have delivered.

Trump arrived in a stretch limousine wearing a striped suit, a red tie, and a benevolent gaze. His divorce from Ivana had just become final. Ivana had finally faced up to her ex-husband's radically diminished circumstances and taken what she could get from the prenuptial agreement. In 1993, on radio shock jock Howard Stern's program, Trump recalled what he considered "the worst day of my life," when the "*New York Times* front page, *Wall Street Journal* front page" focused on his financial failings. "All of a sudden," he remembered, "she called up and she said, 'I'll take the twenty-five million.'"

That was all behind him now, and that day at the Breakers, beside him walked twenty-six-year-old Rowanne Brewer, the 1989 "Miss Snap-On-Tools." The *National Enquirer* had outed Brewer's relationship with Donald in their current issue ("TRUMP DUMPS MARLA FOR SEXY MODEL"). She sat a dozen rows away from Trump, and whenever reporters sought to talk to her, she said, "I'm sorry."

Brewer saw that if she wanted to be around Trump, her job was to exude sexuality yet signal she was Trump's alone. At a party around the pool at Mar-a-Lago, where there were almost twice as many models as male guests, Trump had asked Brewer to try on a swimming suit. When he approved of how she looked in the bikini, he had her parade around the pool. Brewer recalls him saying, "That is a stunning Trump girl, isn't it?"

As Brewer sat watching the elaborate auction, the thirty-five units sold for an average of 40 percent less than the initial offering price, bringing in a total of $8,815,000. Subtract the marketing costs and sales commissions, and Trump walked home that day with no more than $7.9 million. That was less than a third of what Trump owed the bank and would have been considered a failure in many scenarios, but not to Trump.

"Auctions are the wave of the future for real estate," Trump said. "In a slow market, rather than holding them for two to three years, it's better to sell them at an auction for lower prices." That may have been true, but it did not explain why Trump had sold relatively few units, leaving him with at least eighty-six apartments he still had to sell elsewhere. "It's been tremendous, very successful," he said. "It's exceeded my expectations. I have never seen anything like this."

Trump's hype was like a helium balloon that eventually deflated and fell to the floor. The buyers had listened to Trump's frenetic hype, but after the auction many of the successful bidders got nervous about their deals and walked away. By mid-February only eleven of the thirty-five successful bidders had closed on their units.

Instead of accepting responsibility for the auction's failures, Trump blamed the auction company. He alleged that the company's incompetent, poorly trained employees had messed up, and he went after them with his favorite weapon: a lawsuit in Palm Beach County Circuit Court that was quietly settled.

Matters at Trump Plaza were in such a precarious state that Trump called in his secret weapon: Marla Maples. For months, Maples had been shuttling in and out of Trump's life so quickly that only the tabloids could keep score. Maples came and left largely at Trump's call. He believed, as he told Howard Stern, that the more desirable you were, the more women enjoyed being mistreated by you. It was a pleasure he rarely denied Maples.

In February 1991, Trump invited seventy-five local real estate brokers to Mar-a-Lago, where he would pitch the newly discounted units at Trump Plaza.

To intrigue them even further, Maples was waiting in the living room. Trump not only promised the agents the full 6 percent commission, but he offered a trip to New York, staying in the Plaza Hotel, to anyone who sold four apartments in March. But the condos were impossible to sell so quickly, and no one even came close to winning.

With his debts ever mounting, Trump struck a deal with the Marine Midland Bank in which he gave them the rest of the condos, and he walked away from his fourteen-million-dollar personal debt. In April, the bank sponsored an auction at the PGA National Resort Hotel a few miles north of Palm Beach, and the remaining sixty-two units sold for a total of $13.56 million.

That wasn't enough for Marine Midland to be close to breaking even, but it didn't matter for Trump how well the auction did. He arrived at the beginning, signed a few autographs, and spoke to reporters. "I came out fine on everything," Trump said just before he left, "but the press doesn't report that."

Trump was facing massive debts, and the only way to save himself from personal bankruptcy was for him to unload most of everything he owned. His Boeing 727 was to Trump what a horse is to a cowboy, and he went everywhere in it. But even the plane had to be sold, putting him in the humiliating prospect of flying time-shares, rental planes, or, God forbid, commercial.

Other than his triplex at Trump Tower, the only personal property he could likely sell for a significant profit was Mar-a-Lago. Many in the Palm Beach establishment took delight in his difficulties and would have loved to see him gone. His circumstances were such that he almost had to give them that pleasure.

The obvious way out of his dilemma was to do precisely what Cerf Ross, one of the unsuccessful would-be purchasers of Mar-a-Lago, had been planning: to break Mar-a-Lago's massive property into lots where separate homes could be built. The town council had given preliminary approval to Ross's plan, and there appeared to be little reason why the body wouldn't give it to Trump as well.

One Sunday, Robert Moore, the town building inspector, and John "Skip"

Randolph, the town attorney, drove over to Mar-a-Lago to discuss with Trump the subdividing of the property. Trump's lawyers had gone over the relevant legal documents, and he told the town officials that he planned to take full advantage of his legal rights to build fourteen homes on the property. The two men advised Trump to back down a little and apply for the same eight house sites as Ross had done in 1984. "Those of us on the town staff were okay with Donald, but what we didn't understand was that he was not liked by the rest of the people in the town," says Moore. "He was new money."

Trump's instincts were always to ask for more than he expected to get. That way he could make it appear he was compromising while still ending up with precisely what he sought. But Trump was still feeling his way into Palm Beach's peculiar ways, and he agreed to follow what he soon decided had been terrible advice.

The Preservation Foundation was full of influential people. Trump had insulted them by twice making them hold their annual event in a tent. After two years, the organization had moved the event to the Flagler Museum. No one ever publicly criticized Trump for his treatment of the prestigious group, but it was hardly coincidental that the Preservation Foundation led the fight to deny Trump the right to subdivide Mar-a-Lago.

This battle wasn't just about Trump. In recent years, almost all the great mansions had been demolished, with several new homes built on each mansion's acreage. Trump said he should be able to do what everyone else had done, but the preservationists saw this subdividing of property as a trend that needed to be stopped, and Trump's estate was where they intended to bring it to a halt. They wanted to maintain the greatest of the Palm Beach estates in all its expansive glory.

Another problem Trump faced was that when he wanted to do something, he wanted to do it *now*. But he was in Palm Beach, probably the most regulated small town in America. A store owner couldn't put a sign in a window or change the color of an awning without getting permission. If a homeowner wanted to renovate, their contractor ended up trekking to the town offices multiple times seeking permission for matters that might have seemed arbitrary, redundant, and unnecessary.

But most people on the island were proud of this onerous process and saw it as crucial to maintaining the town's unique character. Like it or not, everyone—including Donald Trump—had to go through this process.

The Landmarks Preservation Commission was the body that would advise the town council whether they should approve his plan to subdivide Mar-a-Lago. When the commission met in May 1991 to discuss the proposal to build eight other homes on the property, a large number of people came forward to express their strong opposition. As the arguments went on for hours, it became clear that much of the opposition was driven by how profoundly Trump was personally disliked.

The four-person commission was so overwhelmed by the critical response to the proposal that they deferred their vote until the next meeting and ended up bringing in Clarion Associates, a Chicago real estate advisory company, to give its opinion and shield the commission from responsibility for the decision.

By the time of the next meeting, in July, Clarion had still not delivered its report and the decision was postponed again. "If anyone else but Donald Trump owned it, they would approve it," Trump told *The Washington Post*. Trump thought he knew what his problem was, and it was not about his plan to subdivide Mar-a-Lago. He believed this was the Preservation Foundation's sneaky way of getting even with him for throwing them out of the mansion for their annual event, even though he felt he had good reasons for doing so. He recalled that no one had ever publicly thanked him for the two times he let the ball be held in a tent at Mar-a-Lago. Instead, they rewarded him by trampling his beautiful lawn.

The foundation's leaders were not the sort to offer gushy tributes to the media. But they said they had thanked Trump privately and had even given him several gifts, including a picture of Ivana in a silver frame. As for damage to the lawn, Trump was the one who relegated the group to a tent on the lawn.

On most issues, Trump saw only one side—the one where he stood. He was not about to squander time worrying about the feelings of those who were against him. "Best thing they could do is oppose it," he said, daring the town council to challenge him. "I have the right to build on my own property. I'll bring a major lawsuit, and I'll win."

Trump might have been best advised to approach the town by showing deferential respect for Palm Beach and its institutions, but he had never done that in his life. Instead, he told the *Palm Beach Daily News* that if he wasn't allowed to subdivide the estate, not only would he sue the town but he would sell Mar-a-Lago to "some interesting people who aren't your usual Palm Beach types."

Trump let it be known that the prospective purchaser was seventy-one-year-old Rev. Sun Myung Moon, the Korean-born leader of the Unification Church. Rev. Moon's church owned all kinds of businesses across America, including the conservative newspaper *The Washington Times*. In 1975, the religious leader had inquired about buying an estate on the island, and it was not unthinkable that he would be interested in Mar-a-Lago.

Rev. Moon's plans supposedly were to use the estate as a retreat for his Moonies, the common term for the believers. Most Palm Beachers knew the sect only through its blissed-out adherents standing on street corners soliciting donations, and the idea that they might soon be roaming up and down Worth Avenue in the guise of religious freedom appalled them. They thought that Trump was the worst thing that could happen to Mar-a-Lago, but he was the rebirth of Marjorie Merriweather Post compared to Rev. Moon and the estate filled with hordes of chanting Moonies.

In the whole history of Palm Beach, nobody had ever threatened the town government in such a belligerent way as Trump. It bordered on blackmail. Some involved with the subdivision issue considered Trump's threat to sell to Rev. Moon a pathetic publicity stunt that should lead to an outright rejection of Trump's plan to subdivide the estate. Trump's story lost more credibility when Rev. Moon's spokesman announced the minister had "absolutely no interest" in the estate.

But Trump actually had been seriously working to sell the estate to Rev. Moon. One of Trump's top executives, Jeffrey Walker, flew down to South Florida and spent a week negotiating with Richard Jorandby, who, despite being Palm Beach County's public defender, did many chores for the Unification Church. Wayne Grover was friends with Jorandby, and Grover attended meetings with the principals not only at Mar-a-Lago but at Grover's home in Lantana. They ended up with a contract ready to be signed, but in the end, the deal fell through, and Trump did not get the vengeance he sought.

Trump's financial troubles were so immediate that he felt he had no time to sit around waiting until the Landmarks Preservation Commission made a decision that might well go against him. Instead, he took his subdivision proposal directly to the town council's June 1991 meeting.

Trump showed that he still had not learned how Palm Beach worked—or he chose not to learn—when he attempted to jump over the commission. The council wasn't about to abrogate the town's slow, deliberate process. As council member Nancy Douthit said, there should be "no breathtaking rush on this thing." The council sent Trump's proposal back to the landmarks commission for its decision before the council dealt with the matter. In the proceedings, he had shown himself to be what many considered a belligerent bully who thought he was better than the town's procedures, and as word of Trump's actions got around, it only created more bad blood in the community.

In August, Trump got some good news when the consultant's report called for the subdividing of the property: "We believe, that if some form of acceptable subdivision is not sought . . . the buildings and grounds could be left to deteriorate through neglect and lack of resources. . . ." The report called for building eight homes on the property that would be somewhat smaller than the ones Trump proposed. When Trump read the document, he decided he could live with that. "For the first time since we announced the subdivision back in February, I felt like a fair decision had been rendered on Mar-a-Lago," he told the *Palm Beach Daily News*.

The Landmarks Preservation Commission had pushed for the hiring of the consulting firm, so the members could hardly formally disavow its report. At their August meeting, they listened to both sides with the appearance of objectivity. When Trump's attorney Peter Broberg spoke, he practically begged the four members for specific changes he could make in the proposal to win their approval. And he requested that if the commission couldn't support the plan as it was, they could at least vote in favor of the principle of subdivision.

Another speaker that day was Frank Chopin, the Preservation Foundation attorney, who practiced tax and probate law. He was a tough adversary in the courtroom and had taken a personal dislike to Trump. Chopin said that Broberg's request for approval of the subdivision was nothing but "hocus-pocus, sleight-of-hand Donald Trumpism at its very best." The exchanges between the lawyers was obviously driven by personal views of each other's client, but Chopin spoke directly to that when he proclaimed that the "Preservation Foundation doesn't care if the property is owned by the Moonies, Donald Trump, or Donald Duck."

Predictably, the Trump proposal was unanimously turned down, prompting him to call the decision "ridiculous" and threaten to sue the town and the commission. But after ranting, he calmed down. He desperately needed the money from the subdivision and to have the town council vote his way. If he said what he truly believed in too bold a fashion, he might lose them, and uncharacteristically he managed to contain himself, at least publicly.

The October town council meeting was full of those ready to applaud anyone who was against Trump. The debate went on for four hours. In the end, the council voted unanimously in support of the Landmark Preservation Commission's rejection of Trump's plan.

Instead of starting over, Trump submitted a Planned Unit Development (PUD). This approach would let the Palm Beach Planning & Zoning Commission decide if Trump had the legal right to build the homes on the acreage before the matter was referred to the town council for a final decision. A four-hour debate at the zoning commission's December meeting ended with the seven members unanimously turning down the plan. Despite the rejection, Trump took the PUD to the town council. In March, after six hours of debate and discussion, the council tabled the vote on the plan until the next meeting.

Everyone in Palm Beach knew the town council was voting on the Trump proposal at its April 1992 meeting. The chambers were full that day, primarily with citizens opposed to Trump's venture. He sat quietly in the back of the chambers. After an exhausting seven hours of debate, the town council unanimously turned down the proposal. Afterward Trump told reporters that he viewed the turndown as a personal attack. "All the others have already been subdivided, and no one has had to do what I've done to get a subdivision," he said. "Constitutionally I can do what I want with my property, and yet the town has blocked me at every turn."

Trump vowed to sue the town for one hundred million dollars. If he won the suit, he could in essence bankrupt the town and destroy the proud certitudes with which it lived. "My only question is whether Palm Beach can afford the ultimate cost of their actions today," he said ominously. If Trump were not already isolated from his neighbors, this was the final blow. He was in essence declaring war on the streets where he lived.

In July 1992, Trump filed a fifty-million-dollar lawsuit against the town in Palm Beach County Court. The suit argued that many of the members of the Landmarks Preservation Commission and the Palm Beach Planning & Zoning Commission should have recused themselves because they belonged to organizations opposed to the subdivision. The primary culprit wasn't named, but it was clearly the Preservation Foundation. Trump's lawyers pushed ahead and began taking depositions, but the town sought to have the suit dismissed and successfully petitioned to have it moved to a federal court.

Trump was in a hurry to get this resolved. He was in deep water up to his eyeballs, and he was not in sight of shore. Along with his triplex at Trump Tower, Mar-a-Lago was practically the only thing of real value he had left. The estate was leveraged over the top and it could be the asset that brought him down. If he didn't find some way to monetize the estate and do it quickly, he might face personal bankruptcy and have Mar-a-Lago taken away from him. If that happened, it would likely write a finish to the saga of Donald J. Trump.

6

The Forbidden City

Soon after the town council turned down his plan, Trump was having dinner in New York with the biggest shareholder of a major bank. Trump had borrowed millions from the bank, and the banker was pleased that Trump had paid back the money. For that reason alone, the man was in a generous mood. When Trump started venting about the Palm Beach establishment and wringing his hands over just what he could do, the man suggested he talk to a friend of his, Paul Rampell, a lawyer who lived in Palm Beach.

Rampell had grown up in the north end of the island. He had gone to Princeton and returned to Palm Beach to practice trust law, a lucrative field that had few risks and low visibility. The Jewish attorney had a reputation for being able to resolve almost any case out of court. He could have been a successful lawyer in New York or Washington, but he preferred the Palm Beach life.

Rampell understood far better than Trump how Palm Beach worked. Even though he was something of an introvert and easily assumed a deferential attitude when it was useful, he possessed a hidden brashness and a willingness to say what he thought. Trump invited him for a meeting at Mar-a-Lago. As a boy,

Rampell remembered Mar-a-Lago as being "kind of like the forbidden city in China that hardly anybody went in or out of," and it was exciting for him to be in the mansion.

"I don't think you should divide the property at all," said Rampell. That was a risky thing to say to a man who had just spent eighteen months trying to do just that.

"What are you talking about?" Trump asked.

"I think you ought to turn Mar-a-Lago into a club."

Not only had Rampell put down Trump's plan for the subdivision, but now he proposed an idea that was obviously absurd.

"What do you mean?" Trump asked in that confrontational style of his. "Like 21 or Studio 54? A nightclub?"

"No, like a private social club," the lawyer said. "Like the others on the island. Like the B&T across the street. Or the Sailfish Club. Or the Palm Beach Country Club."

"I just don't see how that could work," Trump said, shaking his head dismissively.

"Look, if you subdivide, you're going to be competing with the Bolton and Blossom estates," Rampell said, referring to two other large properties on the island. "They've got about ten lots each, and they're not selling. That's how slow things are."

"But this is Mar-a-Lago," Trump said.

"That's the point," Rampell said. "Your buyer is going to have to submit his plans to the Landmarks Preservation Commission. And they're going to have to have Spanish tile roofs and stucco walls."

Trump was silent.

"Look, when people come down here and buy a lot for two or three million dollars, they want a trophy property," the lawyer continued. "Here their homes will look like cottages compared to your mansion. And what about the air traffic? The Blossom and Bolton lots are farther north. They don't have that problem."

Trump, who fancied himself an expert on all things real estate, had apparently never thought about any of this. His plan to subdivide the property looked like it had been put together with the same level of due diligence that had gone into the purchase of Trump Plaza in West Palm Beach.

Trump turned the discussion back to the idea of a club. "What will these club members do?" he asked. He wasn't somebody who hung out, and he couldn't quite figure out what a guest would do at this so-called club.

"Club members will come and have dinner, lunch," Rampell said enthusiastically. "Look, you could put in more tennis courts. They can use the beach, the swimming pool, have receptions, weddings, bar mitzvahs, all kinds of stuff."

After thinking about this a little, Trump decided it just didn't make any sense. "Look, Paul, it's a crazy idea," he said, shaking his head definitively. "I just don't like it. It's just not right."

When Trump called Rampell the next day, he squandered not a moment on small talk but carried on as if they were continuing their discussion at Mar-a-Lago. "The memberships will never sell," Trump said.

"The town of Palm Beach is probably about half Christian and half Jewish," Rampell said. "There are five clubs right now. Four of those clubs are restricted. No Jews. No African Americans. And there are about four or five thousand members. There's one club only where Jewish residents can go, and that's the Palm Beach Country Club. It only has three hundred membership slots. They're all full, and it's very expensive. So, you've got an island with a lot of Jewish residents who have no club to go to."

"Well, maybe," Trump said and hung up.

In the early years of Palm Beach, any number of German American Jews came down to the island from New York City each winter and were welcomed in the exclusive clubs. That all changed in 1944, when a Jewish American Boston businessman, A. M. Sonnabend, attempted to purchase two hotels on the island, a beach club, and a run-down golf course that he planned to renovate. Everyone in Palm Beach society viewed that as nothing less than a Jewish beachhead that would change the island forever. A few Jews had been fine, but too much spice ruined the dish.

A group of Palm Beach gentleman calling themselves the Committee of the Select 100 met at the Everglades Club to decide how to deal with this threat.

The group decided that if ten of them put up fifty thousand dollars each, they could pay Sonnabend off, buy the properties themselves, and keep Palm Beach as it was. These men could have easily written checks for that amount, but most of these Palm Beach WASPs had one trait in common. Generously they were called frugal, but more accurately they were cheap, and they were not about to write checks for an uncertain venture.

When news of Sonnabend's purchase spread, Jews from all across the eastern United States began making Palm Beach their winter home. Most of their families were originally from Eastern Europe, and for the most part, they were not as sophisticated as the German-American Jews who had preceded them.

To the old Palm Beachers, it was not just that there were so many of these new arrivals, but they seemed Jewish in a way their predecessors did not. And they made part of Palm Beach their own. They transformed the golf course into the Palm Beach Country Club. The Sun & Surf Beach Club became a massive condominium project with mainly Jewish residents. The tall condominiums that rose up along the ocean on the southern part of the island had almost exclusively Jewish residents. The buildings looked nothing like the villagelike atmosphere of the rest of Palm Beach. Those who lived north of Sloan's Curve, where the condominiums began, referred to the area derisively as "the Gaza Strip."

As more Jews continued to come to the island, old Palm Beach retreated back into its own clubs and customs, tightening its restrictive policies. The membership committees at the restricted clubs defined whether someone was Jewish in a more all-encompassing way than the Nazis' Nuremberg Race Laws, which had said a person was Jewish if he had at least three Jewish grandparents. The Palm Beach establishment barred anyone who had even one Jewish ancestor from the premises of their clubs.

Few of the Everglades and the B&T members used the word "Jew." It was "them," and everyone knew who "they" were. "They" had gone far enough. It was time to hold the line and to ensure that all the main clubs on the island stayed true to their Christian identity. If some Americans condemned Palm Beach as a place of institutionalized anti-Semitism, that was a small price to pay not to have dinner in the same room with "them."

Even though Trump continued to say that turning Mar-a-Lago into a club was a bad idea, he kept calling Rampell to talk about it. In these conversations, Trump put down almost everything Rampell said. The lawyer could have hung up anytime he wanted. After all, he wasn't being paid for this verbal onslaught. But he liked a good battle, and he had fun going back at Trump with his own retorts.

Almost anyone considering starting a club that would likely be identified as overwhelmingly Jewish would have wondered if doing that in Palm Beach was such a great idea. Trump didn't think about this at all. He'd never demonstrated that this issue was of any concern to him. And he didn't fancy himself a social activist contemplating opening up a repressive society. To Trump it was just another business deal.

Growing up in Queens, Trump had many Jewish neighbors. About half the children in the private Kew-Forest School were Jewish, and he attended the bar mitzvah of one of the boys. When Trump's father took his family on vacation for a few days, it was often to the Concord, one of the largely Jewish resorts in the Catskills. In Trump's business life, many of his closest advisers and most of his competitors were Jewish. When Trump wrote about the men he admired in *The Art of the Deal,* he named three prominent Jewish show business executives: Sam Goldwyn, Darryl Zanuck, and Louis B. Mayer. And as the young businessman rose to success, he emulated several of his Jewish competitors in the New York real estate world. So Trump didn't see why it was a big deal for a club's membership to be largely Jewish.

Beyond that, the proposed club was in some ways an extension of what Trump had done in Manhattan. When he was building Trump Tower, upscale Manhattan living was largely co-ops, where owners had to be approved by a committee. Many of the best Park Avenue apartments regularly rejected potential buyers whom they considered not part of their particular class or social grouping. Trump considered his Fifth Avenue building the finest residence in the city, and the residential units were condominiums, which did not have these committees. If you had the money, you could buy your pick of the available apartments.

Trump's calls to Rampell continued for several weeks, and each time Trump said how crazy or stupid it was to turn Mar-a-Lago into a club. Then one day Trump said, "You know what, I'm going to do it. I'm going to try."

The first thing Trump needed to do was to hire an attorney versed in property law (Rampell was a trust lawyer). But this idea of creating a new, largely Jewish club in Palm Beach was so controversial that he couldn't find anyone local to represent him. The lawyers turned him down because they felt that being associated with Trump on this project might lose them clients. It simply wasn't worth the risk. In the end, Trump had little choice but to ask Rampell to take the job.

Rampell was concerned enough about what his association with Trump might do to his practice that he went to his professional mentor, who told him, "Think of it like you're a criminal defense lawyer. You can defend the worst scum bag, and it doesn't spill over on you. There's no guilt by association. But one thing I would consider is getting a retainer where you're paid in advance."

Trump's financial troubles had been widely reported in the press, and he had a reputation for stiffing his creditors. Rampell decided that if he asked for a large enough retainer, he would be okay no matter what happened. Trump surprised Rampell by immediately sending a check for the full amount, making Rampell the public face of the proposed club.

In May 1993, a reporter for the *Palm Beach Daily News* visited Rampell's office on Worth Avenue to profile him. The attorney had no interest in publicity and cringed at all the attention Trump was bringing him, but he knew that talking to reporters was now part of the job. This interview was supposed to be about turning Mar-a-Lago into a club, but the reporter started talking about how Rampell couldn't be admitted to certain clubs.

"I don't think anti-Semitism and bigotry are likely to be resolved by my remarks to you," Rampell said and pushed on to other subjects.

Rampell had watched closely as Trump and his attorneys treated the fight for permission to subdivide Mar-a-Lago as a legal matter and failed. Rampell knew that winning approval to turn the estate into a club would instead have to be a political battle. As they began their campaign in earnest, the lawyer thought

Trump understood what he must do and how he must act. But it wasn't in Trump's nature to bow in obeisance to what he considered the corrupt leaders of the town. He had a better idea—sticking it to them on their night of nights.

Free of Ivana at last, Trump decided to host a "Bachelor Ball" at Mar-a-Lago on the last Saturday in January 1993—which, not so coincidentally, was the same evening as the International Red Cross Ball, the epitome of the old Palm Beach world.

Trump's guests were not the aging socialites and their tottering husbands or closeted escorts, the ubiquitous "walkers" who escorted the ladies of the island as long as they pretended they were straight. Instead, there were pro football and basketball players, many of them black, busloads of models, Miami Dolphins cheerleaders, a smattering of the usual social suspects, along with scores of reporters and paparazzi. Not invited were the gentlemen sitting at the bar next door at the Bath and Tennis Club having a few stiff ones before heading over to the Red Cross Ball at the Breakers. They could condemn Trump's garish vulgarity all they wanted, but what man didn't want to be at the Bachelor Ball?

One member of the press who had no intention of attending was the Shiny Sheet's society editor, Shannon Donnelly. Society reporters usually came from the class of people whose social lives they chronicled. Donnelly was the daughter of a Newport, Rhode Island, cop. The closest she got to the American upper class was when her father caddied for Jackie Kennedy at the Newport Country Club. Donnelly had been a copy editor at the paper when she had been pressed into duty to write about society.

Before long, Donnelly had a firm grasp on all the nuances of the Palm Beach social world. It might have been expected that given Donnelly's modest background, she would favor a social inclusiveness Palm Beach didn't have, but instead she had become a strict defender of the old order, and she was not amused by the Bachelor Ball.

"What, what, WHAT was *Donald Trump* thinking when he scheduled his party the same night as the Red Cross Ball?" she asked in her column. "Was he thinking at all? Or was he thumbing his nose at Palm Beach society by hosting a get-together the same night as what remains the most prestigious gala of the season?"

Donnelly thought Trump threatened everything she deemed important. She may have realized what was at stake, because she declared war on any islanders so foolish as to attend. "And those—if, in fact, there are any—who abandoned previously made plans for a last-minute invitation to Mar-a-Lago are neither polite nor society," she wrote, drumming those so gauche as to attend the Bachelor Ball out of her social world.

Frank Cerabino of the *Palm Beach Post* was delighted to attend the Bachelor Ball. After graduating from Annapolis and serving on an aircraft carrier, he had entered journalism with the dream of having his own column. The *Post* had given him that a little more than a year earlier, and his humorous, often edgy writing had become a must-read for many in the county. He figured he'd hang out at Trump's blast for a couple of hours Saturday evening and deliver his words by 10:30 P.M., just in time to make the Sunday paper.

Cerabino arrived at 7:40 P.M., twenty minutes before the event's start time. He drove an ancient, battered Toyota, the kind of vehicle more often driven by household help and gardeners. Valet parkers were notorious snobs, and they figured the person driving this wreck had no business there. When Cerabino told them he was a reporter, one of the nineteen valets moved his car out of sight and directed him to a spot near the front door.

Other reporters began arriving. Many of the women wore gowns suitable for the loftiest of Palm Beach social events. Even so, they were treated no better than Cerabino and were told to join him a good distance from the massive, ornate front doors. Meanwhile, the *National Enquirer*'s Wayne Grover got out of his car, handed his keys to a valet, and walked right into the event.

Then came the first of the models, a category of humanity Trump ordered up by the score. When he beckoned them, they came, arriving from Miami, where they were as ubiquitous as palm trees. He invited 350 of them, probably as many in one place as anywhere but New York during Fashion Week.

While the guests continued arriving, much the same scene was taking place three miles south at the Breakers hotel. There the men were in white tie and tails or at least tuxedos; the women wore ball gowns and some had tiaras on their heads.

The evening at the Breakers celebrated a social order unchanged for decades. The great hall was filled with old Palm Beach as they fox-trotted and waltzed the night away. Founded by Mrs. Post in 1957, the ball was staid and formal in every way. The gala had gone on much like this for thirty-six years in a row. The grande dame Sue Whitmore was chairing the event for the twenty-second straight time. The charity ball was as much a statement as a party.

To Donnelly, this evening was the epitome of everything she venerated. "Come on, admit it," Donnelly wrote. "There is still nothing that epitomizes Palm Beach like Saturday night's International Red Cross Ball. All those tiaras. All that blue blood. All that tradition."

Donnelly praised the elegant dress of some of the couples and commented that these ladies and gentlemen were "far too properly deported to end up at Donald Trump's house." After making their mandatory appearance at the annual evening, some of the older guests had already started to leave the Red Cross Ball for home by 10:00 P.M.

That's when things were just beginning at Mar-a-Lago. As the journalists— an unruly brood when they feel they are being kept unfairly from a story— stood outside listening to the sounds of the party, they grew restless and upset. Finally, Trump came out to talk to them.

"We're just having a great time in Palm Beach," Trump said. "Everybody is coming. This is going to be a wild party."

As Trump turned and went back inside, he left the reporters like orphans with their faces pressed up against the windowpane. Watching Trump retreat, Cerabino realized the game Trump had played on them, attempting to create a sense of excitement for the other guests as they ran the media gauntlet into the event.

Cerabino glanced at his watch and saw his Cinderella moment had come, and he hadn't even gotten inside the palace. "Trump's inside the door talking intently with a woman wearing a dress with a gaping cutaway up the middle," he wrote in his column the next day. "I tell the valet, I'm not staying to watch the arrival of the three buses full of models. And I was all set to like Trump."

The ball inside wasn't proceeding quite as Trump planned. He had given ABC's *Primetime Live* a television exclusive on the event. At one point, ABC correspondent Judd Rose asked Trump how he could stage such an extravagant party when he was said to be almost broke. "He went nuclear on us," Rose said. "Ripped his mike off and threw it across the lawn."

Trump hated it when journalists didn't do what they were supposed to do, but he knew he had someone covering the event who always got it right. That was Wayne Grover. The *National Enquirer* reporter had his camera ready when personal trainer Jimmy Franzo jumped into the pool nude, and Trump pushed Franzo's fully clothed date, Kelly Hyler, in to join him. The angry, dripping Elite model would have pushed the tuxedoed Trump in, too, but his security held her back. Trump loved it. He was doubly happy since his Boswell from the *National Enquirer* was chronicling every moment.

When Grover quoted an "insider" in his Trump stories, it was almost always Trump, the greatest insider of them all. In this instance, the "insider" told Grover, "Kelli's [*sic*] gown was a mess. Trump joked, 'Go ahead, take if off. I'll get you a robe—later.'" That was the leering Trump at his best, but it got even better. Franzo told Grover, "Kelli [*sic*] later disappeared with Trump. I don't know what that guy has, but it works."

Trump had tried to get the model to take off her wet dress, and then her date said she had gone off with him, presumably to one of the bedrooms on the estate. What could be sweeter than having the whole world—at least the part that read the *National Enquirer*—know about this supposed assignation?

One guest not taken in by any of this was the ABC correspondent Rose. "It was all for our benefit," Rose said. "Pretty pathetic."

Grover also wrote that after midnight, many of the guests coupled up and roamed over the seventeen acres having sex. That was not the only unusual use of the property that evening. Kennedy cousin Anthony Shriver had not been invited, but he showed up anyway. When he left, instead of driving his Jeep Cherokee out the main gate, he turned to use the massive property as his personal Indianapolis Speedway.

The couples lying around the property looked up to see looming headlights bearing toward them as Shriver sped wildly across the lawns. "He was acting like a psycho," Trump told a pal, that pal being Grover. "He refused to let a valet get the Jeep. He got it himself and drove around the estate at speeds up to 90 m.p.h, destroying plants, trees, hedges, and a pole."

Cerabino missed all the excitement, but he felt his words were strong enough for the front page, and his editor agreed. The next morning Palm Beach County woke up to read "Party Pooper Trump Snubs Press 'Guests,'" describing how Cerabino had stood outside "bemoaning the lack of portable toilets at Mar-a-Lago and looking longingly at a shadowy corner of the manicured lawn."

Cerabino got a call that morning from his brother Tom in New York. Tom Cerabino was a big-time mergers-and-acquisitions lawyer. Trump was one of his best clients.

"Did you write something about Donald Trump today?" Tom asked.

"Yes, I did."

"Well, he just called me. He asked if I had a brother named Frank in Florida, and I said I did. He's going to call you tomorrow morning."

Sure enough, Monday morning Trump called Cerabino. "There's a huge misunderstanding," Trump said. "You should have told me you were Tom's brother, and everything would have been fine."

"Are you kidding me?" Cerabino said. "I want to thank you. I've been to a lot of parties before, and when you've seen one, you've seen them all. But I've never been to a party like this where I didn't get to go inside. You did me a favor. You gave me a much better column."

Trump hung up. Five minutes later the phone rang again. "Trump just called me," Tom Cerabino said. "He said you're an even bigger asshole than he thought you were."

The weekend after the Bachelor Ball, Trump flew west for the AT&T Pebble Beach National Pro-Am. Trump was an excellent golfer. He proved it on the first day of the tournament by scoring a hole in one on the 3-par twelfth hole while shooting a 3-over-par 75, equaling his pro partner, Paul Goydos.

That wasn't an everyday occurrence for anyone, and Trump called Wayne Grover at the *National Enquirer* to tell him. Grover had gotten used to calls from Trump whenever he felt the need to brag or was feeling lonely. Sometimes Trump pretended he was someone else, usually a mysterious gentleman named

John Barron. On those occasions, there were no holds barred on his boasting, as "Barron" went on and on about the great Donald Trump. He apparently liked the name "Barron" so much that he later gave it to his youngest son.

This day Trump used his own name. "Wayne, I just scored two holes in one," he said. Grover wasn't a golfer, but he knew it was unheard of to get two holes in one in a single game. Trump talked in detail about his shot on the twelfth hole. Then he described his second hole in one. What he meant was that Marla Maples had come out to be with him.

When Trump flew to Palm Beach the next weekend, he was a different person. It was time for him to begin the first political campaign of his life, to attempt to convince the Palm Beach Town Council to vote in favor of turning Mar-a-Lago into a club, and he threw himself totally into the battle. This man who had been so indifferent, even disdainful toward the local community transformed himself into everyone's favorite neighbor, a jocular, backslapping buddy with time for everybody.

Paul Rampell had already begun the work. He believed that the two Jewish members of the town council would vote for the club, and the two Christians would likely vote no. That left a fifth member who hadn't been elected yet. Rampell decided to focus on one of the three candidates, Michele Clarke Royal, a third-generation Palm Beacher and a member of the Bath and Tennis with no political experience.

If Trump personally contributed to her campaign, he might appear to be trying to buy her vote. Rampell's money would be almost as bad, so the lawyer came up with other ways of helping Royal, including running a phone bank from his office and asking friends in the Northeast to donate to Royal's campaign.

While Rampell was working to win a majority of the town council, two prominent members of the Everglades came to the lawyer's office. The Palm Beach gentlemen told him there was no way the town council would approve Trump's plan. The sooner he and his patron realized that, the better. They represented a group with whom the town authorities had the highest confidence, and they wanted to buy Mar-a-Lago and turn it into a club themselves.

Although the two men were not so frank in declaring their intentions, they were trying to do what the Committee of the Select 100 had failed to do in 1944: buy up property to prevent the influx of large numbers of Jewish Americans. Rampell had no doubt but that their club would have the same restricted policies as the Everglades, and he would not be welcome.

Rampell had no choice but to take the proposal to Trump. "Fuck them," Trump said. "They're assholes." The lawyer did not disagree.

Trump invited 215 members and guests of the Historical Society of Palm Beach County to Mar-a-Lago for the society's annual award presentation in February 1993. For the special occasion, the organization charged a heady $125 a person, more than four times the thirty dollars the event had cost the previous year.

To get his way, Trump was willing to say anything and embrace anyone, including the honoree, Professor Donald W. Curl, who had attacked Trump's plan to subdivide the estate. Trump remembered every slight and forgave nothing, but he was beyond cordial to Curl and treated him as a dear friend. Trump acted as if his idea of a good time was hanging out with a bunch of local historians. "Maybe we'll do this on a yearly basis," he told the group. That was a neat touch. If he got his club, the Historical Society might be welcomed back.

The Historical Society event was not the only occasion on which Trump wooed the locals. For eight years straight, the Palm Beach Round Table, a popular luncheon group, had invited Trump to speak, but he had always said no. Now he was available. The February event took place in the grand ballroom at the Ramada Resort in West Palm Beach, with space for five hundred guests. To make sure the event was a sellout, the Round Table ran ads in the *Palm Beach Daily News* and the *Palm Beach Post* two weeks before, announcing the luncheon was open to the public.

The ballroom was full to hear the first speech Trump had ever given in Palm Beach County. Trump spent most of his half-hour talk promoting the idea of a club. "It will guarantee the future preservation of Mar-a-Lago beyond Donald Trump," he said. When he finished taking questions, Trump invited everyone present to come over to Mar-a-Lago, where he had soft drinks and wine ready to greet them.

Most of the luncheon guests were thrilled about visiting the famous estate. Some didn't even wait for the program to end before they jumped up, headed out to their cars, and drove across the Intracoastal Waterway to Palm Beach.

One of the guests was Etonella Christlieb, a Dutch-born woman who lived with her South African husband, John, and their three children on an estate facing the Intracoastal Waterway. A member of the Palm Beach Round Table board, she was also raising money to upgrade the Palm Beach County School of the Arts in West Palm Beach.

"I've heard what you're doing with this school," Trump said. "I'd like to help. I'll give you a party here at Mar-a-Lago for seventy-five people."

"That's wonderful, Mr. Trump," the young socialite said.

"What do you charge for your fund-raisers?" Trump asked.

"We've been charging thirty-five dollars."

"Well, you're charging a thousand dollars, and they'll come," Trump said.

That was an almost unthinkable amount of money to ask for what was a decidedly unchic charity, but Trump had an astute understanding of Mar-a-Lago's value when coupled with his name. Christlieb wasn't so sure. She went back to her fellow board members for the school foundation, and they said yes, enthusiastically.

Hosting the benefit was a smart thing for Trump to do as part of his public relations offensive, and it gave him cachet with a powerful community group. During those few weeks when Trump courted Palm Beach, he learned something invaluable. When he wanted people to like him and ratcheted up his charm, something magical happened. It didn't matter what he had said before, he could turn his auditors around with a few well-placed words and have them lapping up his utterances.

Trump was on such a roll with this new persona that he did something he almost never did. He apologized. He accepted some of the blame for the problems he'd had with the Preservation Foundation. "It may have been my fault," he told the Shiny Sheet in February. "Maybe I wasn't diplomatic enough. I'm not saying I should be representing the United States in the United Nations." Then Trump said he was "inclined to probably let them use [Mar-a-Lago] again if they wanted to." Left unsaid was that first Trump had to get his club.

Though none of the three candidates for the open town council seat won a majority of the votes in the initial election. Royal triumphed in the March run-off by two votes, and Trump and Rampell had a town council member in their debt. That gave Trump even more incentive to play the gracious politician.

That same month, Trump got news that changed his life. On a weekend visit at Mar-a-Lago, Maples told Trump that their get-together at Pebble Beach had been memorable beyond a hole in one. That was when she believed she became pregnant.

As he was still trying to digest his impending fatherhood, Trump filed a 150-page application with the Palm Beach Planning, Zoning & Building Department to establish the Mar-a-Lago Club. The document laid out plans for an establishment that would include everything on the estate's seventeen acres, including the pool, golf course, and tennis courts. There would be ten guest rooms, a small ballroom containing a movie screen, a dining room that could seat up to seventy-five guests, and a seventy-five-person staff. He planned to transform a storage area into fitness rooms, a sauna, and massage tables.

In April 1993, Trump told Grover that after Maples signed a prenuptial agreement, he planned to marry her at his Taj Mahal Hotel & Casino in Atlantic City in "the wedding of the century" before a thousand guests, including high rollers. In May he told the tabloid that the prenuptial hadn't worked out, and the marriage was off. He sounded immensely relieved. Trump told Grover he felt it would be fine to walk down the aisle again if he could be with Marla five days a week but could go off and do his bachelor thing the other two days. That wasn't exactly Maples's ideal marriage.

Trump had other matters on his mind. In the days before the May 13, 1993, town council meeting that would decide the fate of the proposed Mar-a-Lago Club, Trump talked to everyone he could about the proposed club. He even met with his nemeses at the Preservation Foundation in an attempt to get their support.

Every seat was filled for this special town council hearing, and Trump and his lawyers arrived early for the 9:00 A.M. meeting. He was often a big talker, but this morning he said only that if he "could leave one legacy to Palm Beach, it would be the creation of a non-sectarian club." This was the first time he or

Rampell publicly suggested that one of the primary virtues of the club was that it would have Jewish members.

In his presentation, Paul Rampell argued that a club was the best solution for an estate that no individual could afford to maintain and was costing Donald Trump seven thousand dollars a day. If a club was not permitted, Rampell said a new owner of Mar-a-Lago would likely come back to the town council to ask to subdivide the estate. The attorney didn't talk about the proposed club being unrestricted.

Most of the criticism of the plan focused on increased traffic and noise. Rampell said they had agreed to limit the club to 611 members and 313 trips a day in and out of the estate. As to the fifty-million-dollar lawsuit against the town, Rampell promised his client would settle if the town council approved the Mar-a-Lago Club.

"Another question that's often asked to me, will Mr. Trump continue to live at Mar-a-Lago?" Rampell said. "No. Except that he will be a member of the club, and therefore he will be entitled to the use of guest rooms."

When Trump left the chambers for a lunch break, he had a good feeling about his chances. But when he came back, he sat for hours listening to representatives of the old Palm Beach, and they were not amused with his proposed club. Louis Pryor, president of the Palm Beach Civic Association, believed Trump was a menace to the island. Pryor referred to "Mr. Trump's close association with gambling interests and business relations with a broad range of people not indigenous to this area or even to Florida."

When Frank Chopin of the Palm Beach Preservation Foundation got up to speak, he began by saying his organization had nothing against the idea of a club. Then he enumerated every problem he anticipated: the lack of smoke detectors, the parking, the ancient drapes that lacked fire retardant, the liquor license, the rooms let out to visitors. "What happens when somebody comes in with a wheelchair?" he asked.

Trump sat through all of this, but he left an hour before the 8:00 P.M. roll call vote. If he had stayed, he would have watched things proceeding just as Rampell predicted they would. The two Jewish council members voted in favor of the club. The two Christian council members voted no. And Michele Clarke

Royal voted yes, providing the crucial vote in passing the measure and allowing Mar-a-Lago to become a club.

This victory was far more important than merely the permission to turn the estate into a club. Much of the origins of Donald Trump's disdain toward what he considers the country's entrenched, unresponsive political establishment originates in this experience in Palm Beach. Trump saw the subdivision of the estate as his right as a property owner. Being forced to seek permission from the landmarks commission, the zoning commission, and the town council was, for him, facing off with an intellectually corrupt elite that had created a farcical caricature of the democratic process. Having to return to the town council to ask to turn Mar-a-Lago into a club was just as demeaning.

This battle provoked in Trump a populist, libertarian reaction. It was always about advancing his interests, but it became the engine that helped to carry him to the White House.

"Mar-a-Lago was Trump's launching pad," said one longtime associate. "It was like a Broadway show opening out of town in New Haven." Palm Beach is a privileged enclave of settled customs and laws. The island is, by many measures, the most socially intimidating community in America. New arrivals did almost anything to be accepted. At first Trump was like everybody else, but then he provoked the establishment the way nobody had ever dared to do. He set out to make enemies as much as friends, and he became the most controversial figure in the town's century-long history. And he reveled in that persona, revving it up ever higher.

Three months after winning permission to open the club at Mar-a-Lago, Rampell appeared before the town council again. This time there was no roomful of spectators and impassioned residents wanting to voice their opinions. A technical matter was being discussed, but it was one with enormous consequences for Trump and much of his future business activity.

In seeking approval for his club, Trump had come to the town council offering to grant an easement that would constrain him from building in the future on the massive property. The preservation-minded council members viewed this as a crucial matter as they debated whether to approve the club.

But Rampell had a problem. Trump wanted to take a massive tax write-off for limiting his future rights with the property, but if he signed a document with the town mentioning the easement as part of the deal for the club, it would be a quid pro quo, not a charitable donation, and Trump wouldn't be able to get the tax break. Rampell told the town council, "If the preservation easements are a part of the contractual agreement, [Trump] is no longer doing it voluntarily or in a charitable spirit, and he doesn't get the donation." Everyone in the chambers knew it was a quid pro quo, but they agreed not to make Trump sign a written document so Trump could take as much as a $5.75 million tax deduction, a sum more than he initially paid for the property.

It was a delicious loophole, obscure and lucrative. As Christine Stapleton and Lawrence Mower reported in the *Palm Beach Post,* in the following years Trump took easements worth more than one hundred million dollars in tax deductions on his golf courses and other properties. That was the source of most of his charitable giving, and it all began in Palm Beach.

Even in his most extravagant fantasies, Trump could not have envisioned just how lucrative Mar-a-Lago would become. In the ensuing years, the estate and soon-to-be-built golf club spun off more than two hundred million dollars in profits while providing Trump and his family with a nonpareil resort.

7

"A T-Bone in a Kennel"

As Marla's pregnancy grew increasingly obvious, the pressure on Trump grew. He told Maples he would take her to Paris over the Fourth of July weekend and marry her in the French capital, but he didn't bother telling her that it was impossible to fly into France and get married in such short time. From what Trump had told Wayne Grover, there would be no Paris wedding, but even so, Grover was there with a *National Enquirer* photographer, clicking away while Trump pushed a luggage cart through Charles de Gaulle Airport, and Maples carried her wedding gown in a plastic garment bag over her shoulder. It would take a while before Trump told her the sad news that they wouldn't be marrying this weekend.

Grover had an almost limitless expense account, but he was staying in a fleabag hotel off the Champs-Élysées and eating in dumps even the most adventurous avoided. He became so sick that he ended up in a hospital. Larry Haley, his editor, called Trump and asked him to visit the reporter. Trump and Maples showed up at the hospital before they flew back to the States.

Trump was not the first Palm Beach man to get his mistress pregnant. If the

birth was not aborted, the young woman was generally shuttled off to an obscure place to give birth. In most instances, the child was either given up for
adoption or brought up far enough away from the island that no one challenged
the father's reputation.

Trump brought Maples to Mar-a-Lago, and at St. Mary's Hospital, in West
Palm Beach, she gave birth to Tiffany Ariana Trump on October 13, 1993. As
usual, the largest audience for this story was the readership of the *National
Enquirer*. Trump's life had become a tabloid story, and he relished it.

This time Trump outdid himself by telling Grover how the loving father flew
down in the middle of the night from New York to be with his "honey" at the
blessed moment. "Watching our baby's birth definitely was the biggest thrill
of my life," he said, the squeamish father having been in the delivery room for
the first time in his life.

No moment seemed too intimate for the tabloid readers. The story described
the moment when obstetrician Dr. Jay Trabin gave Trump a pair of scissors
and asked him to cut the umbilical cord. At first the new father was reluctant,
but he took the shears and with a quick snip separated Tiffany from her mother.
"Welcome to the world, Tiffany," Maples told her daughter. As poignant as this
moment was, it could not be forgotten that even though the baby bore Trump's
last name, the mother did not, and Trump gave no indication that he planned
to marry Maples.

The *Palm Beach Daily News* had little choice but to write about the birth,
considering that it had occurred in a West Palm Beach hospital. The editors
avoided scandalizing their readers by not mentioning that Trump and Maples
were unmarried.

Trump had other concerns than the blessings of fatherhood. One was a spirited rewriting of the history that he had failed at business. In November 1993
Trump ran a full-page ad in the Shiny Sheet trumpeting the success of his West
Palm Beach condominium. "When I look at Trump Plaza from Mar-a-Lago,"
Trump said in the ad, "I am proud that even in the horrendous real estate market of the early 1990s, I was able to rescue this previously troubled and unsold
development, add management, construction expertise and the name Trump . . .
and make it into one of Florida's great success stories."

Never mind that there had been two auctions to get rid of unsold units, that he had welched on mortgage payments and had walked away from a fourteen-million-dollar loan. These were minor matters unworthy of discussion.

Trump challenged Palm Beach's moral standard in a way nobody ever had. He flaunted his busloads of models, his pregnant girlfriend, and then his new-born daughter born out of wedlock. His profligate lifestyle was chronicled in places no one of substance wanted to be—not the always discreet *Palm Beach Daily News* and *Town & Country*, but the *National Enquirer* and the *New York Post*'s Page Six.

Trump had become an acute observer of Palm Beach and its ways. A vocif-erous reader of the dailies, he paged through looking for mentions of his name. On the first Sunday in November 1993, the Shiny Sheet published a forty-four-page preview of the upcoming season. In the old days, there had been only a few charity events, including the Red Cross Ball and a couple of other formal occasions. Now there might be three or four competing affairs in an evening. The list of forthcoming events went on for five pages.

An article in the supplement offered "tips on how to maintain the social pace" and made the season seem less a time of pleasure than an endless ordeal. "I pace myself as much as I can," said Hermé de Wyman Miro. "Make sure you take your vitamins, exercise and get plenty of sleep," advised Etonella Christlieb.

And then there was the question of who would be the next social queen lead-ing Palm Beach society. Donnelly handicapped her ten candidates, giving nine of them odds that ranged from 20–1 to 2–1. The tenth candidate had no interest in the honor, but this was an opportunity for the *Palm Beach Daily News* society editor to show Trump that he and his blond playmate could not bull their way into Palm Beach:

"**Marla Maples:** Miss America looks and Mar-a-Lago, too. Still, mistress to a married, then divorced man and mother to his love child. A T-bone in a ken-nel has a better chance. **ODDS:** 1,000,000–1."

Trump would try to get even with Donnelly in his own good time, but he was faced with one problem that would not go away, and that was what to do with

Maples. His parents were of a generation that looked on a child born out of wedlock as moral dereliction of the highest order, and they implored their son to marry the woman. Her parents were equally insistent that Trump do the right thing.

Early in December, Trump phoned Maples in Palm Beach and asked her to marry him. He sold the photo rights to the December 20, 1993, nuptials to the *National Enquirer*. Grover and his editor, Larry Haley, flew up to New York from Florida. The day before the wedding, Trump called Haley to discuss the event.

"Larry, do you really think I should get married?" Trump asked.

"If you're asking me if you should get married, you shouldn't get married," Haley said.

For the wedding, the two tabloid journalists sat in some of the best seats in the Grand Ballroom of the Plaza Hotel. They were among an array of celebrities that included Bianca Jagger, Rosie O'Donnell, O. J. Simpson, Howard Stern, boxing champions Joe Frazier and Evander Holyfield, boxing promoter Don King, and New York mayor David Dinkins.

Trump and Maples had only a few weeks to prepare for the service, and the couple went for the greatest hits, everything from "Ave Maria" to the Lord's Prayer. Trump stood at the front of the ballroom in his tuxedo as Marla, in a white satin gown by Carolina Herrera and a borrowed two-million-dollar tiara, walked down the aisle on the arm of her father.

The forty-seven-year-old groom looked at his thirty-year-old bride with what appeared to be adoration and blissful happiness. A few years later, he admitted his feelings were somewhat different. "I was bored when she was walking down the aisle," he said. "I kept thinking: '*What the hell am I doing here?*'" As the newlyweds walked up the aisle after saying their vows, Howard Stern shouted, "I give this marriage a fucking four months!!"

When the newlyweds went up to their suite at the hotel, Maples wanted to do the traditional wedding night ritual and make love. Trump had something more significant to do first: check out the coverage. He turned on the television, and there was Stern repeating his ominous prophecy.

It wasn't all bad news. Trump had the honey half of the world lusted over, or so it seemed. He placed Maples's life-size cardboard image in a bikini behind his desk. Every man who came into Trump's office to talk to him had no choice but to look right at Marla and know she was Donald J. Trump's wife and she was hotter than Death Valley.

Trump had won approval to turn Mar-a-Lago into a club, but the people of Palm Beach were still deriding him and hoping he would go away, taking his bride and baby with him. "What's going on?" the *Palm Beach Daily News* asked in an editorial. "There seems to be a wave of hysteria sweeping the town over Donald Trump and his Mar-a-Lago Club plans."

Challenging the idea that developments at Mar-a-Lago weren't being carefully monitored, Mayor Paul Ilyinsky insisted that "the town government is in full control of the situation." Members of the town council wrote memos to town officials imploring them to make sure Trump followed through on every promise he had made. These enforcement officers then zapped off memos to Trump reminding him of everything he had to do before he could open his club.

Trump believed his Mar-a-Lago Club would be different because anyone who had the money could join. He saw himself as creating populism for the well-to-do, democratizing the top ranks of American wealth. A new class with more and more money stood ready to buy their way into what they considered the establishment.

Trump's victory had stirred up an island full of venomous enemies who deplored his vision for Mar-a-Lago. "There's a lot of resistance," socialite Tamara Newell told the *Palm Beach Post*. "To a lot of people, it's more a Boca idea than a Palm Beach idea." Boca Raton was full of Jewish residents. No one missed what Newell was saying.

It hardly helped Trump's cause when he gave another party full of busloads of scantily clad models from Miami. To many on the island, Trump was creating an estate of sin and salaciousness. He was bringing in the sorts of people who had never before come to the island. Trump had shown his disregard for the laws of the island. Soon the locals feared he would want to bring gambling to Mar-a-Lago and other vices that the good gentry of Palm Beach thought had no place on their beloved island.

Civic groups began to put forth resolutions condemning the town council for making "concessions" to Trump. No group was more vocal and personal in its criticism than the Palm Beach Civic Association. Their newsletter described Trump as "the notorious New York developer" who might destroy the most precious relic of the island's glorious past. "What would Marjorie Merriweather Post think?" they asked.

Civic Association board member Stanley M. Rumbough Jr. knew best what Mrs. Post would have thought. He had been married to her daughter, Dina Merrill, for almost two decades and had been to Mar-a-Lago innumerable times. Tall, handsome, and lean, he had impeccable manners and a graciousness that rarely faltered.

A graduate of Yale and a champion tennis player, Captain Rumbough flew a Mustang fighter plane in the Pacific during World War II on more than fifty missions. He was the recipient of eight Air Medals and two Distinguished Flying Crosses. In Palm Beach, the Colgate heir lived within a world he knew and understood and possessed a self-confidence that some friends thought veered occasionally into arrogance.

Rumbough loved the old Palm Beach profoundly and was devoted to maintaining its unique quality. To him, Trump symbolized a vulgar new world, a wrecking ball smashing everything he touched. Rumbough believed that Trump's intention to turn Mar-a-Lago into a club was another of his commercial ventures that would exploit the island's social life to make money.

Trump sicced his lawyers on the Civic Association, claiming "that by your actions, words and deeds, you have libeled me and seriously damaged my reputation." The group backed off on some of its criticism, and Trump never followed through on his threat to sue.

As workers proceeded with the physical changes to turn Mar-a-Lago into a club, Trump signaled how different things would be. In January, he hosted a fund-raiser at Mar-a-Lago for the 1994 State of Israel Bonds. This was the first time a Jewish organization had held an event at the estate, and it signaled to the community how serious Trump was about soliciting Jewish members.

Trump was hands-on in transforming Mar-a-Lago into a club. While keeping everything as true to the estate's original vision as he could, he managed changes such as altering the property for heavier traffic and addressing the enormous dining room table, which had no place in a room that would seat all kinds of smaller parties. Unlike so many of the restorations on the island that destroyed the souls of the classic buildings, Trump stayed true not only to his vision but to Mrs. Post's.

Every Saturday morning, Trump sat down on the living room sofa with project director C. Wesley Blackman to discuss the previous week. If things had not gone well, even if the failures had nothing to do with Blackman, Trump raged against the project coordinator in words so fiercely intemperate that many employees would have scurried away.

"It was a challenge to work for him," says Blackman. "He was visiting every week, and we had construction that was not always a straight path. Sometimes permissions didn't come through, and you can't fool him. He has such attention to detail. He's brilliant in being able to juggle a lot of things at once and know pretty much what everyone else is doing."

Paul Rampell had an equally high opinion of his client. He became so close to Trump that he began to identify with him. When Rampell noted Trump's eternal struggle with weight, he rashly bet Trump two hundred thousand dollars that he could not lose twenty pounds in a month. Rampell was not just a judicious lawyer. He was a judicious man, not given to taking wild chances. He was successful, but he could ill afford to cough up such an enormous amount of money. Just after issuing the challenge, he realized that winning wouldn't be so great, either. Trump wouldn't be happy, and where would that leave Rampell?

Trump took the bet seriously. He came over to Rampell's house wearing enough clothes for a winter evening in northern Maine, got on Rampell's professional scale, and jiggled the lever until it balanced perfectly at 235 pounds. Trump brought a Mar-a-Lago employee as a witness. In the next days, Trump kept checking in with Rampell, letting him know how he was doing on the Atkins diet. The first pounds were the easiest, and after about ten days Trump had lost as much as ten pounds. He kept losing more, and Rampell began facing the horrendous possibility that Trump might win. Then Trump started gaining weight, and Rampell took an easy breath. Then, on the final day, Trump called from Philadelphia to say he had lost twenty pounds.

Rampell couldn't let the verdict rest on that assertion. He insisted that Trump fly down to Florida for a weigh-in on the same scale he had used the month before. Trump arrived with his Mar-a-Lago assistant and the scale used for his victorious reading. If the clothes he was wearing were any thinner, he might have been arrested for public nudity. Sure enough, his scale indicated a loss of twenty pounds, but Rampell's scale read nineteen. The two men had a lengthy debate over who had won. In the end, they decided to call it a draw, with no money changing hands. Rampell was one relieved lawyer.

That's where it should have ended, but Trump was going to win one way or another. It took him a while before he called the *National Enquirer*'s Wayne Grover and told him about the bet. "I lost 25 pounds and gained $200,000—and even Marla's friends are drooling over me!" Trump said in a story in the tabloid. "I never do anything halfway, and I knew I could lose the weight and gain the money. When I collected my $200,000, the guy could hardly believe his eyes—or the scale!"

Now that Trump had the renovation of Mar-a-Lago under control, he moved on to his next obsession: to build his own golf course. Mar-a-Lago had a nine-hole pitch-and-putt golf course that, for a golfer with a swing like Trump's, was more like playing miniature golf than a game on a real course. He wanted to expand the course into eighteen holes. One potential green would be a mere two hundred feet from a tee on the back lawn to the ocean, and Trump realized it just wasn't going to work.

Trump decided to acquire a course elsewhere. When he learned that the Palm Beach Polo and Country Club was for sale, he drove out to Wellington with Paul Rampell to check the club out. The place wasn't bad, though not the world-class course Trump wanted. Worse, it was a sixteen-mile drive from Palm Beach, and he couldn't subject his club members to such a long, unpleasant trip. Palm Beach Polo was crossed off his list.

"You know, there's some other properties we could take a look at," Rampell said as they headed back toward the island. Just west of the Palm Beach International Airport, they saw the Palm Beach County Jail, a twelve-story concrete and steel slab, rising high above the horizon. Around the facility was scruffy, forsaken land that appeared fit only for storing dangerous chemicals or dumping abandoned cars.

Trump looked across this miserable two hundred acres owned by the Palm Beach County Department of Airports and saw a great international golf course. "This might work," he told Rampell, asking him to check out acquiring the land.

When the Department of Airports said it would lease the land to Trump only if he dropped his threatened lawsuit over the airport noise, he reared up and ran off in a huff, seeking other sites. But with Trump a no was never definitive, and he would be back when the wind was behind his back.

Meanwhile the Mar-a-Lago kitchen was reconfigured to serve seventy-five dinner guests at a time. Trump thought of the ten guest suites as big money-makers, and he made sure they were ready. A new gate was needed on Southern Boulevard, the back entrance to the estate, and that work was done.

Trump turned the library into a bar and kept his portrait, *The Visionary*, as the centerpiece of the room while removing the unread leather-bound volumes. Any of Post's furniture that was too fragile to survive the heavy use in a club was taken out and replaced by sturdy replicas.

Sundays became a dreaded day for Mar-a-Lago employees. That was the day Trump had the unwanted furniture and other possessions hauled down to the ballroom. Mrs. Post had a Costco-like attitude toward belongings. One was never enough, and even the two bomb shelters were full of furniture. On the weekend, a massive array of goods moved through the ballroom, yet even that represented only around 4 percent of Mrs. Post's belongings.

Trump squeezed every nickel he could out of the possessions for which he had no use. He shipped the best of the lot to New York for an auction at Christie's. The items on view a few days before the March 1995 auction included an eighteenth-century Russian altar panel, a seventeenth-century Spanish carpet, and several Italian gilt wood tables.

Dina Merrill, Mrs. Post's daughter, was among those perusing the objects before the sale. Sometimes those who inherit wealth assume their riches are a part of them and always will be. Merrill had a hurt expression as she looked across the large room. "If I'd known he was going to do this, I would have taken more when I had the chance," Merrill said, and walked away.

On auction day Trump watched as some of the items sold for ten or twenty times the expected price. Christie's had expected to net around a million dollars, but the auction took in $1,535,973. Observers attributed the sum to what was called "the Streisand factor," recalling the previous year when the singer had auctioned art and furniture. Nobody better understood the monetary value of celebrity than Trump. As he saw the world, his and Mrs. Post's names rightfully merited a 50 percent increase in what people were willing to pay.

Any items that Trump didn't think worthy of Christie's were shipped twenty miles south to Arthur James Galleries in Delray Beach. Scores of people wanted their connection with Trump and Mrs. Post, and these doodads and minor collectibles sold for a total of $140,000.

The rest was a motley array of Christmas lights with broken bulbs, golden reindeers with smashed necks, lampshades yellow with age, and other similar items. These items were sold at Adam & Eve Architectural Salvage, along the railroad tracks in West Palm Beach, to more than two hundred casually dressed Floridians who clambered through the chain-link gate. It was just another indication that what Trump was truly selling was a connection to the growing power of his fame.

To market the club, Trump pushed his own celebrity as far as he could take it. When membership director Kathy Merlin told the Shiny Sheet that the world's most famously estranged couple, Prince Charles and Princess Diana, had each become charter members at the Mar-a-Lago Club, the editors put that on the front page—though they knew Trump well enough to add a minor caveat to their headline: "CHARLES, DIANA JOIN MAR-A-LAGO CLUB, *TRUMP SAYS*."

This was an amazing story for the day after Christmas 1994, and it ended up in papers and on television all across the country. The reports noted that Charles and Diana had not hit up Trump for a two-for-one membership. The separated couple had each apparently paid the full fifty thousand dollars. They were smart to have done so, because Merlin said that on New Year's Day, the initial fee was going up to seventy-five thousand dollars and soon after one hundred thousand dollars.

Merlin even addressed the problem of what to do if Charles and Diana showed up at the same time. "I assume they would work that out themselves, her people talking to his people," said the membership director. "I don't think that would be our job."

Charles and Diana were not the only charter members announced that day. The list issued by the club's PR office was so incredible that for once Trump didn't have to pump it up with hyperbole. It was exciting just imagining what it would be like.

Maybe the royals would come at the same time on occasion, but if they did, they would likely stay on opposite ends of the living room. In the middle, Henry Kissinger might be talking to former President Gerald Ford about their days in Washington. Kissinger liked being around Hollywood types, and he could have his pick from fellow members Bruce Willis, Arnold Schwarzenegger, Robert Wagner, Elizabeth Taylor, Denzel Washington, and Steven Spielberg. Norman Mailer was not a club kind of guy, but even he had joined, and there was no telling what he might say.

Four days after the Charles and Diana story, Shannon Donnelly's column ran on the paper's front page. "Buckingham Palace has a message for Donald Trump," the column began. "'Liar, liar, pants on fire.'" Donnelly had phoned a spokesman at Buckingham Palace, who told her, "This story is nonsense—absolutely, utterly untrue. Neither of them is a member. This story was concocted by Mr. Trump to secure publicity for his club. It is a matter of regret that he feels he can use the names of the members of the royal family to do so."

The movie stars, former secretary of state, and former president had not joined the Mar-a-Lago Club, either. But getting caught at this didn't seem to bother Trump. Some of what had been announced stuck even if it wasn't so. It wasn't his fault anyway. He had people working for him, and he blamed them. Trump claimed the membership director misunderstood him when he said he was sending honorary memberships to a long list of celebrities.

The story was widely considered an outrageous fib, and the media took the opportunity to mock Trump. *The New York Times Magazine* published a satirical send-up in March 1995 that included a picture of Trump as Gloria Swanson in *Sunset Boulevard,* dressed in a scarlet and white gown, elbow-length gloves, and an extravagant boa, obviously distraught that her guests have not come to her haunted mansion. Michael Rubiner wrote the piece as a mock screenplay in which Joe Gillis, a "young, down-on-his-luck screenwriter," talks to a distraught, lonely Trump:

> JOE: It's a farce. Look around you. There's no Jimmy Carter here. There's no Mike Ovitz. You couldn't get . . . (searching) Steve Lawrence in this room . . .
> *(Trump throws himself on the chaise longue and buries his head in a pillow.)*

It was over-the-top funny, but Trump was incapable of understanding that it was satire. His reaction spoke convincingly to the fact that when it came to himself, he had no sense of humor. "I can state with great authority that the author of your piece is a third-rate talent who, unfortunately, never even called to check his incorrect facts," Trump wrote in a letter to the editor.

Trump may not have been able to laugh at himself, but his life was going great again. He had a new wife and baby. Marla had slimmed down and was the same sexy honey who had driven him half crazy. He had beaten the Palm Beach mandarins without ever compromising, and he had his club now. Trump intended to turn Mar-a-Lago into the club of clubs, a venue so spectacular that the old Palm Beach elite would salivate at the mention of the word "Mar-a-Lago." They might think that his wife had less chance than a "T-bone in a kennel" of being accepted at the heights of Palm Beach society, but he would show them who was the true king of Palm Beach.

8

The Promises of Life

The Mar-a-Lago Club held its grand opening in December 1995. The theme was "Déjà Vu." Trump re-created an evening in the late twenties, from when the estate had been the scene of the most exclusive social events in the wealthy resort community.

To foster Trump's fantasy, twenty workers spent six months turning the ballroom into a black-and-silver cabaret that resembled a nightclub during the Jazz Age. That evening a moon would be shining down on the formally dressed guests standing and sitting around the swimming pool, but Trump wanted to light up the scene like day itself, and he brought in seventy-two thousand watts of additional lighting. Parked along the Intracoastal Waterway were vintage Packard automobiles, another nod to the Roaring Twenties.

The club had actually been open to members since April, but Trump wanted a spectacular evening to shine attention on his accomplishment and lift him even higher in the mass consciousness. "People can't believe how many members we have," Trump told a reporter, looking out on the 350 members and guests. "The place sells itself."

Trump believed that boasting about hundreds of Palm Beachers throwing their checks at him would cause a stampede for memberships. His enemy was always the literal truth, and what he was saying wasn't quite what had happened.

Despite Trump's assertion that he initially charged fifty thousand dollars, raising the amount to seventy-five thousand after the informal opening, most of the first one hundred members paid twenty-five thousand dollars. The money had been kept in escrow, and if the club never opened, they would have gotten their money back.

For some, it was cheaper than that. "I had half a dozen clients that didn't pay to get in," said CPA Richard Rampell, whose brother Paul was Trump's attorney. "Trump comped them because he thought that they would bring in other people." Trump gave one man free membership in return for carpeting and cut almost as many different deals as there were members. For all his braying and boasting, Trump needed to attract new members who would shell out major money, and this showy gala was one way to do it.

Trump was still rising out of a financial debacle that included four business bankruptcies and a sale of most of his assets. "Half of his body was out of the quicksand, but the other half was still there," says one early member. "Several New Yorkers warned me not to join. They said Trump was going down, taking Mar-a-Lago with him."

The invitees entered the driveway past a gauntlet of cameramen filming for CNN, Fox, and other television outlets. No one else but Trump could have gotten national television networks to cover a party promoting a private club, but there they were in the driveway with their cameras. As the guests arrived through the main gates, they were serenaded by a row of violinists culled from classical musicians in South Florida, and as new arrivals entered the mansion, waiters offered cocktails, flutes of champagne, and hors d'oeuvres. The guests moved outside, where professional dancers dressed as flappers and their beaus danced the Charleston.

Once guests filled their plates with fresh jumbo shrimp, filet mignon, and lobster in a pastry shell, they sat down at tables around the pool. For dessert, there was a deliciously tart lemon torte, a rich chocolate mousse cake, and other pastries so beautiful that it seemed a pity to eat them.

After dinner, the crowd flowed into the ballroom. The room was not large enough for everyone. Those who could not squeeze in watched on screens set up on the lawn as the cabaret singer Karen Akers got up on top of the grand piano. Akers's songs evoked feelings of the long-gone era. Afterward, out on the verandah, Tony Bennett sang a few more songs.

Trump wore black tie and walked through the party alongside his wife; Marla wore a brocaded flapperlike gown, elbow-length white gloves, and a white headpiece from the twenties. Trump greeted one guest after another, never stopping for long, moving on with nervous intensity and then moving on again, rarely letting anyone touch him.

"It was a scene out of *The Great Gatsby*," the *Palm Beach Daily News* began its front-page story on the gala. It was natural to compare Trump to F. Scott Fitzgerald's greatest creation, and Trump may have planned the evening with that in mind. He did not have Gatsby's mysterious aura, but he did share Fitzgerald's description of his character that there was "some heightened sensitivity to the promises of life." Trump also possessed Gatsby's restless quality as described by Fitzgerald: "He was never quite still; there was always a tapping foot somewhere or the impatient opening and closing of a hand."

By the measure of those in attendance, the evening was a splendid success. Two town council members, Jack McDonald and Leslie Shaw, were there that evening, along with county commissioner Carol Roberts and U.S. representative Mark Foley. They came to show Trump public deference. "I'm very pleased that the club is in full operation," said McDonald, who, along with Shaw, became an early member. "I think it will be an asset to the town of Palm Beach."

Trump had begun to claim that the club had been his idea, even though it was very much the vision of his lawyer Paul Rampell, who was present that evening. A majority of the members were Jewish, but there were many Christian members. At the party, the two groups melded seamlessly together, and for that alone, the evening was a seminal event in Palm Beach history.

Members who attended the opening received a glossy magazine, *The Mar-a-Lago Club: The Jewel of Palm Beach*, that included a section titled "Five of Clubs," profiling several prominent club members. Never before had one of the island's private clubs promoted itself by touting the accomplishments of individual members. That was another signal that Trump was something new in almost every way.

Celia Lipton Farris was featured in the magazine. Her late husband had been a prolific inventor who made his fortune creating the milk carton. Farris was probably the island's wealthiest widow and was as close as Trump got to having someone from the old Palm Beach establishment join his club.

Farris was Scottish-born and had been a star in the West End and on Broadway in the forties and fifties before she married. Her showbiz career made her unlikely material to join the restricted clubs. She had been a guest at the Bath and Tennis, but now that Mar-a-Lago had opened, she said, "I don't want to go back there. The food is delicious here, and let's face it, it's much more fun."

Farris had been a regular guest at the estate during the Post era, but she thought life at Trump's Mar-a-Lago would be even better. It had troubled her that Mrs. Post's events ended at 11:00 P.M. Farris also loved publicity, especially seeing her picture in the Shiny Sheet. Unlike at the B&T and the Everglades, photographers would be welcome at this new club. She was delighted to be in Trump's magazine promoting her Salvation Army benefit, to be held at the club in a few weeks.

Another charter member profiled in the magazine, attorney Robert Montgomery Jr., had earned $206 million in his historic suit against the tobacco industry and lived in a grand mansion south of Mar-a-Lago. He was far from the only liberal Democrat in the new club. In fact, although Palm Beach was a Republican enclave, Mar-a-Lago probably had as many Democrats as Republicans. Montgomery was one of the three or four Christian members of the Palm Beach Country Club. The attorney joined the fight to end restrictions against Jews and blacks at the Sailfish Club and the Beach Club. He saw Mar-a-Lago as his kind of club. "It's quite simple. If you've got the dough you can join," Montgomery said. "What more could people want than a club with a setting more beautiful than anywhere else on earth and a backdrop steeped in history."

Montgomery was a notable philanthropist, but it was a stretch for Trump to say in his magazine that he "seemingly has done more to enhance the quality of life for South Floridians than anyone but Mother Nature herself." Trump liked hyperbolic assertions of praise. They didn't cost anything and often reaped big rewards. The magazine noted that the next month Montgomery was chairing a benefit at Mar-a-Lago for the Miami City Ballet.

Helen Boehm was also profiled in the magazine. She had a store in the atrium at Trump Tower where she sold limited-edition porcelain birds. Boehm had marketed her brand for three decades by giving her inspired kitsch to celebrities. Her endless self-promotion made her undesirable in the old Palm Beach world, but she and Trump were kinfolk. "Donald and I are cut out of the same cloth," she said. "We've seen both sides of everything. We're success oriented, and we love to work." Boehm would soon be hosting the Adam Walsh Foundation dinner at Mar-a-Lago.

The members profiled were all chairing upcoming charity events at the club. Mar-a-Lago's three-hundred-person ballroom might not compete with the Breakers' massive facilities, but Trump wanted the estate to become the preferred venue for all but the largest events in Palm Beach. These bookings could be reliable moneymakers, bringing in all sorts of added revenue that would be crucial to Mar-a-Lago's bottom-line success. Promoting these five members was pushing that plan along.

Moira Wolofsky and her much older husband, Kenneth, were not featured in Trump's magazine, but Moira was useful to Trump for another reason. Trump liked a winner by his side, and when he played mixed doubles, he often chose Wolofsky. She was a finesse player who lobbed the tennis ball if her opponents came to the net and drop shot them if they stayed back. Trump always hung back, waiting to drive the ball back with his forehand. That fierce shot was most of his game. The twosome played together in the club's mixed doubles championship, losing in a close match.

Rare was the opponent who challenged Trump's inspired line calls. He used the same approach on the golf links when the game mattered. "In championships, he's a chronic cheater," says one of his caddies. "He gave me a ball and said, 'Keep it. If we don't find my ball, drop this one. It's marked the same way.'"

As in his golf game, Trump was willing to do almost anything to make Mar-a-Lago the premier club in Palm Beach. "Those early years, it was Camelot on steroids," says one charter member. "It was Richie Rich playing with all his toys. Donald was under the gun to make everything first class, and that's what he did. We'd say, 'Holy cow, look who Donald has coming!' For $120 you had a fabulous buffet dinner and a show with a fifty-piece orchestra and a world-class performer like James Brown or the Temptations. Many of the performers stayed around and you could talk to them just like anybody. I had lunch with Tony Bennett once and played tennis with Regis Philbin."

Not all of the charter members were happy. Thirty-one-year-old Joseph Visconti paid twenty-five thousand dollars to join a club that he thought would be part of the "new Palm Beach." But according to Visconti, "It's turning out to be The Donald Trump Club, which I don't want to be a part of."

Like everybody who joined, Visconti had signed an agreement saying that he could sell back his membership once the club had its full complement of members. But Trump kept the membership list a secret, and Visconti discovered what any number of unhappy members learned. Trump did not live by the business adage, "The customer is always right." He preferred the used-car salesman's axiom: "You bought it, you own it."

Trump said about Visconti probably the worst thing he could say about a person: "Obviously, he needs money. It's our policy that we don't give money back. I can't be extorted."

When Visconti sued to have his twenty-five thousand dollars returned, Trump countersued for one million dollars, claiming that Visconti had made "false and defamatory statements." Visconti caved and agreed to an undisclosed settlement.

Trump and Maples and baby Tiffany flew down almost every weekend to Mar-a-Lago. Instead of staying in a guest room, as Paul Rampell had promised to the town council, they took over the suite of rooms that had once been Mrs. Post's quarters.

Trump regularly used Mar-a-Lago to advance his other business interests. He found that even the fiercest dealmaker could sometimes be won over by a visit to Mar-a-Lago. When Trump attempted to build a casino in Florida in association with the Seminole Indians, he brought members of the tribe to Mar-a-Lago and set out on the stage an enormous alligator, a species as familiar to the Native Americans as pigeons were to New Yorkers. The alligator's jaws had been clamped shut with masking tape, and some of the guests went up and petted the denizen of the Everglades swamps.

When *New York* reported that Trump was wooing Seminole leaders in Florida so he could work with them in building casinos, Donnelly asked in the *Palm Beach Daily News* "whether Florida's Native Americans will forgive or forget his past indiscretions—such as his reported references to Connecticut's dark-skinned Pequots as the 'Michael Jordan Indians' and his observation that 'organized crime is rampant on the Indian reservation.'"

As Trump's fortunes began to revive, he faced the painful problem of his parents' slow demise. Fred and Mary Trump were well into their eighties, and neither was doing well. His father had Alzheimer's, and his mother was suffering, too. Trump could not stand sickness, pain, hospitals, dying—all of which confronted him. He could have afforded to shuttle his parents off to caregivers, rarely allowing them to interrupt his busy life. However, that's not what he did.

"Every time we flew to Palm Beach, we'd carry Trump's mother up the stairs and set her on a chair in the back of the plane," recalled Mike Donovan, his personal pilot. "Then we'd bring his father on board, too. And we'd sit on the tarmac for an hour and a half while Trump talked to his parents. His father couldn't fly. We'd bring him down the ramp and put him in his car, and then we'd take off for Florida carrying his mother with us." Trump would have done almost anything to have his father fly with him, but Fred Trump's health did not allow it, and it gave him some measure of pleasure just to sit and talk to his son before the plane flew south.

Although Donovan saw nothing but a touching tableau of love between a father and son, there was another drama playing out between the two Trump men. In 1990 as Trump's empire crumbled, he presented his sickly eighty-five-year-old father with a twelve-page document making Trump the only executor of his will.

Fred Trump had as cynical a view of human beings as his favorite son. The old man had the sickening fear that if he signed the document, when he died Donald would strip his empire bare to save his own faltering fortunes.

"This doesn't pass the smell test," Fred Trump told his only daughter, Maryanne Trump Barry, a federal judge, as she recollected in a deposition. It was an odorous document reeking of possible betrayal. Fred Trump's lawyer presented him with a very different sort of codicil to his will, making sure Donald did not have sole control of his father's fortune. That one he signed.

Trump enjoyed his weekends in Palm Beach, but Marla couldn't stand parts of her life there. The very things her husband loved about the estate appalled Maples. She sought privacy, but unless she huddled alone with Tiffany in the family quarters, wherever she went she ran into people. She also wanted a true husband and father, someone she could talk to and someone who would walk down Fifth Avenue pushing a baby carriage.

There was an immense sadness and loneliness about Maples. Like Ivana, Marla tried to please her husband by becoming what he wanted, and in doing so, she destroyed what he had first loved about her. What first drew Trump to Marla was her apparent guileless innocence. With that quality, she seemed even younger than she was (always a plus in Trump's book). There weren't many women like this in Trump's world-weary New York scene, and initially he was enchanted. But as his significant other and wife, he wanted not a blond naïf but a decked-out woman whom he was proud to have on his arm.

"Putting on gowns and going out hosting events and having Harry Winston put jewelry on my hands was always uncomfortable for me—that was me playing a role," Maples told *People* in 2016. "I felt that's what the job called for." And so it did. In the end the woman Trump loved disappeared, and Marla turned into just another Trump girl.

The Trumps' marriage was soon so troubled that Maples often stayed in Florida when Trump flew up to New York to spend the week. The staff reported seeing Trump on his plane with models. It was clear theirs was not a marriage for the ages.

In mid-April 1996, while Marla was still at Mar-a-Lago, the *National Enquirer*'s Wayne Grover called Trump in his New York office.

"Look," Grover said, "we've got this story." He knew what Trump's reaction would be, but he had to forge ahead. "Marla was caught by the cops under this lifeguard stand on the beach near Delray in the middle of the night having sex with your bodyguard."

Trump was disbelieving. The cops might have caught *him* on the beach a few miles south of Mar-a-Lago having sex, but not any woman who had felt the Trump touch. And not his wife. And not with his employee.

"No, no, that's not the way it was," Trump said, as if he had been on the beach that early morning. "Goddamn it, I'm going to sue you guys for fucking lying about this. I'll have your ass ten times over."

Trump and Grover were like an old married couple to whom squabbling had become the preferred means of communication. Grover had felt Trump's wrath many times. The tabloid reporter knew whenever it happened, the best thing was to look Trump in the eye and talk him down from his rage. That's why he flew to New York with his editor Larry Haley to see if he could make Trump see reason. He wasn't going to be able to hide this forever, and Grover would spin it about as well as it could be spun.

Trump wouldn't even see Grover and Haley. He agreed only to talk on the phone. By then Trump had his tale straight. "He made up a bullshit story that Marla was with her girlfriend," Grover says. "And they stopped every fifteen minutes to call him, and she had to pee real bad. So she went to pee under the lifeguard stand, and the bodyguard was just watching over to make sure no-body came back and caught her."

Grover was sure about what happened because the police officer had come to the reporter's house and told him the whole story about catching Marla with thirty-five-year-old Spencer Wagner. That's why the tabloid's lawyers ultimately let the publication run a cover story with the headline: "SHOCK FOR TRUMP! MARLA CAUGHT WITH HUNK / COPS INTERRUPT LATE NIGHT BEACH FROLIC." The piece was carefully written with enough innuendo that readers would conclude that the couple was having sex.

Trump's beautiful young wife had been on the beach with a handsome young man at 4:00 A.M., and to make it even uglier, the man was Trump's employee. Marla had done to Trump what Trump had done many times to Ivana. It was devastating beyond imagination to a man of Trump's macho self-image, and the worst thing about it was that he couldn't do anything. His only choice to avoid endless public humiliation was to deny this had happened and stay married to Marla.

Trump flew down to Palm Beach, where Marla released a statement that she had needed to relieve herself that evening, and Wagner had stood a respectable distance away. Trump's spokesman issued a statement: "Along the lines of Elvis sightings and Martian invasions, the *National Enquirer* has once again fabricated a wholly unreliable story for this week's issue."

Despite having excoriated the *National Enquirer,* for the next week's issue Trump gave Grover an interview where he played the loving husband, loyal and trusting beyond measure: "Any man would be shocked to hear his wife was stopped by the police at 4:00 A.M. with another man on the beach—but I am not just any man, and Marla is not just any woman. I love Marla, and I trust her."

For the first few days, Trump kept Wagner secreted away in a house he owned near Mar-a-Lago, where the assistant club manager Nicholas "Nick" Leone Jr. brought him food. Then one day when Leone took Wagner a meal, he discovered that the bodyguard was gone and never returned.

Trump didn't fire the bodyguard for four months. Soon after that, Wagner sold his story to the one of the *National Enquirer*'s competitors, the *Globe*. After he passed a lie detector test, the tabloid published a front-page story headlined, "MY SECRET AFFAIR WITH MARLA." Trump sued Wagner in Palm Beach County Circuit Court, not for libel but for violating a confidentiality agreement.

The bodyguard's life was already ruined. Nobody wanted to hire him any longer, and he fell lower and lower. In 2012, he died of a drug overdose in a likely suicide.

As Trump pretended he was married to a loyal and loving wife, everything irritated him. His club was shackled by onerous rules he had agreed to in order to get the town council to approve the club (and that the Bath and Tennis and the Everglades did not have to follow). The Mar-a-Lago Club was limited to 500 members (the B&T had nearly twice as many) and events were limited to 390 guests.

Trump wanted to go back to the town council to get the regulations changed. Rampell cautioned Trump that they should wait two or three years until he had built the club membership into a political constituency to support him before going back and presenting their arguments to have the restrictions lifted. Rampell also said that making anti-Semitism a part of their argument with the town council would backfire on them.

Trump didn't listen. He saw the anti-Semitism at the other clubs as a handy bludgeon at his disposal for attacking his enemies. He intended to claim that the only reason his club had such harsh rules was because he allowed Jewish members. By making that argument, he would ensure that even if he didn't get the rules changed, he would have harmed his enemies. Thriving on controversy, he relished going back into the fray, berating the town as a bastion of anti-Semitism, casting a full measure of shame and embarrassment across the community.

Trump saw himself as the wronged party—having been singled out with restrictions that didn't apply to the other clubs—and his revenge came from being at the center of what to him was an exhilarating controversy. He enjoyed unsettling the island and dividing it into those who esteemed him and those who loathed him.

Trump had never before demonstrated any affinity for antidiscrimination issues, so it's hard to imagine that he suddenly became a crusader for the rights of Jewish Americans for purely noble reasons. Instead these charges of anti-Semitism at the private clubs on Palm Beach conveniently served his battles with the town council while at the same time helping to drive Jewish membership in his club.

Rampell was in an untenable position. He thought Trump's approach was wrong in any number of ways, but what could he do? To preserve the relationship, he had to do what his client wanted him to do, but the whole thing was making him increasingly uncomfortable.

In the spring of 1996, Trump called the restrictions on his membership numbers "discriminatory, unfair and unconstitutional." He told the *Palm Beach Daily News*, "We've always felt that it was discriminatory and very unfair." "I always felt I would bring it up at the appropriate time, when the club was a proven success."

Trump wrapped the banner of anti-Semitism around the rules, many of which had been put there for clearly legitimate reasons. Mar-a-Lago was in a part of town that was zoned as residential. People living there feared what increased traffic and noise might mean for their neighborhood. It turned out that the club created almost no problems, and Trump could have gone to the town in a straightforward way and made a strong case that such rules were not needed. But he sought to stain his enemies with charges that would stay.

Trump went to war to overturn these restrictions. "TRUMP RIPS PALM BEACH JEW-HATERS" ran the headline in the *New York Post*. The story told how Trump not only raged against the so-called anti-Semites but socked it to them by having Rampell mail town council members, community leaders, and local journalists videotapes of *Gentleman's Agreement*, the classic 1947 film about a reporter who pretends he's Jewish to understand anti-Semitism in post-World War II America.

"Sending out *Gentleman's Agreement* was a horrible idea, horrible," said Robert Moore, the longtime Palm Beach building inspector who had been supportive of most of Trump's efforts at Mar-a-Lago. "It had the reverse effect of what he wanted." Trump ended up insulting any number of Palm Beachers, many of them Jewish. One of them, William Guttman, an executive committee member of the Palm Beach Civic Association, said that he was "deeply offended" by the "crude effort to interject anti-Semitism into a hearing on a zoning matter."

Trump probably fancied himself a version of the film's star, Gregory Peck, fighting the good American fight against discrimination. "We proudly have Jewish members, and if I didn't have Jewish members, the Mar-a-Lago Club wouldn't be going through what it's going through with regard to discrimination," he said.

Jewish members of the town council had almost always voted as a bloc on any issue that even peripherally involved their religion. That was no longer the case. Allen S. Wyett, one of the two Jewish councilmen, was Trump's most intransigent foe. Wyett was not hostile to his religious brethren but felt that much of what Trump was demanding was wrong. The council member had been the CEO of a major corporation, and he brought all his abilities to his first elected position. Realizing the danger Wyett represented, Trump tried to ingratiate himself with the councilman by offering him a free Mar-a-Lago membership and rides on his jet to and from New York. Wyett always turned them down.

Making matters worse, word got around that Trump wanted to build a massive ballroom on the estate. He also announced plans to construct a two-hundred-slip marina on the Intracoastal Waterway behind the estate that would be big enough for two-hundred-foot yachts. He had also recently agreed to drop his lawsuit against airport authorities in exchange for a lease on 214 acres of scrubland for $438,000 annually, where he planned to build a world-class golf course. Although for him, the amount was a pittance, this proved to be the biggest deal he had made since buying Mar-a-Lago. For a man with his gigantic appetite for deals, there was no telling what he would try to do next.

On September 16, 1996, the town council debated whether the restrictions on Mar-a-Lago should be removed. The old-fashioned white-paneled council chambers had a waist-high banister that separated the council members from the 143 seats for the public. It could have been the setting for a New England town meeting.

Even though the debate took place at a time of year when there were few people in town, every seat was taken and at least seventy people stood around the back of the room. The chambers were packed in part because the Preservation Foundation had placed two full-page ads in the Shiny Sheet declaring "THERE IS NO DISCRIMINATION" and imploring residents to attend to show their support for maintaining the regulations concerning Mar-a-Lago.

As the meeting started, Trump walked to the front of the chambers to address the council. "I'm very proud of what's happened at Mar-a-Lago," he said. "A few of you know that prior to my purchase, we were close to seeing the wrecker's ball into the property." That was not true, but to Trump history was an inventive reconstruction to help him get what he wanted in the present. He also claimed he had saved the estate in a "non-discriminatory fashion," a dig at the restricted clubs.

When Trump finished, Paul Rampell got up to speak. Like so many people who got close to Trump, Rampell was losing his sense of being and had become his client's one-man claque. The lawyer understood how uncomfortable it made the people of old Palm Beach to listen to a man's achievements effusively celebrated in public. Rampell was a restrained man, not given to excess in word or deed. But he had been around Trump enough to know his employees were expected to praise him with accolades so extreme they might have embarrassed Stalin.

Rampell began by saying many on the island had become so obsessed with Trump, they couldn't look straight on at the issues at stake or at this extraordinary man. He said that Trump was a wildly successful businessman, bestselling author, movie star, political activist, television entertainer, and financial genius.

"You forgot scratch golfer," said Council President Lesly Smith.

"I love Donald Trump," Rampell said, as if anyone doubted this.

Rampell said Trump's troubles in Palm Beach resulted from him not going along with the "gentleman's agreement." The difficulties began when Trump stopped letting the Preservation Foundation have its events at Mar-a-Lago when "the property was essentially trashed, and he had to have it cleaned up."

These were harsh charges. Rampell eventually presented reasons why many of the stipulations should be ended, but few in the audience listened to this as much as they had to his accusations. Of the 156 letters received in Town Hall commenting on the debate, 134 opposed Trump's attempt to end the stipulations. The reaction to Trump was so overwhelmingly negative, he might have been well advised to be conciliatory, but he and Rampell did just the opposite.

Rampell pointed to Mayor Paul Ilyinsky, council president Lesly Smith, and town attorney John Randolph and said they should step down from any further role in the hearings because they belonged to restricted clubs. Trump's attorneys also accused the town of partnering in discrimination when it included the restricted private clubs to meet its requirement to provide public open space, considering that half of the town's citizens couldn't set foot there. Palm Beach quickly took the private clubs out of their totals, but the whole thing had nothing to do with what Trump wanted, and it was intended only to embarrass the community. The rancor had reached an unprecedented level, and the last veneer of civility was shredded.

"To listen to the trash coming from you and Mr. Paul Rampell, frankly, is going to make me throw up," Mayor Ilyinsky told James Green, one of Trump's other lawyers.

"Do so, sir," Green replied.

"I may do so on you," the mayor said.

America's leading authority on anti-Semitism, the Anti-Defamation League (ADL), was inevitably drawn into this high-profile squabble. The group asked Trump to back up his allegations and gave him two weeks to submit the promised evidence. When he did not do so, Arthur Teitelbaum, the ADL's southern regional director, issued a statement: "In our view, raising the specter of anti-Semitism without credible evidence is reckless and harmful to the entire community."

Trump didn't seem to understand the danger involved in throwing out claims of anti-Semitism just to get his way. Nor did he back down, as he now pointed his finger directly at the Everglades and the Bath and Tennis. "All they [ADL] would have to do is look at the other clubs to see the flagrant anti-Semitism," said Trump. That was true, but the restrictive clubs' membership rules had no direct connection to what Trump wanted from the town council.

Trump took his case to Abraham Foxman, the ADL's national director, who was based in New York. "Who the fuck is this guy Teitelbaum?" Trump asked. "Abe, it's anti-Semitism. All my members will be Jewish."

"Donald, *that's* anti-Semitism," Foxman said. "You don't know who your members will be." Foxman was trying to explain to Trump that by saying that gentiles would not want to be in a club with Jews, he was the one acting in a blatantly prejudiced manner.

By invoking anti-Semitism, Trump and his attorneys had put the town council in a position where they would be admitting to prejudices if they did away with the eleven stipulations. When the matter came to a vote in November, the council removed only three minor restrictions, leaving eight others intact.

After all he went through with the town council, Rampell just couldn't do it anymore. He no longer could live overwhelmed by Trumpian reality. He went to Trump and said he wanted to back off and no longer would be his lead lawyer.

9

The Contest

Trump was a multitasker of the first order. He was always managing many things, promoting new projects, working for the ascendency of Mar-a-Lago in the Palm Beach world, advancing his name in the media, and settling scores with his innumerable enemies.

Trump wasn't going to sit back and let the town council think they had won. Mar-a-Lago was not allowed to put on commercial events to make a profit or to promote a business. Trump dealt with that rule by asking charities to lend their names to occasions that had overwhelmingly commercial purposes. Then he went ahead and advertised them in ways that might have further violated the agreement with the town. Sometimes he didn't even bother with such transparent facades. Oprah Winfrey staged a three-day eightieth birthday bash for author Maya Angelou in April 2008. Another weekend Mercedes took over the club. These events brought in millions of dollars, and Trump didn't care that his actions outraged town officials.

Few things made Trump so angry as the way Shannon Donnelly mocked and belittled him in the *Palm Beach Daily News*. For Thanksgiving 1996,

Donnelly's column was about Palm Beachers giving thanks for their blessings, but she couldn't resist a dig at the grand master of Mar-a-Lago. "Donald Trump will be giving thanks that arrogance isn't a crime, otherwise he'd be doing life without parole," she wrote.

Trump forgot little and forgave less. "I love getting even with people," Trump had told Charlie Rose in 1992.

The time had come for Donnelly to feel Trump's sting, and he had an unfailing way of knowing what would most hurt a person. In Palm Beach, staying skinny is an obsession, but not for Donnelly. As the society editor made her social rounds, she was sheathed generally in inexpensive black gowns that did little more than shroud her size. People at these events noticed her stoutness and how she ate and drank, but nobody said anything. Not until Trump.

"Let's make a deal," Trump wrote in a letter he sent to her and top executives at the *Palm Beach Daily News* and Cox Enterprises, the parent company, "if you promise not to get 'personal' with me, I will promise not to show you as the crude, fat and obnoxious slob which everyone knows you are." The attack had the opposite effect from what Trump intended and instead elevated Donnelly in the minds of her superiors, including the top Cox executive, who wrote a letter to Trump supporting the society editor.

Unusually for him, Trump did not go immediately back on the attack flinging a series of savage ripostes at Donnelly.

Trump had a Palm Beach matter far more important than Donnelly's unseemly rants. It was time to name a managing director for Mar-a-Lago who would help to elevate the club to where Trump felt it belonged. The first of two candidates was German-born Bernd Lembcke, who had been the food and beverage director of the Breakers and was doing much the same at Mar-a-Lago. The other was Nick Leone, who had also spent years in the hospitality industry before joining the staff.

Trump asked members which man they preferred, and Leone was the overwhelming choice. The members went on and on praising him. Leone heard about this and thought he was about to be chosen the top executive.

One day, Lembcke walked into Leone's office. "Mr. Trump has made his decision," Lembcke said.

"I'm sorry to see you go," Leone said, not meaning a word of it.

"No, it's you who's going," Lembcke said. "Can I do anything for you?"

"Yes, get the fuck out of my office."

Trump didn't like how much praise Leone had gotten. With Lembcke, there would never be that problem. Beyond that, Trump was not about to do what others wanted him to do. "Trump's ego is everything," Leone says. "He's number one. I understand that and why he chose Lembcke."

The next day Leone received a call from Marla Maples Trump. "I want you to know, Nick, that Donald is getting rid of everybody who has goodness in their heart," she said. "And I'm gone, too."

When Trump gave Lembcke the job, he said he had tossed a coin, and Lembcke had won. The clear message was that Lembcke had been chosen not because Trump thought him best but because he had won in a lottery of two. But the two men worked well together. Lembcke even got used to Trump reaming him out like a marine drill sergeant.

Nothing in his life hurt Trump as much as having his wife cheat on him, and it was a mark of his immense shrewdness that by staying married to Marla he had hidden his shame from the world. Her time would come when she would be sent off into banishment. But what better tonic for Trump's hurt soul than hanging around with scores of gorgeous, svelte women?

In 1996 Trump, in partnership with CBS, purchased the Miss Universe, Miss USA, and Miss Teen beauty pageants from ITT. Not only did this appear to be a good business deal but it ensured that he would no longer have just Miami models filling his Palm Beach parties.

Not long after Trump became emperor of these beauty pageants, he was faced with a problem—one that would come back to haunt him in later years as he entered politics. The reigning Miss Universe, nineteen-year-old Venezuelan Alicia Machado, had gained a large amount of weight, taking her from an ultra-lean 117 pounds to around 170 pounds. Some pageant executives wanted to fire her, but Trump insisted that the woman he called "an eating machine" get down to an appropriate weight in time to crown the next Miss Universe in May 1997.

Trump considered fat a mark of moral failure in women, representing spiritual slovenliness and lack of self-discipline. He didn't seem troubled by corpulent men. He saw a publicity opportunity in Machado's battle to lose weight quickly. In February, he flew her to Palm Beach to begin a serious regimen of diet and exercise.

On Machado's first day at Mar-a-Lago, Trump called a press conference. Dressed like a spa trainer in white sneakers, a white golf shirt, pale yellow pants, and a baseball cap, Trump had gotten pudgy himself. It could be argued he needed laps in the pool and a carefully monitored diet more than Machado did. She had already lost considerable weight. At 158 pounds, and in T-shirt and tights, she appeared Rubenesque.

Trump was in an expansive mood. "There are a lot of people out there who have similar problems," Trump said, glaring no farther than the first row of reporters to find examples. "It is obviously not healthy to be overweight."

Even with Trump seeking to control her, Machado dared to combat the self-image that had been projected onto her. "I am no cow or something like that," she said.

Early in May, the Trumps issued a short statement announcing their divorce. "After a long relationship and a 3½ year marriage, we have decided to separate, as friends," they said. "For the sake of our family, we ask that the members of the media will accept this statement, respect our privacy and move on to coverage of more important issues of this time."

Trump had stayed with Marla for a year after the notorious beach incident, long enough that the media did not cite that as the cause for the divorce, and Trump faced no public threat to his manhood. Instead reporters accepted the story that Trump was divorcing his second wife now because their prenuptial agreement called for him to pay Marla dramatically less if the marriage lasted fewer than four years. That didn't make Trump look great, but in his mind, better cheap than cheated.

Marla had been scheduled to cohost the Miss Universe contest in May alongside movie star George Hamilton. Removing her at this late date would focus more attention on the divorce than going ahead as planned. In the United States, the televising of the pageant generated about as great television ratings as *Cops 2,* but Trump bragged two and a half billion people worldwide would watch the new Miss Universe being crowned at the Miami Beach Convention Center. Trump invited a number of Mar-a-Lago members and drove them down in a fleet of limousines.

As the co-owner of Miss Universe, Trump considered it a perk and privilege to enter the contestants' dressing room and observe the half-naked women as they dressed. Miss Utah Temple Taggart recalls Trump coming up to her and kissing her on the lips, a story Trump says is not true.

Alicia Machado had fulfilled her pledge and lost more weight at Mar-a-Lago, but it hardly seemed to matter. She came onstage to crown Miss Universe 1997, then was largely forgotten.

At the party afterward, the room was full of beautiful women. It was Trump's kind of event. He kissed Marla on the cheek and was warmly affable, but this would be the last time Trump had anything to do with her in public. She walked away with the two million dollars stipulated in the prenuptial agreement.

After Trump had gotten rid of Ivana, he threw the Bachelor Ball. Now he held a "Freedom Party" at Mar-a-Lago and invited around 250 models from Miami, who arrived on buses too large to go through the estate's entryway. The women got out and walked up the driveway. "They were like zombies as they piled in," one witness recalled. "And they were pretty innocent. Inside they drank champagne and talked about their modeling careers."

Trump invited only a few men, and they were married and not party guys. Three of the men sat in wicker chairs on the verandah, looking at the hundreds of women.

"Nice party, huh, guys?" Trump said, with an impish look in his eyes.

"I'll say," one of the men replied.

"Wait until you see my date," Trump said.

"Date? What do you need a date for? There are women all over the place."

"Wait until you see her," Trump said. To Trump, nothing proved you are a real man more than being with a tall woman, and six-foot-tall Victoria Silvstedt had just been named *Playboy*'s Playmate of the Year. Silvstedt would later be turned into a sixteen-inch-tall, $49.99 doll featuring "a smooth, soft outer layer of skin . . . to create unparalleled realism in a toy." And Trump had the real thing to himself. The evening was not complete until he threw Silvstedt into the pool and watched as she climbed out, every curve showing through her drenched gown.

Maples wasn't the only person Trump had waited until the time was ripe to get his revenge. His new book, *Trump: The Art of the Comeback*, was in part a place to attack those who had offended him when he was down. He had taken special umbrage at Mrs. Post's daughter, the former movie star Dina Merrill, writing that she "would constantly criticize me and say things behind my back." She did complain about him to her friends, but more significantly, she had written him a letter saying it wasn't good for Palm Beach to turn her mother's home into a club.

Trump wrote that Merrill was "born with her mother's beauty but not her brains." (In addition to her acting career, Merrill was a successful businesswoman and philanthropist and sat on several boards of directors.) Trump went on to say that Merrill lived "in a terribly furnished Palm Beach condominium, thinking about her failed acting career and how she can make me look as 'nouveau' as possible." Most people who visited Merrill's home thought that it was done in perfect taste. As for her career, she had starred or been a featured player in scores of movies and plays.

Merrill's ex-husband Stanley M. Rumbough, the perfect model of the old Palm Beach gentleman, got an early copy of *The Art of the Comeback*. He knew she was going through a difficult time and was about to divorce actor Cliff Robertson. Knowing Merrill as he did, he was convinced she would be devastated by Trump's brutal comments. Rumbough wanted to get to her before a reporter did, but he was a little late. When he reached her, Merrill had just spoken with Shannon Donnelly. It turned out his ex-wife had handled the situation with aplomb. Donnelly wrote in the *Palm Beach Daily News* that when she read the passages to the actress, she "began to giggle."

"How lovely," Merrill said when Donnelly finished. "He's a charming man, isn't he?"

❧

Trump wasn't always tossing out nasty asides to his declared enemies. He was immensely proud of Mar-a-Lago and was concerned with every aspect of the operation. Trump made a habit of walking around greeting members during dinner. At those times, he came off as a robust extrovert, but those who knew him best realized how much work that was for him. He was not comfortable standing around with people for very long. Like Swede Levov in Philip Roth's *American Pastoral*, Trump was a man "who used himself mainly to conceal himself."

When Trump walked through Mar-a-Lago, he had a proprietary gaze on his face, scanning every aspect of his club to see that things were right. Once he came upon two employees seated on the grass.

"What are you guys doing?" Trump asked.

"Well, we don't have anything to do right now."

"Then you're fired," Trump said.

That sent a shiver of apprehension into everyone who worked in the estate. That's how he was with almost everyone. Mess up in front of him and it was over, creating an atmosphere of constant nervousness among his employees. Forgiveness just wasn't part of his business credo.

And yet Trump was a man of the most astounding contradictions. You could say one thing about him and five minutes later he would be doing the opposite. Yes, he was a tough boss, but he could be incredibly understanding.

Trump walked into Mar-a-Lago's Super Bowl party in January 1998 to find that things were in a terrible state. Twice as many people had showed up as had been anticipated, and the lone cook struggled to keep up grilling hamburgers and hot dogs. The game was about to start and a number of the members were not amused.

Trump had made a big fuss out of making it known that anyone with money could join Mar-a-Lago. That helped drive memberships, but he ended up with some members who thought that flashing their money was entrée to everything. They berated the employees and endlessly complained. In many clubs, they would have been shown the door, but not at Mar-a-Lago. There were a number of those members present at the Super Bowl party, and they were obnoxiously loud in their gripes.

Trump had expected nothing more than a pleasant afternoon of football. He had been known to ream out employees, even in front of the members, but in this case, he could see the job was too much for the man at the grill.

"Give me your apron," Trump insisted. "Let me show you how to make burgers." The cook took off the apron and handed it to Trump. "Now tie it around the back for me real tight."

As a grill man, Trump was a natural, lecturing as he moved the burgers and hot dogs around the grill. "You know you can get sick if it's not cooked enough," he said, using a spatula to press down on a sizzling burger. Then he cut into the patty to make sure it was cooked through. "Yeah, that looks pretty good," he said as he placed the burger on a roll and looked up. "Is it okay now? How's it taste? All right then. Next."

Trump was so busy grilling that he missed much of the Denver Broncos defeating the Green Bay Packers in a thriller by the score of 31–24, but he hardly appeared to care.

That was the kind of scene that never would have taken place at the Bath and Tennis or the Everglades. So much was different at Mar-a-Lago. Trump invited people to the club who in the past would never have come to Palm Beach, including African Americans. The island was inhabited largely by northern transplants living with southern customs. In the island's early years, the hotels had largely been built by black workers. African Americans lived in a grubby little shack town. By 1913 their tiny homes had been torn down, and blacks were required to be off the island by dusk. There was no formal law, but few were so foolish as to try to circumvent the custom. Even in the last years of the twentieth century, African Americans were nervous about coming over onto the island.

In April 1998, Trump invited the black rap artist Sean Combs, aka Puff Daddy, to spend the weekend at the estate. Combs was as much a businessman as an artist, and like Trump, he was obsessed with money. One of his songs was "It's All About the Benjamins," referring to Benjamin Franklin on the hundred-dollar bill. Both men thought women were put on earth for their distinct pleasure. Puff Daddy's longtime girlfriend, Kim Porter, was in Miami with their newborn son. But he was in Palm Beach.

On Sunday afternoon, Puff Daddy and a woman friend took the tunnel underneath South Ocean Boulevard to the beach. No demarcation set off where the Mar-a-Lago beach ended and the Bath and Tennis began, but it was fairly obvious to anyone that the canvas cabanas just to the south were part of another property. Puff Daddy would have seen the families and children on the beach, but Combs was a man of the moment, and he decided one of the little shelters was perfect for his favorite leisure-time activity.

A guard came over to ask the rapper to cease and desist, a request Puff Daddy apparently found premature. As the rapper stroked away, the guard became louder and more strident in insistence that Combs stop.

When Trump learned about the incident on the beach, he was royally amused. Boys will be boys, and Puff Daddy had enlivened a lazy Sunday afternoon. Trump's first thought was to call Page Six at the *New York Post* and give them the story. That would get everybody talking Monday morning and it would be great publicity for Mar-a-Lago.

When Trump's longtime butler, Anthony "Tony" Senecal, heard what Trump intended to do, he didn't know what to do. He had been a footman for Marjorie Merriweather Post in her last years and had stayed on during those years when the mansion resonated only with the shadows of the past. He had revered Mrs. Post, and though he was too savvy to ever say this publicly, he believed something precious was lost forever when the mistress of Mar-a-Lago died. As far as he knew, in all the years Senecal had been at the estate, nobody had ever fornicated on the beach, and he hardly thought it an occasion for celebration.

"Mr. Trump," Senecal said finally, "I don't know if it's a good idea for you to call Page Six."

"What are you talking about, Tony, got some problem with news?"

"No, Mr. Trump, I just don't think it will make Mar-a-Lago look that great."

"Oh, what the fuck, maybe you're right."

Trump had all kinds of ideas how to make Mar-a-Lago an even bigger source of income. He set up a ten-thousand-square foot white tent large enough to stage major galas. The tent was large enough for elephants and clowns to prance around a ring, but Trump hung chandeliers, covered much of the cloth sides with massive arrays of flowers, cooled the tent with giant air conditioners, and set up the tables with settings worthy of a fine restaurant.

Trump did well booking galas there, and he took in as much as two hundred thousand dollars at a time, but as soon as the tent was up, he decided to replace it with a permanent ballroom that could draw the biggest events on the island and make millions of dollars each season. His plans also included building a new large swimming pool on the beachfront, along with two buildings and fourteen air-conditioned cabanas. But he could do none of this without the town council's approval.

Some of the members felt Trump was way over the five-hundred-member limit imposed by the town, but they weren't about to say anything. Unquestionably, he often skirted the limit of 390 guests at events, violating the rule eleven times in two years. In February 1997, he hosted a charity event for the Cystic Fibrosis Foundation featuring diva Céline Dion. More than a thousand people attended, almost three times the maximum permitted by the town. The traffic was so horrendous that residents along South Ocean Boulevard couldn't get in and out of their homes.

A month later, the club's new speakers blasted a cacophonous noise far beyond the estate and it lasted until around midnight. Mar-a-Lago's director of projects wrote a letter of apology to Robert Sterling, who lived a quarter mile away and had been bothered by the noise.

Alyne Massey lived just across the street. The widow was upset that the club was sometimes as boisterous as a Shriners convention. Trump was furious when he found out that she wrote a letter of complaint to Mayor Lesly Smith.

Trump wrote to Massey: "After you asked to come to the Beach Boys concert and then brought with you a group of sixteen people and after giving you and your friends a tour of the club, your letter was highly insulting."

For not ending the restrictions at Mar-a-Lago, Trump had sued Palm Beach for one hundred million dollars in December 1996. He was convinced he would beat the town hands down, forcing Palm Beach to pay him royally for its misconduct.

Trump went back to the Palm Beach Town Council in the spring of 1999 to petition once again for permission to build the club the way he wanted to build it. Everything appeared the same, but almost everything was different. Trump's lawyers and consultants presented proposals similar to what they had put forth before, and Trump's foes repeated the same arguments they had been making for several years. But the belligerent, in-your-face Trump did not show up. He dropped the anti-Semitism charges and stopped berating the town government. He called off his hundred-million-dollar lawsuit against the town and was remarkably polite as he soldiered through an onerous process that went on for six months, with sessions going on sometimes for eight or ten hours. Trump even sat through a marathon twelve-hour session.

Something else was different. His lawyer Rampell had cautioned him to wait to go to the town until there were enough club members to form a political constituency that could lobby the elected politicians. He had that now, and the club itself had become to most people an accepted, appreciated part of the community.

In the end, the town council gave him almost everything he sought, from being able to build a giant pavilion ballroom in the same Moorish style as the mansion to an increase to seven hundred guests at events in the new building. Nobody said it but everybody thought it: if he hadn't gotten his way, he would have thrown a fit, filed another lawsuit, and embroiled the beleaguered council members in a battle royal.

A ballroom of this magnitude had not been built on the island since the 1920s, and this was being constructed in a residential neighborhood. Council member Allen S. Wyett was not sanguine about the prospect. "If I were to write a newspaper headline, I would write, 'Rape,'" he said.

Trump seemed to see everything as competition, with winners and losers, and he was determined always to be in the winner's circle. Every Palm Beach club had a New Year's Eve event, and Trump made an extra effort each year to make the B&T's and the Everglades' evenings seem like dreary relics of a forgotten past.

Trump set the price for New Year's Eve 1999, celebrating the beginning of a new century, at two thousand dollars a person. That was several times what anyone had ever charged for a New Year's event in Palm Beach. Trump believed the price was part of what made it the most desirable invitation on the island, and perhaps he was right. Four hundred members and guests happily shelled out their money to spend the evening with Donald J. Trump.

Trump hired party designer Bruce Sutka to decorate Mar-a-Lago as a fantasy. The formally dressed guests entered the great white tent and they could have been on a cruise ship. There were Grecian columns, scores of balloons shaped like champagne bottles and glasses, and black and white table settings. Thirty pounds of caviar rested in the bed of an ice sculpture weighing five thousand pounds. Dinner was not only such delicacies as truffles and foie gras, but mashed potatoes sprinkled with what was said to be gold dust.

Trump stood at the entrance greeting guests. Next to him was his latest squeeze, Melania Knauss. Trump had a thing about Eastern European women, in part likely because with their foreignness there was a part within him they could never venture. The twenty-nine-year old, five-foot-eleven-inch tall model came from Slovenia, in the former Yugoslavia. She had a reserved, dignified manner and seemed to float through the room.

Melania had hardly begun dating Trump, a man twenty-four years her senior, and already she had survived one excruciatingly difficult evening at Mar-a-Lago. In a development only slightly less extraordinary than the wolf dwelling with the lamb, Trump had become friends with Ivana. As a mark of this renewed relationship, he invited his ex-wife and her mother to dinner at Mar-a-

Lago and seated Ivana one place away from his new girlfriend. "Melania was quiet to begin with," said one guest, "and she was especially quiet that evening. It was kind of surprising that Donald would do that to her, but the two women seemed to get along okay, though they didn't talk much to each other."

Ivana and Melania were both beautiful woman, and both model tall. Ivana had a lush figure, while Melania kept herself impossibly lean, her discipline led by eating tiny portions of food. While Ivana had been known at Mar-a-Lago for her swearing, Melania's language was sedate and proper. Her father, Viktor Knavs, had been the gigantic figure in her young life. A chauffeur and a Communist Party member in Yugoslavia, he did well for himself in their little town of Sevnica. Melania would later say that Donald reminded her of her father.

Trump was never going to let the New Year's Eve that rang in the new century go without a full helping of publicity. CBS and NBC had set up their satellite trucks so Dan Rather and Tom Brokaw could get Trump's take on the millennium. *People* had also sent a reporter. All that media was a measure of how famous he had become and what a draw his name was. He was an alchemist who could turn celebrity into gold, and he had good reasons for every interview he gave.

When the Mar-a-Lago Club first opened, Celia Lipton Farris had prophesized that it would be like no other place on the island. That was true, and the tipsy Farris did her part, strolling up onstage and singing with R&B singer Gladys Knight, whose "Midnight Train to Georgia" was the perfect New Year's Eve song.

Farris couldn't stand that Palm Beach rolled up the sidewalks when things would just have started hopping in London or New York. At the other clubs, as soon as the midnight hour struck, the guests rushed out to their valeted cars as if the building had caught on fire. Not at Mar-a-Lago. Trump served a buffet breakfast, and some of the guests danced to disco music until just before dawn. As usual, Trump had outdone everybody else in Palm Beach.

Trump's best new profit center was not his massive tent but the Trump International Golf Club, which was built in 1998–99 within sight of the Palm Beach

County Jail. Trump had spent forty million dollars building what was probably the most expensive golf course in America. And when he got things cheap, he was as proud as when he paid big bucks. For the landscaping, he finagled the royal palms for only three hundred dollars a tree when they usually cost at least two thousand dollars and often a lot more. The canary date palms generally went for a good five thousand dollars, but he pounced on a bankrupt tree farm and bought ninety-six of them for only $637 each.

Trump had played Steve Wynn's ultraexpensive Shadow Creek Golf Course in Las Vegas and had been blown away by its waterfall. Wynn was one of Trump's major competitors in the casino business, and Trump tried to best Wynn any way he could. His waterfall would be twice as tall as Wynn's, at a cost of three million dollars. Trump also moved nearly three million yards of dirt to form a landscape of gentle dips and ascents rising to fifty-eight feet, the highest elevation in the county. A golfer riding the course might imagine himself in northern California or Scotland until he spied in the distance the jail rising above everything.

Trump's perfectionism was seen in the final details. He brought over his artist in residence, Richard Haynes, to work on the clubhouse exterior, especially designing the TRUMP sign at the entrance. Trump appreciated the work of the talented artisan, who was also a decent golfer. Trump bought him a set of golf clubs and once the new course was open often invited him to play with him. Many Palm Beachers would have considered it beneath them to play a round with a worker, but Trump always did what he wanted to do.

When Trump flew down in January 2000 for the official opening, he had just broken up with Melania shortly after New Year's Eve. But that didn't last, either. As in his relationship with Marla, Melania bounced in and out of his life like a careening golf ball. Either way, life went on, and Trump with it.

When Trump surveyed the golf course, everything looked great except for the grass. He insisted upon a surface as smooth as a pool table but the grass looked pockmarked and was full of bald spots. The golf course superintendent, Roger Fink, had been instructed to mow the grass at such a low height that this was the result. It would do no good to say this was the reason. Trump fired Fink and sent him on his way.

Trump believed that columnist Frank Cerabino, who had mocked his Bachelor Ball on the front page of the *Palm Beach Post*, had some kind of vendetta against the golf course. When the bulldozers were only starting to clear the land, in February 1998, Cerabino had commenced writing in the *Palm Beach Post* what Trump considered nasty, smart-ass pieces. Then Cerabino instituted a mock campaign to move the new high-rise jail away from the golf course so Trump's guests wouldn't be subjected to such an unseemly distraction.

Trump had promoted the golf course by saying it would raise up the area, and that May, Cerabino visited the neighborhood and wrote about T's Lounge, a downscale strip joint, Tommy Richards Bail Bonds, and Condoms Galore, where, in the back room, he found a "3-foot-long rubber item" for fifty-eight dollars. When the pseudocampaign to move the jail ran its course, the columnist asked readers in May 1999 to rename it instead. One of his favorites was Breakers In, playing off the Palm Beach resort hotel.

A few days before the golf course opened, Cerabino wrote: "The green fees for one round of golf cost more than a month's rent at Cotton Bay, the rental complex to the west of the course. And the signs are everywhere that the $40 million golf course is an irrelevant luxury to people with more urgent, and less splendid needs: The bus benches on surrounding streets advertise criminal defense lawyers. The Burger King advertises '2 Whoppers for $2,' and the sign on the La Placita Grocery says 'Aceptamos Food Stamps.'"

Trump wrote a letter to the *Palm Beach Post*: "Doesn't Post columnist Frank Cerabino have anything better to write about than my golf course? . . . Perhaps Mr. Cerabino has problems with the fact that his brother, Tom, is a highly paid lawyer whose firm works for the Trump Organization or that he forgot to thank me for the free meals he received at Mar-a-Lago."

Trump was a client of Cerabino's brother, but the columnist was perfectly happy with his lot and would likely have slashed his wrists if he had been sentenced to serving a lengthy term as one of Trump's lawyers. As for the free meal, that was true. Cerabino's brother and his wife had been visiting Mar-a-Lago for the weekend, and Tom had invited Frank and his wife for dinner. Toward the end of the meal, Trump approached and asked, "Can I join you guys for dessert?" When the bill came, Tom had reached to pick it up, but Trump said, "I've got this."

When authors and journalists took rides on Trump's plane and free perks at Mar-a-Lago, Trump felt he owned them. Cerabino had accepted Trump's largesse and went on to write just what he would have anyway. Trump despised people who didn't stay bought.

10

A Proper President

Donald Trump thought he would make a great president, if only the system wasn't so screwed up that he couldn't get there. In 1980, when he was only thirty-four years old, he did an extended interview with Rona Barrett for an NBC special in which he said that the best candidates wouldn't run for president. The media scrutiny was overwhelming and destructive, and a man like Abraham Lincoln was too ugly and didn't smile enough and wouldn't have had a chance. "One man could turn this country around," Trump said. "The one proper president could turn this country around." Was there any doubt who that man was?

In 1987, Trump toyed with running for a few months, even going up to New Hampshire to give a speech. A series of ads he ran in *The New York Times* set out his main themes. They weren't based on polling or consultants testing the wind. They grew out of Trump's gut feelings and would resurface when he won the presidency in 2016. He asked, why did we continue to pay for the defense of Japan and Saudi Arabia when these rich nations should pay for themselves? He was all for lowering taxes and revving up the great engine of American capitalism. And he was tired of other nations making America the butt of their jokes. "Let's not let our great nation be laughed at anymore," he said.

In 1992, the white knight that Trump had prophesized came riding forth on his trusty steed. The bad news was that it wasn't Donald Trump. Billionaire businessman Ross Perot spoke in a populist idiom that resonated with millions of voters. As a straight-shooting independent, the Texan won a startling 18.9 percent of the vote that year in an election in which Arkansas governor Bill Clinton defeated President George H. W. Bush. Four years later Perot ran on the Reform Party ticket and netted 8.4 percent of the votes. That was enough of presidential politics for the iconoclastic Texan, and four years later Trump was mentioned as the possible Reform Party candidate.

In those days, Trump was in some respects a true populist, hardly a popular position among the wealthy gentry. His big idea was to hit anyone worth more than ten million dollars with a onetime 14.25 percent tax on their assets. That went over among the well-to-do like rotten caviar. "He's going to have fewer friends in Palm Beach than he already has—which isn't saying a lot," said John Rau, an estate attorney with many local clients.

That wasn't Trump's only problem. He hadn't enamored himself with his neighbors and was an unwanted native son. The *Palm Beach Daily News* wrote: "It is nonsensical for someone who wants to be chief executive of the United States, someone who is supposed to uphold and follow the law of the land, to be unwilling to follow simple rules—rules that he agreed to—in his own home town. His word can't be trusted in his own back yard . . . it would be best if Americans never hear: 'Here he is, Mr. President.'"

In January 2000, Trump invited leaders of the Reform Party to Mar-a-Lago. Many of them were the down-home folks Trump would presumably be spending time with if he hoped to use their party as a springboard to reach the White House. They shook his hand, and some even wrapped their arms around his waist and hugged him. That was part of the price the germophobic Trump would have to pay if he entered politics. The Reform Party was desperately looking for a viable candidate, but Trump asked, "If you don't win, what is the point?" He promised them an answer in a few weeks.

The next evening Trump was spotted in the VIP room at the Liquid Room nightclub in West Palm Beach, with the leggiest lovelies in hot pursuit. The club's owner, Chris Paciello, wasn't there to greet Trump. He had recently been indicted for murder and robbery.

It would hardly seem a fit environment for a future president. Indeed, the next month, Trump opted out of a presidential run, saying, "The Reform Party is a complete mess." Despite withdrawing his name, he was on the ballot in Reform Party primaries in California and Michigan, where he won, suggesting that Trump's presidential quest was not totally quixotic.

Even while he was tinkering with presidential politics, Trump kept a close watch on Mar-a-Lago, including the perennial quest to find a great chef. In August 2000, Bernd Lembcke showed the recent hire, French chef Bernard Goupy, where he would be spending his time. Lembcke led Goupy to a kitchen that was little changed since Mrs. Post had lived there. Goupy wondered how anyone could prepare hundreds of meals a day with only four stoves and eight burners. But he was a master chef of France, a title he had won by cooking everything from a buffet of culinary delights for six hundred at the Hilton International Hotel in Key West to onion soup served to the king of Bahrain in his palace.

Considering Trump's grandiose taste, he might be expected to appreciate classic French food, with its succulent sauces. But Trump was a man of simple, direct tastes. His favorite meal was a blackened burger or his mother's meat loaf. The first time the chef prepared a meal for his patron, he tried a compromise between Trump's taste and what Goupy viewed as authentic cuisine. But he came up short, or, more accurately, long. Trump didn't say a word, but Goupy could tell he was not happy. From then on, Goupy served Trump the food he liked without embellishments or artful additions.

Goupy became convinced that Lembcke wanted to replace him with a German chef, but he decided to fight this war on his terms, preparing food that was so memorable he could not be fired. A few days before New Year's Eve, Lembcke handed Goupy the evening's menu. Goupy wished he could have chosen the courses, but he could see Trump's hand and taste on everything. As the chef saw it, the worst was the salad—nothing but lettuce, tomato, and cucumber.

This was particularly galling since Goupy was known for his signature Caesar salad. Starting with an edible bowl of parmesan cheese, he added the freshest lettuce, caper berries as large as small marbles, special croutons, and his secret dressing. Club members praised the dish, sometimes enjoying it more than the main course.

A few days later, Céline Dion and her Svengali-like elderly husband, René Angélil, arrived at Mar-a-Lago with ninety of their friends flown down from Quebec. The couple had a home in nearby Jupiter, and the occasion was a baby shower before the birth of the couple's third child. Goupy put on a show, ending with exquisite dessert pastries. Dion insisted that Goupy come out of the kitchen to take a bow, and he did.

In February, after Goupy had been working at Mar-a-Lago for six months, he saw Trump and Lembcke talking around the pool. Lembcke kept looking at the chef, and Goupy felt it was ominous.

That evening Trump marched into the kitchen and shouted at Goupy, "You and your fucking Caesar salad. I'll show you how to make a fucking Caesar." Goupy recalled that Trump was "swearing like a truck driver." But truck drivers are generally inventive in their profanity, while Trump settled on a single word in almost every part of speech. A verb ("Fuck you"). A noun ("You old fuck"). An adjective ("fucking idiot"). An interjection ("Fuck!"). An adverb ("fucking screwed up").

Trump grabbed a bowlful of lettuce. After tossing in a handful of croutons, he sprayed the concoction with salad dressing. "Now that's a *fucking* Caesar!" Trump said triumphantly.

Goupy was fired the next morning. The chef saved most of his bile for Lembcke and believed he was the evil whisperer in Trump's ear. A few days later, Goupy received a phone call from a man who said he was René Angélil, and he wanted to know if Goupy would like to cook for Céline Dion. Goupy had no use for this cruel prankster. "Yes, and I am President Clinton," he said and hung up.

A few minutes later, a friend called and said Angélil couldn't understand what had just happened. Goupy called Angélil and later that day drove out to the couple's estate in Jupiter to cook dinner. It was a test to see if they wanted him full time, and it was quite a test, preparing a meal for twenty friends and family.

Before Goupy walked to the kitchen, Dion asked about his experiences at Mar-a-Lago. "It was my Caesar salad that was my downfall," Goupy said.

"Well, Bernard, why don't you serve it this evening?" Dion said.

The dinner was a success, and Dion proclaimed that the notorious Caesar would be called the "Trump Salad." It was a regular on her table for the two years Goupy worked for her in Jupiter and Montreal.

The Mar-a-Lago chefs tended to have lifespans shorter than that of mayflies. A number of years later yet another chef took over duties at the club. Intending not to duplicate the fate of his predecessors, the young American knew he must give Trump exactly what he wanted. Knowing that steak was one of his patron's favorite foods, the chef ordered a number of wildly expensive Kobe steaks, the most succulent, tender beef in the world. After grilling one of the steaks until it was the way Trump liked it, as black as the devil's soul, the cook proudly served it to the master of Mar-a-Lago.

Looking down at the plate with anticipation, Trump picked up a steak knife, and started to cut into the meat. "What the fuck is this?" he asked throwing the knife down on the table. Then he reached for a butter knife and sliced the beef in half. "Nothing but fucking mush!" Trump shouted. "I asked for a steak."

That was the last Kobe beef ever served to Trump at Mar-a-Lago.

Trump had come back financially. At the same time, Palm Beach was evolving into a town more in his image. In this new Gilded Age, money poured into Palm Beach in torrents beyond anything the community had previously known. This new class may not have craved his media exposure and tabloid lifestyle, but they shared Trump's attitude that money was the key that opened all doors. They assumed their wealth afforded them great deference, and many of them flashed their money to get their way.

What is a hundred-dollar bill to the maître d' at the island's best restaurants, such as Café L'Europe or Jean Pierre, if it means you get a fine table? And if valet parkers remember that you always give a twenty-dollar tip, they salivate at your arrival. If people see the money being passed out, it carries special cachet. "Trump tips well if someone is watching," one of his caddies said. "If he's got a big crowd around him, he starts throwing out the hundred-dollar bills. If there's nobody special around, well, the tip's not special, either."

Nowhere did money speak louder than at the Trump International Golf Club. The caddies there had no benefits and lived largely from tips. When they got together, they were full of stories about the golfers and how much money they had, and yet how they seemed to be restlessly pursuing a happiness that was always just beyond their reach. The caddies couldn't understand why the club members acted as badly as they did, considering that they had what appeared to be everything.

The stories of the Trump club golfers spread throughout the Palm Beach community. One guest bludgeoned a black swan to death at the waterfall on the seventeenth hole. He said the bird threatened his life. A female member drove her cart over a caddy and, instead of stopping, left him on the ground bleeding while she drove on to tee off. Some golfers descended onto the lawns by helicopter, the backwash of the blades signaling their arrival to any and all.

Trump rarely did anything about this egregious behavior—unless it risked his bank account. "You have been abusing numerous caddies, other members and representatives of the club in general," he wrote suspended Greek shipping heir Harry Theodoracopulos. "Now it has come to my attention that you exhibited intolerable behavior toward guests and members on the driving range. At least one of the guests (and possibly three) who were preparing to join the club have decided, after watching your deplorable conduct, not to join. Please be advised that I am holding you personally liable for the amount of money lost by the club due to your antics." Trump couldn't force Theodoracopulos to cough up that money, but he held on to his two-hundred-thousand-dollar deposit fee.

Trump was always looking for real estate deals, and when he purchased and then sold one of the grandest estates in Palm Beach in 2004, it linked him financially to the world of Vladimir Putin's Russia. The home had been built by Abraham D. Gosman, who achieved a grand fortune as he moved from industry to industry and deal to deal and was worth between five hundred and six hundred million dollars when he came down to Palm Beach. As one of the richest men in Palm Beach, he built a humongous eighty-four-thousand-square-foot mansion on six and a half oceanfront acres on the island's north end.

Gosman gave dinner parties for 200 to 250 people and millions of dollars to local charities, too, making sure that his contributions were richly celebrated. Then it all started falling apart rapidly, and in 2004, the U.S. Bankruptcy Court was auctioning off Gosman's home. Trump smelled a special deal and bought the house for $41.35 million. Four years later he resold the property to Russian fertilizer oligarch Dmitry Rybolovlev for ninety-five million dollars, which was then the highest price ever paid for residential property in the United States.

Trump fancied himself the toughest of businessmen, but the Russian oligarchs traveled far deeper into the dark world than he had ever ventured. As a boy Rybolovlev watched the 1987 film *Wall Street*, which Americans viewed as a cautionary tale on the evils of avarice ("Greed is good"). The young Russian saw it as a guide to success. In 1996, he was put in prison accused of murdering one of his former colleagues. Rybolovlev's attorneys made a strong case that he had been falsely accused by business opponents willing to say almost anything to destroy him and after eleven months he was freed. It was just business by another means.

It was a bewildering puzzle why the Russian would pay such a high price for the Palm Beach estate. It would have been one thing if Rybolovlev had visited the estate, but he never did. He said he purchased the property as a business investment.

Rybolovlev tore down the massive home and divided the oceanfront property into three lots, two of which sold for a total of $71.34 million, suggesting that in the end Rybolovlev may break even.

Bewildering beyond the incredible price Rybolovlev paid was why Trump didn't brag about the $53.65 million (minus commissions) he was pocketing in one of the most profitable residential real estate sales in American history. Instead he complained about having to spend twenty million dollars preparing the estate for sale, even though it was probably no more than one million. Despite all his efforts and disavowals, both the media and government investigators have kept a focus on the sale. Even the most dogged reporters have been unable to link Trump to something untoward in the Russian deal, but it still sits there, a reality that one day may have secrets to disclose.

Trump and his family had other Russian connections in Florida far more intimate than those with Rybolovlev. The central figure in this is Elena Baronoff, a Russian-American woman who in the years before Trump ran for president was a familiar figure at Mar-a-Lago.

In 2001, Trump signed a deal with Florida developers Michael and Gil Dezer to be the public face of six massive condominiums in Sunny Isles Beach, a small resort town a few miles north of Miami Beach. Instead of taking the risk constructing a building, Trump preferred to slap his celebrated name on someone else's work, do a measure of quality control, and take a percentage without a penny of risk.

Two years later Baronoff's real estate company moved into the Trump Grande, where she had the exclusive right to sell the upscale condos. Baronoff had been brought up in Tashkent, the capital of the Central Asian Soviet Republic of Uzbekistan, in the last decades of the Soviet empire. As a young woman, she worked for the Uzbekistan Friendship Society. One of her duties was to report on foreigners, a common practice in the Soviet Union. Not long before the breakup of the Soviet Union, Baronoff and her family received exit visas and came to the United States, where they eventually settled in Florida.

The Russian-American woman brought tour groups from Russia and traveled often to the former Soviet Union. She was so successful marketing the Sunny Isles apartments to wealthy Russians and promoting the enclave that, in good part because of her efforts, the resort town got the nickname "Little Moscow" and she was given the honorary title "International Ambassador of the City of Sunny Isles Beach."

As Baronoff became the public face of Sunny Isles Beach, she described herself as "a cultural attaché in public diplomacy with the Russian government." Baronoff never discussed in detail just what she did as a "cultural attaché," but she surely used her acumen and attractiveness to advance Russian interests in America.

Russians purchased condos throughout the town. As of March 2017, sixty-three Russians had spent $98.4 million dollars buying luxury condos in seven Trump-branded buildings along the ocean front. The true figure may be several times that since over 700 of the 2,044 purchasers did so with limited liability companies, effectively disguising the owners. Many of these purchases were likely vehicles for money laundering. Two of the buyers, Anatoly Golubchik and Michael Sall, were later indicted for their alleged membership in Russian-American organized crime and running gambling and money-laundering businesses.

There was nothing better to promote sales than the Trumps themselves, and Baronoff became close to the family. She drove up from Sunny Isles to spend evenings with the family at Mar-a-Lago. A stunning woman of exuberant charm, she fit perfectly into the social scene in Palm Beach.

And Baronoff traveled to Russia with Ivanka, Don Jr., and Eric. Elena and Ivanka looked like sisters as they stood together in their matching chinchilla coats in the Russian winter. Everyone knew that Baronoff was the way to Trump, so much so that a Russian magazine put the Realtor on its cover with the title "The Russian Hand of Donald Trump."

"Putin's policy has always been: where there are Russians, that is where Russia is," says John Sipher, who ran the CIA's Russian operation. Most Russians may have come to South Florida only for the sun and bacchanalian rites, but they were still part of *Russkiy mir* (the "Russian world"). And as the Trumps and Baronoff worked to sell Sunny Isles condos to residents of Moscow and Kiev, they were expanding potential Russian influence in the United States. If Baronoff had not died of leukemia in 2015, she likely would still be "The Russian Hand of Donald Trump," working to extend the Russian presence.

A key victory for Trump in managing his public image occurred in 1999, when David Pecker, the CEO of the investment firm Evercore, oversaw the purchase of American Media Inc., publisher of the *National Enquirer*. Pecker knew Trump and sought to be close to him. Pecker joined Mar-a-Lago and sometimes flew with Trump in his plane from New York to the tabloid headquarters in Florida. He declared Trump off limits from any scandal-seeking coverage and was ready to do whatever else Trump needed.

It was great news for Trump that from then on the tabloid would only celebrate his life. Trump seemed to have the upper hand even as he battled with his neighbors at the Bath and Tennis Club. The club confronted Trump when he built an Olympic-size pool and glassed-in cabanas right next door to the

B&T on the oceanfront. As the work proceeded, the din of hammers and drills echoed across the property line. The worst were the workers' boom boxes blasting music. When Trump put in a request with the town for the construction to continue into the season, the B&T successfully petitioned to stop the work.

Trump found a way to take his revenge. Just south of Mar-a-Lago on the east side of South Ocean Boulevard was a loading dock that served the Bath and Tennis. It had been there for decades, and no one at the B&T paid it any attention. For members of the B&T, if you didn't see it, it didn't exist. The same was true of their un-air-conditioned kitchen, a torture on hot days to cooks and waiters.

In January 2002, Trump sent a letter to Douglas Egem, the B&T's general manager, complaining about the loading zone. He wrote that "the Bath & Tennis Club's deplorable truck dock loading area" forms the initial impression visitors have of the island. "Lately, the conditions have become far worse," he went on. "Workers are sitting on the platform listening to loud music and drinking beer while watching all the cars go by. Never has the filth and noise been greater than it has this season."

Initially, the town council wanted nothing to do with this dispute between next-door neighbors. But the B&T's attitude that this was the way things had always been wore thin. Council member Allen Wyett pointed out that the workers were on the dock because they needed breaks from the insufferable B&T kitchen. "You should air-condition the kitchen, so they don't have to come outside," Wyett told Egem in a town council meeting in October 2002.

The B&T manager wasn't buying any of that. "Air-conditioning won't solve the problem," said Egem.

"Yes, but it would help your employees," said Councilman Jack McDonald.

In the end, the B&T agreed to put up hedges along the roadway, the Palm Beach solution for all kinds of problems.

Most businessmen in Trump's position would have delegated such minor matters as dealing with an unkempt neighbor to a subordinate, but there was nothing so small that it didn't catch his attention. That said, he was far from merely a creature of Palm Beach. As he dealt with the minutiae of management, he was negotiating a deal that would take him to the highest level of celebrity in America.

11

The Apprentice

O n a January evening in 2004, members and their guests were invited to the bar at Mar-a-Lago to watch the premiere of Trump's new television program, *The Apprentice*. There were two television screens and between them, at the same eye level, the large portrait of Trump in tennis whites that was practically a signature at Mar-a-Lago, which meant that wherever you looked, there he was.

Waiters served cappuccino and chocolate and raspberry soufflés as the guests watched sixteen contestants vying to survive the weekly gauntlet and win the prize of working with Trump for a year at a $250,000 salary. They quivered under his gaze, worried they would be the one at the end of each episode to whom Trump said, "You're fired."

The scenes on television were extensions of what people at Mar-a-Lago had seen in the club. During the commercial breaks, the guests in the small bar discussed the show. "He's very good at catching the right angle of the camera," said Thierry Morel, a European filmmaker visiting Florida, as he watched Trump dominating the program. "He knows what to say and when and how.

He probably could have a film career. He has that charisma. He's full of energy and inspires others."

Reality television was almost always ensemble television, but NBC realized immediately that Trump was so good he became the singular star of the show. As popular as the show was, peaking at twenty-seven million viewers that first season, that wasn't good enough for Trump. He talked about how it was eternally number one when it had never been that. But that wasn't what mattered. The morning after the first showing, when Trump made the rounds of morning television, there were crowds greeting him not as a distant celebrity but as their new virtual friend. He was no longer this often-mocked Page Six personality, but an iconic figure for the masses. During his fourteen years hosting the weekly program, he became a reality television performer like no other, learning techniques that he easily transferred to his successful presidential run.

The popular show gave Trump ample opportunity to display himself and his children as American royalty. When his three children with Ivana were growing up, he used the limited time he spent with them to impose his value system on them. Mike Donovan, his longtime pilot, saw Trump interact with Don Jr., Ivanka, and Eric in those years. "It wasn't easy being his child," Donovan said. "He made the kids toe the line. They wouldn't be what they are today if he didn't have so much to do with that."

Now that his children were adults, they had a place beside him as his heirs. They were too young and sheltered to have done much on their own, but that didn't stop their father from sitting them beside him on *The Apprentice* and having them criticize and judge people older and far more experienced. They were Trumps, and the would-be apprentices were not.

As Trump's celebrity grew with the success of his TV show, he grew more distant from the people at Mar-a-Lago. The burger-grilling Trump was gone. As he walked through the club at a brisk pace, he looked down and asked, "How am I doing?" There was only one answer: "You're doing great, Donald."

Trump had achieved a magnitude and longevity of celebrity rare in modern America, and he believed he possessed an ability to handle it better than others. "From what I've seen, it's fame itself that bends people out of shape," he had written in his 1990 book *Surviving at the Top*. "In fact, the more celebrities I meet, the more I realize that fame is a kind of drug, one that is way too powerful for most people to handle." He thought he was different.

Trump asked Melania to marry him on the night of the Met Gala in May 2004. Melania arrived wearing a $1.5 million Graff diamond engagement ring. Most newly engaged men would have said nothing if they had gotten the fifteen-carat diamond ring at a Filene's Basement price, but Trump boasted that he had paid only $750,000. The company replied that whatever he asserted, Trump had paid the full amount.

Trump had no problem merchandizing the rest of his wedding to Melania at Mar-a-Lago in January 2005 to upscale merchants who wanted to be associated with the spectacular occasion.

Top chef Jean-Georges Vongerichten picked up the dinner bill for five hundred guests and received free publicity for doing so. Guests arriving on private planes at Palm Beach International Airport walked on a red carpet into the general aviation terminal and were greeted with flutes of champagne, all thanks to Jet Aviation. Braman Motors, a local luxury car dealer, coughed up two Rolls-Royces. Getty Images had the rights to sell the wedding photos. Melania's Christian Dior gown retailed at around two hundred thousand dollars, but one knew without being told that Trump had likely not paid anything like that.

The best Palm Beach venue for a quasiroyal wedding was the Church of Bethesda-by-the-Sea, Palm Beach's Episcopalian place of worship. Built in 1925, the Gothic Revival structure was one of the oldest buildings on the island. The pews on Sundays were a weekly gathering of Everglades and B&T members and their ilk, dressed with a degree of formality rare any longer in American churches.

Rev. Leo Frade, the bishop of Southeast Florida, insisted that the twice-married Trump sit with him for counseling before he would agree to let Trump marry Melania in the church. A few years earlier, members of the church would likely have protested Trump's request to stage the nuptials at Bethesda-by-the-Sea, but there was not a public peep in opposition. "The wedding may come to signify that the old social order has fully given way to something new," wrote the *Palm Beach Post*. "A tad gaudy perhaps, but new nonetheless."

Still, Trump didn't get everything he wanted. He hoped to have a glorious display of fireworks bursting into the nighttime sky above Mar-a-Lago, but the town council squashed that idea. When they voted unanimously against the proposal, members of the audience applauded, signifying that an undertone of Trump resentment still existed that even his wedding could not undo.

Trump didn't care if guests were on the right or the left as long as they were famous. So, there was former Democratic president Bill Clinton with his wife, Senator Hillary Clinton, in the pews, along with Republican New York governor George Pataki and former New York City mayor Rudy Giuliani. Trump's guests from the world of business were mainly media types like boxing impresario Don King, music mogul Russell Simmons, and two network presidents, CBS's Les Moonves and NBC's Bob Wright. The television personalities included Matt Lauer, Barbara Walters, Katie Couric, Simon Cowell, Billy Bush, and Gayle King. Most of these guests weren't real friends. They were fellow celebrities, and it was a glorious meeting of the clan.

When sportscaster Pat O'Brien arrived at Palm Beach International Airport by private plane, a chauffeured Rolls-Royce was waiting for his use during his stay. O'Brien had been one of the few major figures who kept up with Trump during his down years, and the luxury car was just one way of saying thank you.

Melania, at age thirty-four, looked ethereal in her Dior gown, which was featured in a fourteen-page spread in *Vogue*. Trump made a handsome groom and looked younger than his fifty-eight years. In that shade of Palm Beach blond worn by half the women on the island, his hair rose above his head like a golden rooster's comb and became a signature statement of his own late-middle-age masculine identity.

Melania had orchestrated much about this day. She insisted that the ceremony not be televised and that journalists be kept across South County Road, where they jumped up on stools and ladders to get a decent glimpse of the crowds entering and leaving. Trump could do little to jazz up the wedding ceremony in the church, and it was a touching, if predictable, exchange of vows that lasted scarcely half an hour.

The reception at Mar-a-Lago was held at the just-opened massive ballroom Trump named after himself, as if it were a football stadium. For the wedding celebration, long tables covered in cream and gold cloths had been laid out throughout the ballroom, and they held candelabras wreathed in white roses and orchids. The thirty-piece Michael Rose Orchestra sat on a stage on the east side of the ballroom, where they accompanied Billy Joel, Tony Bennett, and Paul Anka, who sang for the hundreds of guests.

The newlyweds entered the ballroom to the strains of Puccini's "Nessun dorma," one of the most famous of arias, performed by soprano Camellia Johnson. Trump's children gave heartfelt toasts, the groom was witty and deeply felt in his words, and the bride was regal. The train of Melania's gown was so long that when the newlyweds danced she could only move forward. Trump was not used to having anyone lead him, but he handled it well.

The evening was long and the liquor limitless, and a number of the guests became inebriated. Pat O'Brien got so loudly drunk, he was asked to leave.

Thanks largely to *The Apprentice,* Trump had become one of the greatest celebrities in America. He did not have the aura of old Hollywood stardom but intimate, reality TV fame in which people felt they knew him and could come up and greet him and start a conversation. Most people who had reached that magnitude of celebrity protected themselves behind a public relations team and traveled from limousine to limousine and one shielded scene to the next, but that wasn't always Trump.

When the Donald J. Trump Ballroom was being built, Trump sometimes drove his Lamborghini over to West Palm Beach to do some shopping. As he crossed the bridge, a giant banner on the side of Classic Chandeliers advertised a 50% OFF EVERYTHING SALE. The sign stayed up year after year, and passersby had to wonder how legitimate the sale was.

Nicholas Jacobsen, the eighty-two-year-old store owner, was a Latvian immigrant who had fought as a mechanic in the Luftwaffe in World War II. After the war, most of his surviving comrades joined the French Foreign Legion and died in combat in Algeria and Vietnam. Jacobsen came to America, but he thought his adopted country was a largely despicable place full of slothful losers. Jacobsen's chandeliers were made in the Czech Republic and were copies of antiques.

One day in December 2004, Trump roared in and chose three chandeliers for his ballroom. The price was $67,994, but with the 50 percent discount that came to $33,997. Someone from the Trump organization arrived immediately with a deposit check for half the money.

Jacobsen's people installed the chandeliers, and two months later, Jacobsen still had not received the remaining $16,998. Jacobsen had been in business long enough in West Palm Beach to know that Trump was a notoriously poor payer. The small-business man said that he went over to Mar-a-Lago many times trying to get his money. Each time they said they would pay him, and they never did. So he phoned Jose Lambiet, the *Palm Beach Post*'s widely read gossip columnist, and got his story about Trump stiffing him into the January 26, 2005, paper. Jacobsen even said, "When Mr. Trump came to buy the things, he didn't want to pay the sales taxes. But I wouldn't let him take them unless he did."

Trump began each morning rummaging through the papers looking for mentions of his name, and he fell upon the *Post* story. Anyone else with his kind of wealth and status would have called his lawyers and public relations team and figured out what to do. They might decide that a PR rep should talk to Lambiet or a lawyer demand that Jacobsen eat his words. But whatever they decided, it was not for their client to become personally involved.

Trump didn't care. He relished a battle, even if it was little more than a knife brawl in the alley. The first thing he did was to call the columnist with a speed he had not used to pay his bill. "You want a story?" Trump screamed into the phone. "I'll give you a story. This guy did a terrible, terrible job. He was late with the chandeliers. He didn't have the proper equipment to install them. His bills were too high. He had to use my people to install them. We're going to end up in court because he's just trying to get free publicity. I'm not going to pay him what I owe him. That's it. I'm not paying."

Trump had no problem with the chandeliers until Jacobsen complained about payment, and he likely either invented or wildly exaggerated his problems. So what? This was war, and you fight with such force that your enemy has no choice but to retreat.

It didn't quite work that way. Jacobsen wasn't running out of the alley in fear. "Mr. Trump wants to belittle me," he told Lambiet. "That's his style. He is 58. When is he going to grow up? I will collect, one way or another."

Jacobsen escalated the battle by telling a dubious tale of his own. He told the New York *Daily News* that twenty-two merchants called him after the *Palm Beach Post* story and complained that they had been "stiffed in the past" by Trump. That story ran in the popular daily and became part of the legend of Donald Trump. Those who admired Trump dismissed the story, while those who despised him had even more reason for disdaining this miserable miscreant cheating a brigade of small-business people in his winter residence. What was strange, though, was that no one else came forward publicly with their complaints.

Trump did have a reputation for not fully paying subcontractors, but how likely was it that more than a score of business owners called Jacobsen with their own mournful tales? One who doubted this was Don Mendyk, Jacobsen's assistant. "It would not surprise me if he made up the number of people who called him," Mendyk says. "He would embellish to fit his situation."

Jacobsen soon faced a double-barreled legal assault from Trump's lawyers. They served him with papers for breach of contract and threatened a second suit for libel. Jacobsen had never faced anything like this. He didn't even have a lawyer, and Trump's attorneys were demanding the names, phone numbers, and addresses of the twenty-two merchants. If he couldn't supply the names, they demanded a letter of apology, saying he "never told anyone at the newspaper that 22 people had called and told you that Mr. Trump had stiffed them" and that he had lied when he said Trump didn't want to pay his sales tax.

Jacobsen ended up getting a lawyer and filing his own suit against Trump for breach of contract. The matter was eventually settled in mediation. The amount of the settlement was confidential, but Jacobsen's lawyer, Ronald Jones, says it was "much less than we sought."

Trying to get Trump to pay him had cost Jacobsen thousands of dollars, as well as endless anxiety. For Trump, it had been an opportunity to stick it to somebody who challenged him and to prove once again that if you picked a fight with Donald J. Trump, you were in for the fight of your life.

Trump had not spent forty million dollars on the Mar-a-Lago ballroom to have its splendor sit barely used in his backyard. He wanted the Donald J. Trump Ballroom to become the island's premier venue for big events. He believed that if he could bring a few of the most prestigious charity events to Mar-a-Lago, the rest would follow. At the top of the list was the International Red Cross Ball, one of the few events attended religiously by the island's old elite, held each year at the Breakers hotel.

Trump had attempted to establish his bona fides with the celebrated annual event by donating his jet to fly the ambassadors from Washington who were such an important part of the event. On one level, it was a generous gesture, but like almost everything else in Trump's life, there was a tax write-off sitting there waiting to be taken.

In January 2004, Trump heard that the Palm Beach County Red Cross had fired its three-time chairwoman Diana Ecclestone, who had done well for the charity but hadn't donated big dollars herself and wasn't bringing in enough major donors. Trump showed his support for Ecclestone by saying he would no longer donate his jet.

Two months later, Simon Fireman, a Massachusetts businessman and philanthropist, was announced as the new chairman, largely because of the $750,000 he was donating. Fireman wasn't the only person to use his financial leverage to get what he wanted. Soon afterward, the Red Cross said the forty-eighth annual ball would be moving to Mar-a-Lago. "The Red Cross said you move from the Breakers to Mar-a-Lago because if we did Trump would let us use his plane," Fireman said.

The old Palm Beach elite refused to make the move to Mar-a-Lago, but they didn't matter any longer. A new class was coming to dominate Palm Beach, and Trump was its leader. In the past fifteen years, the number of people in the

United States having assets valued at ten million dollars or more had risen from 65,000 to 430,000. The richest 1 percent of Americans owned 33 percent of the nation's assets, and that percentage was constantly growing. This massive increase was mainly new money. In 1989, 23 percent of the assets controlled by the tiny financial elite had been inherited, but that was down to merely 9 percent.

This new money cared little for the ways and reasons of the old Palm Beach or the homes that the traditionalists revered. Between 1987 and 1995, more than a hundred of the old homes had been razed. In their place often rose massive mansions overshadowing even the grandest homes of the past.

Cosmetics magnate Sydell Miller, an early Mar-a-Lago member, tore down one of the grand old houses to spend a hundred million dollars building an 84,626-square-foot structure. It looked less like a home than a giant resort hotel or a major library.

In 2003, billionaire cofounder of the Blackstone Group Stephen A. Schwarzman purchased Four Winds. Other than Mar-a-Lago, it was the greatest of the remaining classic mansions and a historic landmark. Schwarzman submitted plans to add a thirteen-thousand-square-foot addition. When he was unable to affix the addition to the old structure as he had planned, he demolished Four Winds. Schwarzman had teams of lawyers and there was little the town could do but bemoan the loss.

A new generation of immensely rich Americans was coming to Palm Beach to live among themselves and be endlessly amused, blessedly separate from the rest of America. "Palm Beach to me is the epitome of everything that's gone wrong in America," Baroness Helene de Ludinghausen told *Vanity Fair* in 2004. "Because it's all based on money, not accomplishment anymore."

Trump had a genius for the deal. Fireman had none of that. He manufactured pool toys during a period when production was moving to China at dramatic savings. Because of his family, he had lots of Reebok stock when that took off, and that put him in the 1 percent. Fireman became a member of Mar-a-Lago, and he set out to become one of the island's leading philanthropists.

Fireman had no role in firing Ecclestone, but he landed immediately in an unseemly mess when the elite islanders decided to boycott the 2005 event. As they saw it, one of their kind had been fired, and one of *them* had taken over. Ecclestone also rebounded quickly, taking a role in a gala for the International Center for Missing and Exploited Children. This event just happened to take place at the Breakers the same evening as the Red Cross Ball at Mar-a-Lago, giving her kind something else to do that night.

To fill the tables at *his* ball, Fireman called in many chits, bringing in outsiders from Massachusetts and elsewhere. That evening everything went in perfect order until Fireman got up to make his talk. "We have twenty-six ambassadors this year; last year they had six," Fireman boasted. "We raised two million dollars at this ball, last year they raised one million dollars." His barely veiled attack on Ecclestone's reign did not sit well, even with Fireman's supporters.

Fireman hoped to chair the ball for its historic fiftieth year, but first he had to get through chairing the forty-ninth. After promising to make up any shortfall so the charity would net at least a million dollars, the Red Cross signed him on again.

Fireman reveled in the way he disrupted the staid old world. "People here are worried that they now have to deal with a powerful force," he told *The Wall Street Journal*. He thought of himself as a noble figure reaching out to soothe the world's woes. "When you see sadness, pain and suffering I want to rise up, and I want to help," he said.

The living room in Fireman's home was full of magazine covers of him in silver picture frames. These were from *Palm Beach Society*, a local weekly magazine that devoted itself to charity and other social events. For as little as two thousand dollars, you could buy the cover, and one week, Fireman splurged and bought the whole issue, with the cover reading, "SIMON FIREMAN: INNOVATOR, LEADER, HUMANITARIAN."

On the January 2006 night of the forty-ninth International Red Cross Ball, the only celebrities in attendance, other than the singer Frankie Avalon, who was performing, were Donald and Melania Trump. Trump greeted people with such enthusiasm that the uninformed might have assumed he was the chairman of the ball.

Christopher Ruddy, the CEO of Newsmax Media, was seated with his guests at a table just beneath the stage. The youthful-looking, rotund businessman had joined Mar-a-Lago at Trump's invitation to get close to Trump and other prominent Americans who might advance him and his business. That's also why he had paid twenty-five thousand dollars for a table at the ball. He had an extraordinary ability to bring all sorts of people together whose only connection was that they knew Chris Ruddy.

Ruddy's website, headquartered in West Palm Beach, was becoming a favorite place for conservatives to get their news. While they were there, this son of a Long Island cop also sold them financial and medical information and put their names and personal information on lucrative mailing lists. Taking in tens of millions of dollars a year, the forty-one-year-old businessman was quickly becoming a wealthy man even in Palm Beach terms.

Shannon Donnelly also was seated at a prominent table. "Yes, these people give money to charity, but nobody gives it anonymously," the society editor reflects. "They don't do things for the good. They do things for their own glory."

Donnelly loved the elegant old Palm Beach, and she fancied herself the arbiter of the island, with power far beyond that of the old Palm Beach society queens. It wasn't enough to attack Fireman in her column. She tried to get him thrown out as chairman. "I took the Palm Beach County Red Cross executive director to lunch, and I said, 'Don't get involved with this man. You're making a mistake.' He ignored me. Everybody was kissing Fireman's ass because all these charity people care about is getting the money so they can get a big bonus."

Almost no one in the ballroom other than Donnelly had attended the ball in the old days. She would later write critically of the evening, comparing it to "the junior prom" and mocking the music used as the twenty-five marines in dress uniforms led the seven ambassadors into the ballroom. Trump was the other critic of the evening. "The marines were there and it was terrible because you know all these rich people, they're not there to support the marines," Trump said. "They're really there to get their picture in the Shiny Sheet."

As the evening wore on, it became increasingly obvious that many of the first-time guests were not regulars at formal affairs. A number of them drank to excess. The ballroom was air-conditioned, but some of them began to perspire. The cummerbunds on a number of the men rose up around their stomachs and twisted up.

Fireman saw the evening as a stunning achievement by every measure. The only problem was the math. He was going to end up owing the Red Cross almost as much as last year. When he saw that the ballroom was emptying out at what he considered an early hour, he walked up onstage, took the baton from orchestra leader Michael Rose, and began leading the twenty-five-piece orchestra. Fireman moved closer and closer to the edge of the stage, flailing the baton with manic exuberance. As he thrust his arms up and down, he stumbled and fell off the stage, hitting his head on the marble floor.

Almost no one paid much attention, and people continued walking out of the ballroom. Only Trump and one other man jumped up and rushed to where Fireman was resting in a pool of blood. Trump looked down with a grimace of revulsion on his face as he looked at Fireman lying there not moving.

Trump recalled the incident on *The Howard Stern Show* in 2008: "I thought he died, and I said, 'Oh, my God, that's disgusting' and I turned away. I didn't want to touch him. He's bleeding all over the place. I felt terrible, you know, beautiful marble floor, didn't look so good. It changed color, became very red. And you have this poor guy, eighty years old, laying on the floor unconscious, and all of the rich people are turning white. And you know they're turning away. Nobody wants to help the guy. His wife is screaming. What happens is these ten marines from the back of the room come running forward. They created a human stretcher, five guys at each side. They ran him out. I forgot to call to see if he was okay. It's just not my thing."

Fireman was taken to a West Palm Beach emergency room, where the doctors determined he had broken his nose. He was recovering with a large bandage when Donnelly's story appeared in the *Palm Beach Daily News*. Not only did she criticize the evening, she even mocked Fireman's accident. "There's a lesson in timing here," she wrote in her column. "Had this been the Animal Rescue League Ball, those first responders might well have been two beagles and a golden retriever."

Like many events at Mar-a-Lago, the ball had been so extravagantly staged that the ticket prices barely covered expenses and left little for the Red Cross.

It took a donor like Fireman for the event to boast about its donations. He owed the Red Cross as much as seven hundred thousand dollars, but he decided not to pay. "There's nothing in writing," he told them.

He was finished as a major player in the social scene.

The old-timers might moan and groan over Trump taking over *their* island, but they didn't matter much any longer, and with his new ballroom, Trump had turned Mar-a-Lago into the most desired location for major events on the island. Some of the charities considered his prices too steep and settled for the Breakers or other venues, but the historic mansion was such a draw that most of the organizations lined up to get their annual date. Trump's presence was a major selling point, and he rarely disappointed. If he didn't feel like sitting through the whole evening, he at least greeted the guests as they arrived.

In the era just before the iPhone turned Trump's life into an endless photo op, the photographer at Mar-a-Lago played a crucial role, and Trump watched over this with the same sense of detailed concern he did most things at his club. He knew that many guests thought the ultimate souvenir of the evening was a photograph with him. During the early years, Trump had given Bob Davidoff exclusive rights to take photos of members and guests at Mar-a-Lago. Davidoff had been the court photographer for the Kennedys in Palm Beach, keeping that position by never showing a photo of them not looking their best. He played that same role for Trump and his club, and when Davidoff died at age seventy-eight, in 2004, his sons Daryl and Ken took over.

For a while, Daryl and Ken's mother, Babs Davidoff, had done the job of taking down the names and addresses of those her sons had photographed, but Trump couldn't abide having an elderly woman standing there. "Bring a pretty girl," he said. They did as he requested.

Trump thought the Davidoffs were making lots of money selling photos to Mar-a-Lago members and their guests. He knew what they were taking home because he charged them 15 percent of their earnings at the club, and his criticism was largely unfair. Still, every year the Davidoffs had to renegotiate, and every year Trump wanted a bigger cut.

"You know, Mr. Trump, the money you're making off of us in a year isn't enough to buy you a pair of shoes and a belt," Daryl Davidoff told Trump one year. "Why do we do this?"

"That's the way it is, Davidoff," Trump said, as if the photographer needed a life lesson.

Trump couldn't stand the idea that anybody was making money off him, and as time went on, he got upset at the Davidoffs wandering around *his* club earning money from *his* members. When Trump became irritated, he was not beyond coming up to one of the brothers and telling him point-blank: "Davidoff, you're fired."

Then there was the problem with Melania. Ivana and Marla had enjoyed having the Davidoffs around, but Trump's new wife did not. One evening the drummer in the small band that played that evening let young Barron hit on the drums. The Trumps' little boy was ecstatic, and Ken Davidoff shot endearing photos of him. He knew to clear them before he tried to sell them. He showed them to Trump, who said, "Go for it, Davidoff. It's great."

Melania was wildly protective of her son, Barron. The next day her lawyer called and said that asking her husband was not good enough. She was the one in control, and from then on, the Trumps owned the rights to every family photo the Davidoffs had ever taken. Ken said they were his photos. The Trumps could buy them if they wanted, but this was his work. The Davidoffs never worked at Mar-a-Lago again.

In the wake of the World Trade Center attack on September 11, 2001, arose a new breed of public patriot. You could see them most any day on I-95 with American flags poking out of their car windows as they went barreling down the road, often weaving back and forth lane to lane to draw more attention. As this phenomenon grew, in contrast, the more sedate patriotism espoused in Palm Beach appeared tepid and half-hearted.

Donald Trump knew where he stood, and it wasn't with weak-kneed ninnies like Stan Rumbough but with other hand-over-the-heart, red-white-and-blue, love-it-or-leave it, dyed-in-the-wool Americans. In October 2006, he erected an eighty-foot-tall flagpole on his estate's front lawn and from it hung a humungous American flag.

Some of the locals felt the heart tugs of patriotism when they saw the Stars and Stripes practically blocking the sky, but others thought it belonged fronting a used-car lot far away from the placid precincts of Palm Beach. A resident two miles to the north of Trump sent a letter to the *Palm Beach Daily News*, complaining that "it surely disturbs the view of the south part of Palm Beach."

The town regulated every nuance of life, including the size of poles and flags. Trump's flag was four times the maximum, and his pole was double the height allowed. He hadn't even bothered trying to get permission because he knew the town would say no. A fight that involved wrapping himself in red, white, and blue and putting Palm Beach in a predicament over patriotism was pure pleasure.

Palm Beach already had a reputation as a bunch of prissy snobs. The last thing the town needed was to be found ordering down an American flag. Smartly, they ignored the flag and attacked the pole—saying it was too tall and was so close to the property edge that if it fell it would land in the road.

Trump pulled out his favorite weapon: a ten-million-dollar lawsuit against Palm Beach for limiting his club's liberties. Trump learned long ago that you could sue anyone for any reason, and your opponent would likely crumble because of the costs involved in defending themselves. But this time his longtime nemesis Stanley M. Rumbough Jr. was ready to confront Trump straight on.

Rumbough was a war hero, and he liked to see the flag flying high, but not if it meant flouting the rules of the town he loved so much. He had risked his life again and again flying above the Pacific against the Japanese, and a generation later Trump had sat out the Vietnam War claiming foot problems. But Trump had gone to a military high school, and he felt that made him as much a military expert as if he had fought in the Battle of the Bulge. As for Rumbough, his war service was a long time ago and half forgotten.

Rumbough had the audacity to lecture Trump in the *Palm Beach Daily News*: "He should know that we play by the rules in America. In this town, and this country, no one is above the law."

Boldly flaunting his patriotism, Trump wrote an op-ed piece in the Shiny

Sheet that appeared on the same day as Rumbough's letter: "Most U.S. cities would be ashamed to interfere with the display of the American flag. This is not the first time the town has attempted to inhibit free expression at the Mar-a-Lago Club. The town's various, ongoing attempts to harass and stifle the Mar-a-Lago Club will be fought vigorously in a court of law rather than the town's commissions, where free speech is subordinate to a few people's opinions. The American flag is a symbol of enormous inspiration; it should fly proudly and freely in the Town of Palm Beach."

The town didn't back down, and neither did Trump, who raised his lawsuit to twenty-five million dollars. His associates also went around town finding twenty instances where flags violated town codes, and nothing was being done against them. Trump saw this whole matter as more evidence of the continuing vendetta against him and his club.

In another shrewd move, Trump promised to donate anything he received in his lawsuit to returning Iraqi veterans. "I think the returning wounded Iraqi war veterans deserve better than to have the American flag ripped down before their eyes," Trump said.

In January 2007, the town's Code Enforcement Board began imposing a $1,250-a-day penalty until the pole was removed. The more appropriate fine would have been $250 a day, but the board wanted Trump to feel its sting.

But what was $1,250 a day to him? The story had reached the national media, and to millions of citizens, the host of *The Apprentice* was standing up for an America that the chardonnay-sipping elitists in Palm Beach had long since abandoned.

The longer the fines went on, the worse the media portrayed Palm Beach. By April, the town council agreed to a settlement. Trump's flagpole could be seventy feet tall. He just had to move it sixty feet south and 140 feet west. Trump did just that and placed the flagpole on a mound that caused the flag to wave as high as it always had.

The town council waived the $120,000 in amassed fines if Trump would give $100,000 to charities involving Iraqi veterans. Trump had his foundation cut a check. Tax records show that little of this money came from Trump. In 2007, the next to the last year that Trump contributed to his foundation, he paid

$35,000 of his own money into his charity, while four other individuals and institutions seeking his blessings contributed $4,055,000 to be given away in Trump's name. These included World Wrestling Entertainment ($4 million); Trump's friend Alfons Schmitt ($25,000); another friend, carpet king John Stark, giving a corporate donation ($20,000); and NBC ($10,000).

Local officials portrayed the flag settlement as a victory, but Trump was the only winner. He had discovered a rich loam of patriotism lying under fallow soil. His TV fans loved anyone who stood up for the flag. Trump had fallen upon something magical, and he was not going to let it go.

Trump's daughter Ivanka loved everything her father did, including his fight for the flag and his far-flung business enterprises. On a Saturday morning in January 2007, twenty-five-year-old Ivanka took the stage at the Palm Beach Convention Center in West Palm Beach to talk about life within the Trump kingdom to a group of people twice her age.

Many in the audience had received letters inviting them to be Trump's "personal guest to hear my real Trump story on wealth creation from my daughter, Ivanka Trump and be trained by '4' self-made multi-millionaire experts" who "will share with you unique wealth creating secrets and strategies." The letters promised they would "learn what others have paid over $20,000 to learn." They would also receive free lunch and a copy of *TRUMP: Think Like a Billionaire*.

Trump was their hero. They had been left out of an economy that had turned Palm Beach into an island of millionaires. Many of them lived in modest town houses, trailer parks, and downscale condominiums far from the ocean. Some were retirees who wanted to supplement their small incomes, while others earned little more than the minimum wage and still others had overextended themselves and were looking for a way out.

Ivanka let the audience enter for a few minutes into her father's world. "The most important thing is that it's a meritocracy," Trump's daughter said. "How can you prove yourself when your parents have accomplished so much? I work for the Trump Organization all over the world. I know that if I don't evolve, he will fire me. If you do a terrific job, fine. I know that if I don't do well, I expect to be fired."

It was hard to believe that Trump would ever fire the dutiful Ivanka, but it was exciting for the audience to hear her talk about the fast-paced world of which she was a part. She had no secrets of wealth, only little anecdotes about her short time in the real-estate-development business, and then she was gone. She was followed by tough, cold-eyed men who said money was out there in enormous quantities just waiting to be taken. One after another, these men pushed the audience to buy largely online courses that cost between $500 and $4,000. People started getting up and giving their credit cards, sometimes going back two or three times.

This went on for most of the day, and when it was over the audience shuffled out to a world outside that was just the same as when they'd arrived.

12

Trumped Again

In the years after their divorce, Ivana always seemed to be competing with her ex-husband. If Trump had his honey, she had hers, too. First, it was fifty-one-year-old Italian businessman Riccardo Mazzucchelli, with whom she had a short, shaky marriage. She had to live in Palm Beach as well, not far from Mar-a-Lago in a mansion designed by the legendary Mizner. And while Trump was forced to sell his yacht, she purchased the 105-foot *Ivana*—against his stern advice.

Trump tried to make up with Ivana as best he could and hoped she would tone down a lifestyle that at times challenged him for space in the tabloids. Thus, he was delighted when Ivana told him she was marrying again, retreating into what he hoped would be quiet, discreet marital bliss.

Ivana appeared to have found somebody permanent this time in a handsome young Roman, Rossano Rubicondi, a semi-employed model and actor. The media was told he was thirty-five years old, but Ivana knew he was really thirty-one, half the age of his fifty-nine-year-old bride. When skeptics criticized her for robbing the cradle, she replied, "I'd rather be a babysitter than a nursemaid."

Trump was so enthusiastic at Ivana's pending nuptials that he agreed to stage the wedding at Mar-a-Lago. He waived the twenty thousand dollars he normally would have charged, leaving Ivana to pay only for food, drinks, and decorations for the three hundred guests. His ex-wife had learned from the master, and after getting Getty to pay her $250,000 for the photo rights, she turned a tidy profit getting married.

The March 2008 wedding included twenty-three bridesmaids in as many shades of pastel, and twenty-three groomsmen dressed in white, prancing down the great marble staircase. The bridegroom entered, with his hands raised over his head, to the theme from *Rocky*, music appropriate for a man about to be in the fight of his life. Ivana wore a shimmering pink and gold gown and almost fell during her entrance, but she was caught by Donald Jr., who was Rubicondi's age. Trump stood behind almost everyone. The invitations asked that the men dress in white, but he wore black. White was not his color except on the tennis courts with their all-white dress code and in his portrait as *The Visionary* hanging in the bar.

At the wedding dinner afterward, Donald Jr. gave a toast worthy of his father. "She's got some mileage on her, but she's still pretty hot," he said. "Yes, despite the body and the boobs, and all that, yes, she is a grandmother." He also had a message for his new stepfather. "And, Rossano, we are in the construction industry. You better be good to her because we have job sites. We can lose people. I have a .45 and a shovel. Nobody's gonna know you're gone."

Two months after the wedding, Ivana discovered that her new husband had a Cuban girlfriend he was keeping in France. That was the end of Ivana's fourth marriage.

Trump could be a great host, but woe betide anyone who criticized Mar-a-Lago. Longtime member Murray Fox learned that in the most painful way possible. Seventy-year-old Fox had joined early, and he was an outstanding doubles tennis player. If you wanted to win among the aging tennis players of Mar-a-Lago, you could do far worse than having Fox as your partner.

All was well until Fox took it upon himself to write a letter to Bernd Lembcke suggesting a number of court improvements, such as a shoe cleaner and better parking. Instead of taking in these suggestions, the club manager sent the letter to Trump, who was infuriated that Fox would dare to criticize. In Trump's restless pursuit of perfection, *he* was the only one with the right to suggest that things were less than flawless.

For example, one day Trump saw ugly metal cubes sitting next to the new water fountains he had ordered installed on the tennis courts. Trump wasn't interested in hearing that the boxes were chillers to make the water cold. Using all his strength, he shoved one of the monstrosities over, rupturing a pipe and setting a spigot of water rising high up into the Florida sky. Trump then walked away fuming, leaving the mess to be cleaned up and for someone to figure out a better solution. That was how you made things perfect, not by whining letters of complaint.

Trump replied to Fox and let him know he could get out. Fox was not without his pride, and he was willing to leave, but wanted his seventy-five-thousand-dollar membership fee back. Trump called that an "extortionist attempt" and promised "a major lawsuit against you for defamation of the club." Quoting the agreement Fox had signed, Trump said the money would be returned thirty years after he joined the club.

"Over the years we have had many complaints about you from people at the club—especially from those people playing tennis," Trump wrote. "You consistently complained that you were unable to get a game, and yet the primary reason for this was that the people did not want to play with you."

Fox talked to his friends, who said Trump's accusations were ridiculous. He felt he had no choice but to sue the club. Fox's attorney John M. Jorgensen argued that Trump couldn't expel his client because the club hadn't gone through the procedures as outlined in the membership documents. No member had written the admissions committee accusing Fox of misbehavior, and he had not been allowed to appear before the admissions committee to make his case.

Jorgensen's other argument stuck it to Trump over the town's limit on club memberships. He said Trump had "continued to issue new memberships in excess of 500 rather than reissue memberships of resigned members, including the membership held by Fox, in breach of the contract and rules of Mar-a-Lago, in order to avoid repayment of membership deposits." That was a sensitive point. Although Trump had gotten almost everything he wanted from the town, the maximum number of members still stood. From the hordes of members running in and out of the club, the last thing Trump likely wanted was a head count.

When it came time for Trump to give his deposition, he escalated even further as Fox sat across from him and beside his lawyer Jorgensen. "Nobody likes him. Nobody wants to play tennis with him," Trump said.

"Who doesn't like him?" Jorgensen asked.

"All the names are in the office."

"Who doesn't want to play tennis with Murray?"

"Names are in the office," Trump said. "Plus, he's a womanizer."

Jorgensen asked Trump to name names, and Trump returned to his assertion that Fox was roundly reviled. At the time, Fox was running for mayor of South Palm Beach. "He's not going to win," Trump said. "Nobody likes him."

Afterward, Fox went up to Trump. "Donald, you're going to get a pimple on your tongue," he said, looking up at the much taller Trump. "Your nose is going to grow. How could you lie in front of me?"

Trump paused before putting his arm around Fox. "I've heard great things about you," Trump said. "Let's settle this thing." The two men sat down with their lawyers and agreed to end their battle, but nothing was in writing.

Back at the mansion, Trump went around asking members what they thought he should do. "You know I've got this thing going on with Murray Fox," he told one man. "I was in this fucking deposition for three hours asking me the same goddamn questions over and over again. Asshole lawyer."

"Didn't your lawyer object?" the member asked.

"A lot of fucking good that did," Trump said. "What do you think I should do?"

The member knew Fox well. "Murray's had two heart attacks and six stents," the man said.

"I didn't know that," Trump said, clearly confounded. If there was one thing he couldn't stand, it was disease.

"And he's still a champion player for his age. He's always in the club finals. He's encouragement for people his age."

"So, what do I do?" Trump asked.

"It's just aggravation and lawyers' bills," the member said. "Maybe you guys should work it out."

Trump turned to Lembcke. "All right, that's it," he told the club manager. "Tell the lawyers to settle. But get every cent of any back dues he owes."

Few people who left the club got their membership fees back. When Mar-a-Lago didn't return Evangelos Kanaris's money, the Palm Beach jeweler put a small ad in the *Palm Beach Daily News*, asking current and former Mar-a-Lago members to get in touch with him for "new information" about getting their money back. He said roughly twenty people contacted him. Nothing ever came of it, in part because five months later the jeweler was charged with grand theft and fled the island.

Trump continued to treat Mar-a-Lago as his private fiefdom, never giving out a membership list and leaving the members knowing that he could bounce them out with a snap of his fingers, without returning their membership fees.

Trump let Paul Rampell keep his free membership at Mar-a-Lago even after the two stopped working together. Rampell didn't go that often, but it was a nice perk to have, and Trump always greeted him warmly. The attorney was a well-remunerated member of the network of lawyers, accountants, and bankers who discreetly serviced the needs of wealthy Palm Beachers.

Then, one day in April 2006, twenty-year-old Melissa Legare walked into the attorney's office and told him a devastating story. The woman was a pastry chef at the Everglades Club. She lived in a cell-like room without a bathroom or running water in one of three buildings across from the club that housed the club's seasonal employees. The workers called the lodgings the "barracks." That was a fitting name for an austere, utilitarian place suitable for little more than sleep.

Legare's quarters at the barracks were among other white Americans. The Latinos were called "Amigos," and they had their own building, while the Everglades housed the eastern Europeans in still another place.

The pastry chef had the feeling that everything was being done to set the whites against the Amigos. When Legare went to work, she had a name tag. The Amigos didn't merit the identification and were rarely referred to by their names.

"It was bred into their heads that the Caucasian employees were supposed to be better than them," Legare says. The single young woman felt uncomfortable in her dormlike arrangement. There was no lock on the door, and one night when she was getting undressed, she saw a group of Amigos staring in her window.

A few evenings later, Legare had a few drinks after work and went to bed. When she woke up at about 4:30 A.M., a man was on top of her penetrating her. She threw him off, and before he fled, she recognized him as one of the Amigos in the kitchen.

Within a little more than an hour, the police sat with Legare, having her look at photographs of the kitchen workers. She immediately picked out Miguel Cardona, a thirty-one-year-old dishwasher from Guatemala. Cardona and his two brothers worked six evenings a week, washing the fancy crystal and fine silver for $7.37 an hour. Cardona, who was an illegal immigrant, was wearing the same brand of white T-shirt that the perpetrator left at the crime scene and had marks on his neck consistent with what Legare said she had done to ward off her attacker. The police arrested Cardona and booked him into Palm Beach County Jail. He was later convicted and is serving a twenty-year sentence.

The Everglades Club wanted this whole nasty business to go away. They abhorred the idea of publicity. The last thing the *Palm Beach Daily News* would do was to write about such a sordid business involving the esteemed club, but the *Palm Beach Post* was onto the story, and they had a number of relentless investigative reporters.

The Everglades kept Legare segregated in the room where she had been attacked and warned her that if she spoke to the press, she would be fired. "They made me feel horrible, as if I had brought this upon myself," she said.

One Everglades employee visited Legare, who was huddled in her tiny room, distraught beyond measure. "You've got to fight back," the person said. "I know a lawyer who wouldn't be afraid of the Everglades Club."

Rampell's office was within sight of the Everglades Club and Legare summoned up the gumption to walk there. Even before the trust lawyer decided whether he would take the case, he got the traumatized woman out of the barracks and put her up in a hotel. "Paul took me under his wing," Legare says. "Paul was my cheerleader, my rock, reaching and trying to get all the resources he could."

Representing Trump had been highly controversial, at one point costing him many clients, but Rampell believed taking on the Everglades Club directly could be worse. That wasn't what worried him, but whether he could win a civil suit against the club. Rampell talked to Robert Montgomery Jr., the most esteemed trial lawyer on the island. Montgomery was a frequent fighter for social justice, but he said this wasn't a winnable case and Rampell should forget it. That was doubtlessly good advice, but Rampell decided he must take on this battle.

When Trump heard about the rape, he was profoundly affected. He lived within a cocoon of privilege from which he attempted to banish anything unpleasant. Trump wasn't used to hearing things like this crime. He extrapolated way beyond the reality of this one terrible incident, concluding that undocumented aliens were a race of rapists and criminals, a plague on American life. The idea obsessed him, and when he ran for president, he made it a main theme of his campaign.

As much as Rampell cared about Legare, he knew he wasn't the kind of lawyer to fight this case alone. To be the lead attorney, he brought in Theodore Babbitt, a personal injury lawyer. "This suit will uncover what I think is a festering sore on Worth Avenue," Babbitt said. "This is a place which should not exist under its present circumstance."

Babbitt's intention was to win by contrasting what he called the meticulous screening of club applicants that weeded out anyone with Jewish ancestry, while hiring employees with such casual unconcern that there were a multitude of illegal immigrants with fake green cards and those with criminal records. And then he said the employees were set against each other in such a way that there inevitably would be a tragedy. "In my opinion, there will be no doubt in the jury's mind that a club comprised of some of the richest people in America intentionally employed illegals at the expense of the security not only of the other employees but also of their members as well," Babbitt said.

The defendant's lawyers argued that the Everglades had no racist intentions in their housing practices. The club was merely placing people of like backgrounds together. But rather than face the embarrassment of a civil trial that would likely have exposed much devastating information about the club's practices, the Everglades settled with Legare. Everything about the settlement is confidential, but it was at least a million dollars.

Legare returned to her native Maine, where she works as a pastry chef in a popular restaurant. Rampell resumed his regular legal practice. Whenever he picked up the Shiny Sheet and read a front-page story of a charitable donation or attended a dinner honoring someone for their philanthropy, he thought of Legare. She was far from a wealthy young woman, but she took the settlement and gave it anonymously to three charities that work for the protection of women's rights, including helping victims of sexual abuse who do not have the resources to fight back.

As a place for charity events, Mar-a-Lago had become a rewarding business. Even if sometimes little went to the charity, Trump made out well. At the 2010 Policeman's Ball, an annual event raising scholarship money for the local cops' children, Trump received the Palm Tree Award for his "selfless support" of the Palm Beach Police Foundation. That evening he announced a $150,000 contribution to the police.

The five hundred Palm Beachers gathered in the ballroom didn't know—as would be reported in September 2016 by *The Washington Post*'s David A. Fahrenthold—that the money came from the Charles Evans Foundation, a small New Jersey charity. Trump had asked the foundation to donate money to his foundation that would be contributed to the Palm Beach Police Foundation. Instead of giving the Evans Foundation the credit, Trump took it for himself.

Two years later Donald and Melania cochaired the annual Dana-Farber gala at Mar-a-Lago, where money was raised for the prestigious cancer institute.

Trump made a magnificent $200,000 contribution, but it was not quite what it seemed. The money was from the Donald J. Trump Foundation, to which he had stopped contributing. The foundation's funds came from others who wrote checks presumably to curry favor with Trump, who then used the money to make donations in his name. Of the $706,000 paid out by the foundation since 2008 in Palm Beach County, almost all of it went to charities having events at Mar-a-Lago. What could be more touching than the namesake of the Donald J. Trump Ballroom standing there before the multitudes personally handing out his check?

Few things were sweeter than being publicly lauded as a noble philanthropist while using somebody else's money. That wasn't the only blessing. Trump was charging Dana-Farber as much as $150,000 to put on the event, which meant that he was making a neat profit while he sat there receiving accolades for what was not his generosity.

Many people in the ballroom aspired to be like Trump and have their names in bold type in the program, hear their largesse touted from the podium, and see their pictures in the Shiny Sheet. That was fantastic news for Trump, because it helped keep the Mar-a-Lago ballroom booked night after night (and often at lunch as well) for charity events.

Trump made Mar-a-Lago exciting, and when he was gone, so was the excitement. Members called the club in the middle of the week to see if he was flying down for the weekend. If he was going to be there, they booked dinner reservations. If he stayed in New York, the club was often half empty. "You can always tell when the king is here," said his butler Tony Senecal.

Some people quit other clubs and moved over to Mar-a-Lago. David and Ronni Fingold left the Palm Beach Country Club and later joined Mar-a-Lago. David played tennis regularly, and often the couple drove up in their Rolls-Royce or Bentley for dinner with friends. Ronni, who owns Forest Hill, one of the top real estate companies in Toronto, said, "It's a slice of a billionaire's lifestyle. When you're there, you feel you are at home."

At Mar-a-Lago, at dinner on the verandah, one table might have a noisy group devouring their food like GIs in a chow line, while next to them could be an elegant European couple cutting their sea bass with a surgeon's skill and subtlety. And so what? The juxtaposition was perfectly fine. As long as you had the money, you were a rightful part of the scene.

Trump loved it. When he was in a convivial mood, he was the host of hosts, moving through the dining room, asking how the food was, expecting nothing but ecstatic responses. One evening he came up to a group standing together. "Which one of you is Thom Smith?" Trump asked, referring to a popular *Palm Beach Post* columnist.

"That's me," Smith said.

"Look at him," Trump said. "He's the best, the greatest writer in Palm Beach."

Smith thought that having someone like Trump appreciate his work was meaningful. Then Shannon Donnelly came into the room, and Trump walked over to her. The society editor had stayed in power so long because each morning she got up, put her little finger in the air, and gauged which way the winds of power were blowing. In recent years, she had realized that Trump had become almost acceptable, and night after night she was going to events in the ballroom. The society columnist had begun to treat Trump like a modern-day Caesar and was no longer savaging him. For his part, Trump had begun to recognize her usefulness.

"Look at her," Trump said. "She's the best, the greatest writer in Palm Beach."

Trump often had dinner with club members if they were powerful, wealthy, or had a celebrity with them. One evening he and Melania had dinner with his old tennis partner Moira Fiore, who had changed her last name from Wolofsky after her late husband died and she married Jon Fiore. Her twenty-nine-year-old daughter Brooke Mueller and Mueller's significant other, Charlie Sheen, the star of CBS's *Two and a Half Men,* were with Fiore that evening.

Sheen was watching a football game and came to the table a half hour late. Trump was a master of hiding his displeasure and saving it for a better time. When Sheen coveted Trump's cuff links, Trump said the priceless items had been made especially for him, then took them off and gave them to the actor. Sheen later learned that Trump had scores of the inexpensive cuff links and handed them out like autographs.

Later when Trump saw Fiore at the club, he told her, "Do not let Brooke marry Charlie."

"Why?" asked Fiore, who was excited that her daughter was marrying a celebrity.

"Bad boy Charlie," Trump said. "Bad boys don't fall far from the tree."

Fiore looked up as if she didn't quite understand.

"He comes from Martin," Trump said, referring to Charlie's politically active father, actor Martin Sheen. "So that's bad right there."

Some of Fiore's friends felt Trump was wrong to interject himself, but Fiore felt differently. She thought it showed that Trump cared about her daughter. Brooke still married Charlie Sheen, and the marriage quickly turned violent and abusive and ended in divorce.

A few years later Trump called Fiore at home. Trump read the local society magazines and was irritated when he saw photos of Fiore eating at local restaurants. "Moira, you're not eating here enough," Trump said.

Mar-a-Lago had an annual two-thousand-dollar food minimum, and she had no trouble paying that and more.

"Are you serious?" Fiore asked.

"Yeah, I'm not kidding with you. Do you still want to be a member?"

"All right, I'll come tonight," Fiore said.

Trump had also not given up his irritation about planes flying over Mar-a-Lago. They were far higher in the air above Mar-a-Lago than when they rose up out of Palm Beach International Airport above middle-class homes, but Trump didn't see that as his problem. The planes had no business flying over him. He claimed that airport director Bruce Pelly was sending the planes over the estate as a personal vendetta after Trump called Pelly an incompetent manager.

In January 2015, Trump sued the airport and Pelly for one hundred million dollars, which was now his favorite amount. Palm Beach County Attorney David R. Ottey had trouble making sense of the enormous figure. In court proceedings, he kept mentioning one hundred thousand dollars, a sum that might have been reasonable. The judge had to correct him that Trump sought a thousand times more.

Trump claimed that the club was losing money because of the noise, but he couldn't supply evidence that anybody had dropped out for that reason. The annual profits at Mar-a-Lago and the golf club were steadily increasing, to a record $29.8 million in 2015. Beyond that, Trump's lawyers weren't able to prove there had been any significant physical damage from the airplanes.

This was another of Trump's personal grievances played out in the courtroom, and it was not without its societal consequences. The suit was costing Palm Beach County hundreds of thousands of dollars, and it was keeping its duly sworn attorneys away from other matters.

Bill O'Reilly came to Mar-a-Lago in March 2011 to be the keynote speaker at the Alexa Foundation benefit supporting victims of rape. O'Reilly remarked that every four years since 1999 Trump had been touted as a presidential candidate, and he took this opportunity to tease out the idea of a President Trump.

"He'd probably run the country from right here," O'Reilly said. "Of course, I'd expect to be secretary of state. . . . But the main reason I'll vote for Donald Trump is that he'd probably deport Rosie O'Donnell to Tonga."

This was the moment when cable television's most popular personality looked over at America's leading reality TV star and asked, "Have you ever been to Iowa? Do you even know where Iowa is? I can't wait to see him in New Hampshire in the middle of winter."

Trump let it be known that he was unimpressed with the 2012 Republican presidential candidates and believed he had a real shot at the nomination. An April 2011 NBC–*Wall Street Journal* poll showed him tied with former Arkansas governor Mike Huckabee for second place, with former Massachusetts governor Mitt Romney in the lead. Even so, in the spring of 2011, Trump announced he was not running.

No answer was ever final with Trump, no contract inviolate, no pledge ironclad, and he and his Mar-a-Lago buddy, Christopher Ruddy, founder of the conservative website Newsmax, continued to discuss his presidential prospects.

In the 1990s, well before Ruddy started Newsmax, he was one of a group of conservative writers producing conspiratorial exposés on the Clintons and other liberals, a lot of it funded by billionaire heir Richard Mellon Scaife.

In 1997, Ruddy published the book *The Strange Death of Vincent Foster,* about the 1993 suicide of White House deputy counsel Vincent W. Foster Jr. Although the exposé did not say outright that President Clinton's childhood friend had been murdered, the mixture of innuendo and conjecture led Clinton haters to conclude that Bill and Hillary had done Foster in to shut him up about the White-water affair in Arkansas.

Strangely, Ruddy had become friendly with the Clintons in recent years. He not only disavowed the excesses in his book, claiming he had gotten "caught up in anti-Clinton hysteria," but pledged one million dollars to the Clinton Foundation and flew with the former president to Africa to further the foundation's work.

But Ruddy's friendship with his Palm Beach neighbor Donald Trump led him back into the world of political paranoia. Emerging from the shadowy cellars of the internet came the story that President Obama had not been born in Hawaii but in Kenya, which meant that per the Constitution he was an illegitimate president. Trump had no reason to believe this story was true when he learned about it on the internet, and he almost never said Obama was lying. Like Ruddy with Vince Foster, Trump just kept expressing doubts and sowing seeds of confusion in the American consciousness "If he wasn't born in this country, which is a real possibility . . . then he has pulled one of the great cons in the history of politics," Trump said on *Today* on April 7, 2011.

The innuendo was brilliantly effective, and it was picked up like wildfire in conservative circles. These claims may not have been directly racist, but they spoke specifically to a white nationalist audience that already believed Obama was an illegitimate president simply because of the color of his skin. Trump's pronouncements provoked a dark part of the American soul, giving this audience a way of saying what they felt without actually saying it.

Trump was turning his back on the liberal and minority audiences that had embraced him on *The Apprentice*. This also signified that he was taking on a distraught white population that believed America was being taken over by minority groups and illegal immigrants. Trump's sentiments were not uncommon in Palm Beach, where he had heard such things for years and was merely publicly embracing them.

Mar-a-Lago had many Jewish members who had grown up poor in a time when "Jewish" and "liberal" were synonymous. They had left their old neighborhoods and even their old politics, too, but no matter how they voted, a residue of those childhood beliefs remained. Most of them were proud that America had elected its first African American president. They knew President Obama had been born in Hawaii, and they didn't understand why Trump was going from cable show to cable show with the false claim that the president was foreign born.

That man on the TV screen wasn't the Trump they knew, the one who called out to them each weekend with good tidings and fellowship. They wondered what else they didn't know about him. They didn't talk about it much, but the whole business made them uneasy.

Trump kept pushing his "birther" campaign to such levels that Obama asked officials in Hawaii to release his birth certificate. But Trump found ways to question even that.

Obama waited until the White House Correspondents' Dinner in April 2011 to take his revenge on Trump, who was sitting in the banquet hall before him. "No one is prouder to put this birth certificate matter to rest than the Donald," Obama said as the audience began laughing, not even needing the punch line to be in on the joke. "And that's because he can finally get back to focusing on the issues that matter—like, did we fake the moon landing? What really happened in Roswell? And where are Biggie and Tupac?"

Trump could handle even the most vicious of attacks. It was only a game, and in politics the blows were about as real as at a World Wrestling Entertainment match. But he couldn't stand to have somebody make fun of him and have others join in the amusement. The cathartic waves of laughter showed just how much the media establishment despised Trump. Obama was trying to drive Trump off the political stage, mocked into oblivion. To a man like Trump, who was incapable of laughing at himself, it was sheer humiliation.

Anyone who had observed Trump's dealings with the Palm Beach Town

Council and with many of his business associates would know he was all about getting even—and in ways the genteel Obama could scarcely grasp. Many have speculated that Trump's campaign for the presidency began this evening.

Obama's election in 2008 had set off a dark conspiratorial mind-set in many parts of the country, including in Trump and a lot of his fellow Palm Beachers. They feared malevolent forces had taken over the White House, destroying everything America had been. One Palm Beach person who has worked closely with Trump for years said, "I thought Obama was the Manchurian Candidate. They had prayer rugs all over the White House, but not a trace of anything Christian. They actually covered the crosses."

This woman and many like her saw conspiracies everywhere controlling our destiny. Take your pick, or more than one if you like, everything from the Bilderberg Group, the New World Order, George Soros, and the Deep State to cultural Marxism.

Trump plucked his ideas out of the air, a snippet from television, a column in the paper, a chat with the myriad of people with whom he conversed, the pieces feeding into a puzzle that only he could put together, inspiring his belief that America had to be rescued from these evil forces.

These conspiracy theories got full play on Ruddy's Newsmax TV. Trump was a key player in Ruddy's world, and Trump was extolled regularly on the Newsmax website. Ruddy aspired to be one of the great media business figures of his day, as Rupert Murdoch or Roger Ailes had been in their time, but his new network was not doing well. If he didn't start getting viewers to tune in, it was going to do nothing but savage his bottom line.

Ruddy's big idea around this time was to have Newsmax cohost the last Republican debate before the 2012 Iowa caucuses and have Trump ask the questions. Trump was still high in the ratings from *The Apprentice*, and this would draw viewers to Ruddy's network. But if Trump moderated the debate, it would signal that he was not a candidate, and that was a problem with his new book. Trump had gone to a right-wing publisher this time, Regnery, yet another sign of his move to the right. Regnery had just released Trump's latest book and was not happy about his dropping out. *Time to Get Tough* was a candidate's book, and people might not buy it if the author was no longer running.

Trump had to promote the book for it to be a bestseller, and early in December, he headed to Boca Raton to sign copies at a Barnes & Noble. Ruddy drove down separately, and he noticed cars backing up on the exit off I-95, the parking lot filled to overflowing, and a line around the building.

Ruddy had been to numerous book signings for conservative authors. It usually looked like happy hour at a continuing-care community. This was different. "In the line, you had an Asian housekeeper, a millionaire store owner, an Asian kid, all kinds of people that are not part of a traditional Republican crowd," Ruddy said. "This was one of the first clues that this guy could have a huge potential reach as a candidate."

Trump was a multitasker of the first order. While he signed personal notes to book purchasers, he kept up a running conversation with the Newsmax CEO. After about a half hour, Ruddy did some simple math and told Trump that if he continued to write whatever a person wanted, he would be there for three more hours. Trump got the message and started signing only his name, but even that took an hour longer.

"You know, Chris," Trump said proudly when he had signed the last book, "the manager told me this is the biggest book signing in the history of this store."

"You're kidding," replied a skeptical Ruddy.

"No, I'm not kidding at all," said an irritated Trump. "Get the manager."

Ruddy hurried to find the manager.

"Tell Mr. Ruddy what you told me about the book signing," Trump said.

The man seemed genuinely bewildered. "Well, what did I tell you about the book signing?"

Trump moved up close to the manager and pressed his chest up next to his. "You told me it was the biggest signing in the history of the store."

"Yes, Mr. Trump," the manager said dutifully.

Trump's book did become a bestseller, but Republican National Committee chairman Reince Priebus did not like the idea of having a man who might still end up the party's nominee host a debate. The other candidates were worried that the grandstanding Trump would turn the event into what former Utah governor Jon Huntsman said would be "show business over substance." Only two of the candidates, former House Speaker Newt Gingrich and former Pennsylvania senator Rick Santorum, agreed to show up. The front-runner, former governor Mitt Romney, acted like a prom queen with a full dance card, saying he would have agreed to attend if he had been asked earlier.

Trump reamed out Romney and several others as gutless wimps unwilling to come to *his* debate. Trump's attacks proved Huntsman's point and certainly didn't help Ruddy's ongoing attempts to soft-soap Romney and his competitors to show up.

"Look, Donald, I think we can get this," Ruddy told Trump on the phone, trying to pull back his assault. "We've got Newt, and we've got Santorum, and I think Michele Bachmann will fall into line eventually, and then everybody's going to have to—"

"You don't know what the fuck you're doing!!!" Trump screamed. "I've been doing this for twenty years. I'm at the top of the ratings! It's all about controversy! This is going to grow the ratings. Trust me! Trust me!"

Ruddy continued trying to put the event together until he heard on the news a few days later that Trump had backed out of hosting the debate. Ruddy was upset that Trump hadn't bothered to forewarn him. But he needed Trump more than Trump needed him, and the irritation didn't last.

Trump also proclaimed that he was leaving the Republican Party and might run as an independent. But he never did come through on either of these threats, and when Barack Obama was reelected, Trump embraced the Republican efforts to retake the White House four years later.

The annual Palm Beach County Republicans' Lincoln Dinner at Mar-a-Lago was the area's most important conservative political event. The 2014 speaker was one likely presidential candidate, Senator Ted Cruz of Texas. Another potential candidate, surgeon Ben Carson, was in the ballroom, and a third, Florida senator Marco Rubio, was there in a video presentation.

After Trump introduced Cruz as "a special guy" who "shouldn't be controversial because what he's doing is right," he sat down to listen to the thirty-five-minute speech. Trump wasn't even listed in the major polls, and Cruz referred to him not as potential candidate but "a tremendous businessman" and "a powerful voice for free enterprise."

Cruz had developed and honed a right-wing constituency across America that he believed made him the natural candidate for hard-right conservatives, evangelicals, and anyone else who despised Obama. "Liberty has never been more under assault than it is today," he said that evening. "It seems like President Obama is trying to go down the Bill of Rights and violate each one of them one at a time."

Cruz proclaimed that he had faith that a "grass roots" movement would rise up to take America back from this interloper. Trump would later call Cruz "Lying Ted," but then he was hearing themes he would appropriate and use to rev up his crowds to a point far beyond what the pugnacious Cruz even imagined.

The Texas senator had one sentimental moment when he waxed lyrical about his father, who had fled Cuba fifty-seven years before and begun living the American dream by first making his way as a dishwasher. Trump considered nothing and no one off limits in political combat, and he would one day outrageously accuse Cruz's father of possible involvement in the Kennedy assassination.

Trump praised the Republican candidates publicly, but behind their backs, he called them a parade of midgets, each one more diminutive than the next. The more he looked at them, the more he saw himself out there in the center of the stage tearing apart these mediocrities and speaking beyond them to a people who adored him.

As Trump contemplated running, he talked to any number of political operatives. Nobody intrigued him as much as Stephen K. Bannon, the head of the alt-right website Breitbart. The rumpled, unshaven provocateur wrestled with ideas as if they were living things and not essays on paper. He got Trump to read all kinds of material in Breitbart that exposed the "Deep State" and the corruption of so-called liberal democracy. Never mind that a lot of it may not have been actually true, but it was wildly enticing material, and Trump ate it up with the speed and efficiency he did soft-serve ice cream.

Trump recognized that the odds of an outsider winning in the primaries were abysmal. That was no big deal. If he ran, he would stay in at least long enough to elevate his brand to a whole other level. Ivanka Trump and her husband, Jared Kushner, told one of Trump's closest associates that his run for the presidency would be a bonanza for their business enterprises. It was about money, and it was irresistible. No way Trump could lose, no matter the outcome.

What Trump wanted and needed was for the people at Mar-a-Lago to tell him he should run for president. Bernd Lembcke didn't have to prompt club members to do this. The air around Trump emitted its own energy, and early in 2015 members started telling Trump he should get into the race.

"Mr. President," someone would shout as he hurried by in his golf clothes. Others would come to him and tell him he was the nation's last, best hope. Some of this was merely playing the game Trump wanted played, but a lot of it was genuine, even if almost no one believed he could win the nomination, much less the White House. For them, it was a win if they got to see the maestro of Mar-a-Lago running on television for a few weeks or even longer.

No member of the club was more passionate about Trump's candidacy than Toni Holt Kramer. She had been friends with Hillary and had given her a fundraiser at her Bel Air home in 2002. Kramer now felt Hillary had changed into a narrow, relentlessly ambitious woman, interested only in herself and her advance. Kramer believed that Trump and only Trump could save America.

Kramer was a woman of far more complexity than most socialites associated with Palm Beach. She had dropped out of high school and lied about her age to get a spot in the chorus line at New York's celebrated Copacabana nightclub when she was only fifteen and a half, and she had lived by her wits and her beauty, both of which she had in ample supply. Seeking a replacement for a father who left home when she was nine years old, Kramer had married one much older man after another until she met Bob Kramer, who had made his fortune selling cars. They lived in estates in Bel Air, Palm Springs, and Palm Beach.

Kramer wrote letter after letter to Trump, imploring him to enter the race. Every time she saw him, she beseeched him to declare his candidacy. He never reacted until one day, in April 2015, she was standing on the verandah at Mar-a-Lago when Trump came breezing by. He slowed down just enough to whisper in her ear, "I'm running," and hurried off again. Kramer told no one, not even her husband of a quarter century. It was that big a secret.

13

The Candidate

On June 16, 2015, Trump rode down the escalator to the marble atrium of Trump Tower in Manhattan to announce he was entering the presidential race. Most politicians announce their candidacy with gravitas while reading from carefully prepared remarks. Trump sounded off the cuff, tossing out a grab bag of ideas and boasts, many of which he had conjured with for decades. There was no beginning, middle, or end—simply an endless verbal outpouring. Some of it didn't make much sense, but that didn't matter because he was quickly on to the next thing.

As Trump set out on the greatest adventure of his life, he had one nasty little problem. To him, marital vows were little more than silly platitudes followed by lesser mortals. Through all three of his marriages, he had endless affairs, liaisons, and dalliances. His playboy image wouldn't go over well with the evangelicals and other morally conservative Republicans without whom he would not get very far in his quixotic quest for the White House.

That's why David Pecker stepped up. During the summer of 2015, according to court documents, Trump's longtime lawyer and confidant Michael D. Cohen got together with Pecker, who offered to have the *National Enquirer* purchase the stories of women peddling accounts of their relationships with the candidate. And then instead of splashing their lurid tales on the front page of the weekly, Pecker would bury the unsightly business for good. With that unpleasantness in the rearview mirror, Trump could focus fully on the campaign.

Most in the establishment media saw Trump as nothing more than an amusing diversion, a bombastic egomaniac disliked by 70 percent of Americans in a Quinnipiac University poll. They expected him to lose badly in the first primaries. But Trump stood first in the polls almost from the day he announced.

With a threadbare staff of largely political novices, Trump applied much he had absorbed in Palm Beach. The only way for him to learn was through experience, and once he learned, he never forgot. On the island, he had taken on a proud, unyielding establishment that largely despised him, and he had never backed off from his attacks on the town council until eventually he won almost everything he wanted. There he learned that no one sat in a seat of power so high and inviolate that he was invulnerable to attack. Trump didn't care about laws, mores, customs, manners—all the means the privileged used to protect themselves. He stuck it to them good and bold.

In his run for the presidency, Trump used all the things he had learned in his life. His themes such as America being ripped off by foreigners and how corrupt Washington was were things he had been talking about for decades. He wasn't running a political campaign as much as an endless reality TV show, and nobody was better at it than Donald J. Trump. He attacked and belittled anyone who raised their head against him. He made himself champion of the beleaguered white working and lower-middle classes.

Using free media as the primary engine, Trump mocked and belittled the other Republican candidates. Dominating every television frame, he became an entertaining spectacle who was so irresistible that the networks covered his every move. He got ratings and sold papers like nobody else. Some in the media realized they were giving Trump a free ride toward the nomination, but what could the cable networks do? If one channel had ratcheted down its coverage, its viewers would have simply gone to a competitor that was showing the endlessly entertaining Trump.

The Republican establishment considered Trump a fifth column within their midst and abhorred his candidacy as much as liberal reporters. At Fox News, media mogul Rupert Murdoch could not abide the idea of Trump's continuing presence in the race. Murdoch was not the kind to let things just happen, and to all appearances, Fox News used the crucial first debate on its network in August 2015 as the device to bring Trump down.

One issue that set Trump apart from the nine other candidates was his unwillingness to pledge support to the eventual Republican nominee. It was a legitimate question to ask in a debate, but co-moderator Bret Baier of Fox News began the debate that way. "Is there anyone onstage, and can I see hands, who is unwilling tonight to pledge your support to the eventual nominee of the Republican Party and pledge to not run an independent campaign against that person?" Baier asked. When only Trump raised his hand, the audience reacted with ringing boos, and the other candidates attacked him.

Then, later in the Cleveland debate, co-moderator Megyn Kelly focused her attention on Trump by commenting, "Mr. Trump, you've called women you don't like 'fat pigs, dogs, slobs, and disgusting animals,'" she said.

"Only Rosie O'Donnell," Trump said, making a joke out of it.

"No, it wasn't," Kelly replied. "Your Twitter account has several disparaging comments about women's looks. You once told a contestant on *Celebrity Apprentice* it would be a pretty picture to see her on her knees. Does that sound to you like the temperament of a man we should elect as president, and how will you answer the charge from Hillary Clinton, who is likely to be the Democratic nominee, that you are part of the war on women?"

"I think the big problem this country has is being politically correct," Trump said, avoiding the question with a response that would get a positive reaction from the voters he was seeking.

Instead of turning on Trump, many of those watching that evening were outraged that Kelly was making these accusations on the network that was supposed to promote Republican candidates. Kelly also experienced what so many before her had—that if you attack Trump, he will come back at you with a force a hundredfold greater. He trashed Kelly again and again and refused to participate in a later debate in Des Moines because she was again co-moderating it. His allies Steve Bannon and David Pecker savaged Kelly in stories published on Breitbart and in the *National Enquirer*.

Trump was still at the top of the polls at the end of 2015, but still most journalists believed his train would go flying off the tracks in the primaries, when people realized the consequences of voting for him. When Trump flew down to Palm Beach with Melania and nine-year-old Barron for the holidays, he was ready for a break. He loved the Christmas season, and the club members were like the best extended family you could have. They didn't get too close to him. They didn't tell him their problems. They didn't hit him up for money. And he could leave them whenever he wanted.

Trump didn't make the distinction between public and private that most people did—not in how he acted or how he felt. As a presidential candidate, he was given Secret Service protection, and he was comfortable having them constantly around him. Their most visible presences were the black SUVs in the driveway, as shiny as if they had just exited a car wash. Other than that, they were remarkably unobtrusive.

On Christmas Eve Trump had dinner at the club with Melania and Barron, who was decked out in a blue suit and red tie that his mother had obviously selected. The great Christmas tree was all lit up, and the club was wonderfully festive. Barron was usually shy, but this evening he walked around and greeted members just the way his father did. After Barron went to bed, Trump and Melania attended late-evening services at Bethesda-by-the-Sea.

Chris Ruddy seemed to be present whenever Trump was at Mar-a-Lago, and he was there on Christmas Day with a table of his guests. Ruddy was one of the people Trump almost always greeted, but he wasn't happy that Ruddy hadn't embraced his candidacy. Newsmax had become important enough to conservative politics that, one after another, the Republican candidates made pilgrimages to Newsmax's Florida offices to give a video interview and commune with Ruddy.

Trump saw that Ruddy's guests this day were not the kind who often frequented Mar-a-Lago. A priest in clerical garb sat with three Latinos. Ruddy had known seventy-five-year-old Father Hugh Duffy for years and thought of him like the good friar in Chaucer's *Canterbury Tales*. The Irish American priest was totally focused on, and speaking in Spanish to, his Mexican American housekeepers, Jose and Gloria Delgaldo, and their thirteen-year-old granddaughter Mildred, who was visiting from Mexico.

Father Duffy had spent thirty years in a parish in Okeechobee (pop. 5,691), a tiny town in central Florida in the midst of the sugar fields, where he ministered to many migrant workers. He observed throughout central Florida a level of poverty far beyond anything he had seen in his native Ireland. People lived in tiny broken-down trailers and small homes that were little better than shacks.

It wasn't just there. West Palm Beach, not more than three miles from Mar-a-Lago, had one of the worst ghettos in America, with a murder and violent crime rate that in 2015 equaled that of Chicago, a city that Trump had condemned as a prison of violence. And as the priest sat in the gilded setting of Mar-a-Lago, he knew no one here had a glimmering of that world.

Trump was a convivial host, taking pictures with the group and leading the priest to the buffet with its fresh shipment of crab legs. At the dinner's end, as Father Duffy drove away from Mar-a-Lago, he was convinced that his housekeepers' granddaughter would never forget this day.

"You're going to be able to show that picture of you with Mr. Trump to everyone in Mexico when you get back," Father Duffy said.

Mildred knew about Trump attacking Mexicans as the scourges of the earth.

"Oh, I can't show that to people in Mexico," she responded to the priest.

After coming in second to Ted Cruz in Iowa, Trump won in New Hampshire, and then there was little stopping him. After winning seven of the eleven Super Tuesday primaries in March 2016, Trump knew he had the Republican nomination in his hands.

At that point, Trump could have held a press conference in a shuttered steel mill or a beleaguered lower-class neighborhood, but instead he celebrated in Mar-a-Lago's opulent White & Gold Ballroom. He was succeeding to a remarkable extent in making his wealth a positive element of the campaign. His supporters saw Trump as a representative of what could be accomplished in America.

One hundred or so reporters from around the world vied for seats with up-scale Mar-a-Lago members who were there to applaud their hero. But one would gather from this row of Botoxed faces a support for Trump in Palm Beach that actually wasn't there. On the island of around thirty thousand winter in-habitants, so far only five residents had contributed to the campaign. Two of them—Trump's former lawyer Paul Rampell and Roxanne Pulitzer, notorious after her scandalous tabloid divorce—gave the most, one thousand dollars. That's how unwanted Trump's candidacy was in his winter home.

Trump's new friend New Jersey governor Chris Christie stood behind him on the podium. As Christie's campaign had faltered, he tried desperately to stay in the race by rudely berating other candidates. But nobody could out-Trump Trump, and Christie exited the race, endorsing his former rival, even though only a few weeks before he had said, "We do not need reality TV in the Oval Office right now. President of the United States is not a place for an entertainer."

As he stood on the stage, Christie's only task now was to look interested, but instead his eyes twitched and darted back and forth, as he appeared to break out in sweat. His bizarre conduct drew more attention than anything Trump was saying.

Christie had vice presidential stars in his eyes, and key to that was staying as close to the candidate as possible. The governor started spending a lot of time at Mar-a-Lago. Christie hadn't played a game of golf for years, and during the day he was often on a lounge in the living room, a perfect position to spy any-one going into or out of the club. Joining Governor Christie in the hunt to be-come the vice presidential nominee, and around the grounds of Mar-a-Lago, was Alabama senator Jeff Sessions, the first sitting senator to endorse Trump for president.

Trump may have been walking no faster than he always did, but those days he certainly seemed to zoom through the club at such a pace that no one could way-lay him with their requests. The week after the press conference, he walked through the club wearing golf clothes and a "Make America Great Again" cap as he headed out to play eighteen holes. He had thought up the slogan in a visionary moment the day after Romney lost in 2012. Trump had a second visionary moment later when he decided to trademark the words. As Trump hurried ahead, his retired butler Senecal, reborn as the Mar-a-Lago tour guide, shouted, "All rise," and the club members and staff jumped to their feet.

For Easter Sunday dinner, Trump went to his golf club, which was an extension of his Mar-a-Lago world. The golden grandiosity would have fit a pasha's palace. His signature was the boldly extravagant décors that set a new standard for displaying wealth in the twenty-first century.

The buffet was a gargantuan feast with giant shrimp, platters overflowing with crab legs, great bowls of caviar, and sushi laid out like an exotic treasure. Many guests roamed the one-hundred-dollar-a-person buffet (plus a 20 percent service charge), filling their plates to overflowing as if they feared the best of the spread would soon be gone.

Trump walked outside to the grill. He didn't ask for special treatment, and when his turn came, he ordered the only hamburger consumed that evening. The grill man knew his employer's taste, and Trump watched as the ground beef was blackened until it had the consistency of a Brillo pad. When the cook dropped the meat gently onto a bun on Trump's plate, he squirted ketchup in perfect circles round and round again. He wasn't going to let them put what he called "garbage" on his burger, either. To him, relish, pickles, and onions were worthless additions that would diminish his inspired dish.

For dessert, Trump passed on the squishy little cakes that he considered ladies' fare and headed for the soft-serve ice cream machine. Twisting the arm until the ice cream came streaming out full blast, he filled his bowl to a level unheard of by Dairy Queen and then covered every bit of it with chocolate sauce.

After dessert, the hyperactive Trump started moving around the room again. Even with his campaign's success, Trump needed constant praise, and he got it at Mar-a-Lago and the golf club. Among the several hundred people present, many were lifelong New York Democrats. They abhorred the idea of a President Trump, but to stay members of his club, they felt they had to flatter him shamelessly. But he was onto them, and he never focused his eyes on anyone he wanted to avoid.

Trump made a point of coming up to Chris Ruddy's table and talking to the Newsmax CEO. Trump was overwhelmingly persuasive when he wanted something, but he could not get Ruddy to come on board and turn Newsmax into a Trump flagship. And it irritated the candidate the way Ruddy kept his distance.

Trump stopped at a group of women wearing bunny ears. These were the Trumpettes, and they resembled a rabbit hutch. Toni Holt Kramer had founded the women's group devoted to Trump's election in September 2015, sitting in Beverly Hills with three of her Palm Beach friends, Suzi Goldsmith, Terry Lee Ebert Mendozza, and Janet Levy. The Trumpettes were not rough-hewn daughters of toil, but aging sisters of the 1 percent, and no one was more devoted to Trump's candidacy than they were.

Kramer had worked on air in television for years in Los Angeles, where she interviewed movie and television stars. Some of their celebrity had spilled over on her. Kramer and her friends were cheerleaders, flashing their false eyelashes as Trump came near them. They were fevered in their support and pure in their devotion. The oldest was ninety-six-year-old Hermé de Wyman Miro.

If the women were younger, they might have done cartwheels for Trump. They didn't care about policy discussions. They wanted nothing from him but a photo or two. He gave them more time this afternoon than he did anyone else, and then, just as suddenly, he was gone.

Trump's butler Tony Senecal had retired in 2009, and a happy retirement it was. Not having to work those endless hours, he looked about five years younger and had a bounce to his step. As Mar-a-Lago's resident historian and tour guide, Senecal was still an integral part of the estate. He loved showing guests around, and he was wonderful at invoking the last years of Mrs. Post, when he had been a footman. He then switched to intimate stories about the Trump regime, always glorifying his patron. Almost everyone liked the retired butler—everyone except Bernd Lembcke.

Despite his gentle demeanor, during the primary campaign Senecal posted on Facebook that he believed President Obama and Michelle Obama should be hanged and that Hillary Clinton ought to be tried for treason. Senecal had heard

Trump suggest that President Obama may not have been born in the United States, and Senecal accepted that as a fact. But Senecal reached a new level when he advocated "dragging that ball-less dick head from the white mosque and hanging his scrawny ass from the portico." As for "Sasquatch," the name Senecal gave the First Lady, if Obama "gets hung, then Sasquatch does too."

In May 2016, *Mother Jones*'s David Corn exposed what Senecal had written, and the Trump campaign was forced to disassociate itself from him. But Senecal was connected to Trump through Mar-a-Lago, and many members worried that there was a dark Trump out there somewhere that they didn't know. Was it possible Trump had inspired Senecal to speak this way and he was only saying things his patron said in private? The Jewish members were especially worried. They knew that if bigotry began, it would focus on them sooner or later.

Republicans and Democrats in Palm Beach had always civilly disagreed, but a polarization had entered the community that divided the island into two bickering clans. People learned quickly to tell where another person stood on Trump and, if they didn't like the answer, to change the subject or move away. For the most part, Trump supporters were highly circumspect and rarely acknowledged publicly that he was their candidate.

Just as Trump wrapped up the nomination and was looking ahead to mortal combat against Hillary Clinton, the first of the allegations out of his past came forward to confront him. A lawyer representing Karen McDougal, the 1998 *Playboy* Playmate of the Year, went to the *National Enquirer* saying his client had a story to sell of her ten-month-long affair with Trump. McDougal was a credible woman, and her tale was buttressed with all kinds of details of a relationship that took place when Trump was newly married and Melania was home with the newborn. The scandalous story represented a major problem for Trump that, after consultation with Cohen, Pecker tried to bury with a $150,000 payment.

In September Cohen brought Trump into a discussion of how to reimburse Pecker. Trump didn't realize the extent he had created a world in his image where nobody trusted anybody. Despite avowing he would throw himself on a sword for Trump, Cohen was secretly taping meetings with his client and friend.

"I need to open up a company for the transfer of all of that info regarding our friend, David," Cohen said.

For Trump, it was always about the money. "So, what do we got to pay for this? One-fifty?" Trump asked.

"You never know where that company— You never know . . ." the lawyer said.

"Maybe he gets hit by a truck," Trump said. But McDougal had gotten her money and that appeared to be the end of it.

Trump's acceptance speech at the Republican National Convention in Cleveland was a dystopian vision of America, *Mad Max* come home. There were "attacks on our police, terrorism in our cities and chaos in our communities," and America finally had to defend itself against its many enemies. Many of the media talking heads viewed the speech as overlong and overly dark. It was a vision of a world dramatically different than what the citizens of Palm Beach and millions of others encountered, yet it resonated profoundly with Trump's supporters. To them the man was a truth teller who was unafraid to speak of the underbelly of American life in all its ugliness.

Hillary Clinton wanted her campaign to be a classroom where, across the debate podium, she lectured her irascible student on his many inadequacies as she took her rightful place as the first woman president. During the campaign, the former Miss Universe Alicia Machado came forward to tell the story of how Trump had shamed her at Mar-a-Lago in 1996. Her words were the kind that would resonate with millions of women, and Clinton brought them up in the late September debate.

"One of the worst things [Trump] said was about a woman in a beauty contest," Clinton said, relishing every instant of the telling. "He loves beauty contests, supporting them and hanging around them. And he called this woman 'Miss Piggy.' Then he called her 'Miss Housekeeping,' because she was Latina. Donald, she has a name: Her name is Alicia Machado."

"Where did you find this?" Trump interrupted. "Where did you find this?"

Trump was haunted by matters that he had thought of little consequence and scarcely imagined would confront him years later. In early October, a lawyer representing Stephanie A. Gregory Clifford, better known by her stage name Stormy Daniels, came forward to tell about a one-night stand the porn star said she had with the candidate during a celebrity golf tournament at Nevada's Edgewood Tahoe Golf Course in July 2006.

Trump had no fidelity in his infidelity. That was the same time and place where McDougal said she was with the man she loved. Cohen got busy again, paid Daniels off with $130,000, and as with McDougal, the matter appeared to disappear for good.

Early that October there was another matter of seeming little consequence that raised its unforgiving head. A 2005 audiotape emerged of Trump saying that if you're famous, you can grab women "by the pussy." This prompted ten women to come forward and accuse him of all kinds of sexual misconduct. Trump met the accusations directly in a speech at the South Florida Fairgrounds, in West Palm Beach, on October 13. The audience wasn't the fancy folks of Palm Beach, but the sort of people who would flock to this venue for a country music concert. This was an appropriate place for Trump to give this talk because four of the claims of sexual misconduct had taken place at Mar-a-Lago.

Cathy Heller recalled an incident that occurred at a Mother's Day brunch in around 1997. Heller lined up to greet Trump, who was shaking hands. But when Heller put out her hand, she says Trump leaned in and kissed her on the mouth. With the quickness of youth, Heller brushed back just enough that Trump's mouth only grazed the side of her lips.

"Oh, come on," Trump said, irritated that she had ruined his game. Heller kept quiet until the slew of charges surfaced.

The second incident allegedly took place on New Year's Eve in 2001. The Mar-a-Lago photographer Ken Davidoff was there with his young assistant Mindy McGillivray taking pictures at a Huey Lewis and the News concert. McGillivray recalled that as she was going to the bathroom, Trump hurried after her down the hall. "Melania followed him," McGillivray says. "She knew what was going on. She was angry. She gave him a look and whipped her shawl behind her back. And I descended down the staircase."

In January 2003, McGillivray returned to Mar-a-Lago to help Davidoff during a Ray Charles concert. As McGillivray was standing around that evening, she says she felt a grab of her butt that she initially thought was Davidoff's camera bag. When she turned back to look, she saw Trump, who quickly looked away.

"Donald just grabbed my ass," McGillivray told Davidoff, an exchange he remembers.

As repulsed as McGillivray was, she said she had come to realize that men like Trump saw this as their right, one of the perks of power and privilege. For years, she said nothing about the incident. Only after she heard Trump on CNN denying accusations against him did she talk to a reporter at the *Palm Beach Post* whose story ran the morning of Trump's speech.

The third alleged victim, Natasha Stoynoff, was a journalist on assignment in January 2005. When the first-year anniversary of the Trump marriage rolled around, *People* was doing a piece on the celebrated newlyweds. Stoynoff was the magazine's resident Trump expert, having written several stories and covered the wedding. She flew down to Palm Beach and drove over to Mar-a-Lago, where Donald and Melania were waiting for her.

Stoynoff, who is tall and blond, had pretty much everything she needed when Melania left to change her outfit for more photos. Trump offered to show Stoynoff the mansion. Trump led her to what he called one "tremendous" room and shut the door behind them. Then he came forward, pushed her against the wall, and jammed his tongue into her mouth. As she tried to extract herself from him, Anthony Senecal, the butler, entered to say that Melania was almost ready.

"You know we're going to have an affair," Trump said, as if his actions were nothing more than a first step in consummating a relationship.

When Stoynoff got back to New York, she told half a dozen colleagues and friends what had happened but asked them to be quiet about it. The incident had been embarrassing for her, but more than anything, it was frightening. Like the two other women, Stoynoff kept her story quiet until all the allegations started coming forward and she felt it was time to speak out.

In the revealing piece she wrote for *People*, Stoynoff said she had not spoken out initially because "like many women, I was ashamed and blamed myself for his transgression. I minimized it ('it's not like he raped me . . .'). I was afraid that a famous, powerful, wealthy man could and would discredit and destroy me, especially if I got his coveted *People* feature killed."

Trump's response was to flail back at these women with every weapon he had, including threatened lawsuits. "These claims are all fabricated," he told his believing audience. "They are pure fiction, and they are outright lies. . . . We already have substantial evidence to dispute these lies, and it will be made public in an appropriate way, and at an appropriate time, very soon." That never happened.

"You take a look at these people," he said, alleging the sordidness of his accusers. "You study these people, and you'll understand."

McGillivray was getting so many calls from media and others that she left her apartment and moved into a hotel. She got so nervous that she said she was leaving the country.

Kramer wasn't fazed by any of these charges against Trump. That was the kind of thing guys did, and if a man tried to plant an unwanted kiss on her lips, she would have torn off his face. She simply didn't care about the whole nasty business. She told her fellow Trumpettes that nothing could dissuade her from supporting "our superman Trump."

Kramer was a sound-bite machine spewing forth one-liners. The lead Trumpette took after her hero in seeing no distinction between good publicity and bad as long as it promoted Trump. When the media covered the Trumpettes, they often mocked Kramer and her showy surroundings and face-lifts. Desi Lydic interviewed her for *The Daily Show.*

"Trump is, in his way, a blue-collar candidate," Kramer told Lydic as she sat on a sofa in Bel Air attended to by her Mexican American maid. "He appeals to the people. He is Superman in a lot of ways. He is this blond, blue-eyed guy flying around up in the air, looking down saying, 'I can't stand this country. I've got to fix it.'"

Kramer said she knew what Trump would do as president. "If he runs America like he runs his club, we'll have America back again. Yeah. Yeah. Yeah . . . There's every kind of dessert imaginable. Cakes and pies and cookies and a machine that makes ice cream. And whipped cream and caramel. And all kinds of layer cakes and pies. Apple crumb cake. Chocolate . . ."

Kramer may have sounded silly, but this was her shtick, and it was an inspired performance. She was no Madeleine Albright or Condoleezza Rice, but she could play a giddy socialite rah-rahing for Trump. It gave her a whole new career.

On Election Night, in early November, more than 250 members filled Mar-a-Lago and sipped champagne while they watched the television screens. Almost everyone went home before the winner was announced—late evenings were rare in Palm Beach no matter what the occasion. But Kramer stayed until after 2:00 A.M., when the networks declared Trump victorious. Most Mar-a-Lago members were as stunned as anyone else.

Some were less ecstatic than Kramer and her fellow Trumpettes. One club member, Cynthia Friedman, had been a Democratic fund-raiser for more than two decades. Clinton's victory would have been the culmination of everything she had worked to achieve for all those years. It was unthinkable to her that Trump had won. She wondered if she could ever come to Mar-a-Lago again.

Although Chris Ruddy had not supported Trump early on, once Trump got the nomination, Ruddy turned all the forces of Newsmax toward helping the Republican nominee win the election. Not only did Ruddy celebrate Trump's candidacy endlessly on Newsmax, but he contributed one hundred thousand dollars to the campaign, at a luncheon at the Southampton home of Palm Beacher and self-described billionaire Wilbur Ross. Ruddy also published a quickie pro-Trump book, and promoted it into a bestseller. Despite his belated arrival, Ruddy saw nothing but opportunity for Newsmax TV. After all, over at Fox, Rupert Murdoch and Roger Ailes, Ruddy's models of what he would like to be, had early on in the campaign played what turned out to be a resolutely foolish hand.

Ruddy's efforts did not go unnoticed by Trump, and by November, the media viewed Ruddy as one of Trump's important confidants. Trump's call to Ruddy on Election Night sanctified their closeness.

"I'm surprised you won the election, and I know you're surprised," Ruddy said.

"Actually, I knew in the last three days," Trump said.

Trump spent the first weeks after the election huddled at Trump Tower in New York, with a few trips down to Washington, most notably an awkward visit with President Obama in the Oval Office. The president-elect wasn't going to let anything change his plans to come down to Palm Beach for Thanksgiving, for decades his first trip of the season.

Trump flew down from New York on his plane on the Wednesday afternoon before Thanksgiving, not just with Melania and Barron but with extended family members. He had four adult children with their three spouses, and eight grandchildren, an enormous family by modern-day standards. It took forty-five vehicles to bring the president-elect and his family from Palm Beach International Airport to Mar-a-Lago. Homeland Security memos seen by NBC News said there were 150 Secret Service personnel assigned to protect them. And along the Intracoastal Waterway sailed heavily armed coast guard boats monitoring the waters.

That day Trump issued a Thanksgiving greeting: "It is my prayer that on this Thanksgiving, we begin to heal our divisions and move forward as one country, strengthened by a shared purpose and very, very common resolve."

Trump invited the immensely wealthy Isaac "Ike" Perlmutter to have Thanksgiving dinner with his family. Trump loved being around his fellow billionaires. He was just starting to fill out his cabinet and he had already named one billionaire, Betsy DeVos, as secretary of education and had decided to name a second self-styled billionaire, Wilbur Ross, as secretary of commerce.

Trump loved rags-to-riches stories, and Perlmutter had begun by selling toys on the streets of New York. In 1996, the Israeli American bought the bankrupt Marvel comic book company and turned it around by making Marvel's make-believe characters the heroes of megamovies. In 2009, Disney purchased Marvel for four billion dollars, and Perlmutter became even richer. He spent the winter months in his $3.2 million condominium at Sloan's Curve, two and a half miles south of Mar-a-Lago. It was a modest home for a man of his wealth, and it was there that he had gotten into a vicious legal dispute that risked his reputation and made him a controversial figure and unlikely presidential soul mate.

Another wealthy condominium owner, Harold Peerenboom, sued Perlmutter, claiming the Marvel billionaire had sent out hundreds of anonymous letters accusing the Toronto businessman of child molestation and murder and saying that he was *dafuk barosh*, a Hebrew phrase for screwed up in the head. Perlmutter's attorneys countersued, claiming that Peerenboom and his allies had sent the letters themselves in an attempt to extort Perlmutter. Despite those charges, Peerenboom's lawyers expressed confidence that they would win by showing that Perlmutter was behind the whole sordid business.

Most presidents would have steered far away from a man in the midst of such a legal wrangle. But Trump seemed not to care. He saw Perlmutter frequently after he became president, and Perlmutter was a crucial private adviser. In truth, with so many people in the new Palm Beach involved in legal proceedings, you couldn't just snub all of them. One longtime resident lived by the axiom "Until you get indicted, you still get invited."

Lois Pope was among those having Thanksgiving dinner at Mar-a-Lago. From her perch as a charter member of Mar-a-Lago, Pope had risen to the highest slopes of the Palm Beach charity world. She spent many evenings at the club, and Trump almost never failed to greet her and hear about her latest endeavor. He had another reason to like her. Her events generally cost between $275,000 and $450,000 to put on, and she had her annual Lady in Red gala in the grand ballroom at Mar-a-Lago. It was no wonder Trump often attended.

Pope's late husband was Generoso "Gene" Pope Jr., the owner of the *National Enquirer*, the crucial element in building Trump's populist base. After Pope's death in 1988, his widow sought to win acceptance in the Palm Beach world. Her problem was that her money came from a man who funded the purchase of his tabloid allegedly with loans from the Mafia and turned it into a downscale weekly abhorred by those of power and substance. Pope dumped her husband into the dustbin of history and built her own brand, stamping her name on whatever she did.

In May 2015, Pope spent hours at the North Palm Beach County Airport, scanning the skies for the arrival of two private planes carrying sixty dogs and pets from shelters in the North where they had been certain to die. Waiting for them were two fifty-foot-long Lois Pope Red Star Rescue vehicles. A crew filmed the scene to be shown during the American Humane Association Hero Dog Awards, presented by the Lois Pope LIFE Foundation on Hallmark Television. "I want to set an example for the country and the world," Pope said. "These animals are part of us. We're all one. The gas chamber days are over."

The scene would make dramatic, heart-rending television, but local shelters were full of animals days away from being euthanized. "How does flying or busing in puppies from other regions help the dogs in this community?" asked county commissioner Shelley Vana at a press conference held in the county shelter. "How does it benefit dogs that are going to die here?"

To Pope, there were always naysayers picking away, but the criticism did nothing to diminish Pope's image. Like Trump, she believed that charity made no sense unless one's generosity was richly celebrated, and no one in Palm Beach was more celebrated than Pope. She was constantly at Mar-a-Lago, either dining with friends or attending charity galas, where the diminutive philanthropist's picture was almost always taken for the *Palm Beach Daily News*.

During the meal, Pope came to the president-elect's table to show him a picture of Patton, a Golden Doodle pup she wanted to give him as the presidential dog. With the help of her expensive public relations team, Pope then told *The Washington Post* that Trump had said, "Go over there and show it to Barron," pointing toward his ten-year-old son. "He's going to fall in love with him. Barron will want it."

When Pope showed Barron the picture, she later said a "big smile came over his face, and it just brought tears to his eyes." That may have been, but the boy's father was not a dog kind of guy. Patton would have to find another owner, and Trump became the first president in over a century not to have a dog.

In Palm Beach, Trump had stood up against the powers that be that no one had ever dared challenge, and he had won that war hands down. In doing so, he had transformed not only Mar-a-Lago but the whole island into a place where his grandiosity and obsession with wealth were the new standard. And now he intended to do the same thing for America and the world, transforming them into his image.

14

The Sun King

During those first weeks after the election, people in Palm Beach discussed how often President Trump would come there and where he would stay when he did. Many thought the problems of security and the incredible demands of the presidency would prevent Trump from spending much time in Florida and making Mar-a-Lago his winter White House and believed he would have to rent another estate. But Trump always did what he wanted to do, and he wanted to live just as he had always lived.

People often imagined Trump living in a massive space at the estate, but the family quarters were a modest twenty-five hundred square feet. "Trump asked me to watch a football game with him once in the family quarters, and I was surprised just how small it is," says one longtime member. "I've had people ask me, 'Doesn't he have the whole top floor, like ten thousand square feet or something?' And I say, 'No, it's not like that at all. Those are suites people rent.'"

The Trumps returned to Palm Beach on December 16 for a sixteen-day visit during the Christmas holidays. The media staked out a preserve for themselves on Bingham Island, a tiny strip of land next to the drawbridge to West Palm Beach. This isolated location provided them with shots of Mar-a-Lago as background for their reporters' stand-ups.

The Trump people treated these reporters like mangy pit bulls; if you got too close, they might bite off your fingers. Campaign manager Kellyanne Conway was handling much of the press chores during the transition and accompanied Trump during his trips to Mar-a-Lago. Conway held court at the media tent sitting in a director's chair.

One evening at Mar-a-Lago, Trump had dinner with Mexican billionaire Carlos Slim, the largest single shareholder of *The New York Times*. During the campaign, Trump had wheeled Slim out to a prominent place in his honor roll of villains. Not only was Slim a Mexican, but according to Trump, he had largely destroyed the *Times*, turning its reporters into "corporate lobbyists for Carlos Slim and for Hillary Clinton." But that was yesterday, and in his world, where water could be turned into wine and then turned back again, Trump transformed his fellow billionaire into what he described as a "lovely man" and a "great guy."

This meeting had been set up by Trump's former campaign manager Corey Lewandowski, who was cashing in by starting a new lobbying firm that advertised its location as "just a block from the White House." Trump had vowed to drain the swamp. Even before he was sworn in, the water was rising in some places.

Trump's life was pure theater, and he had long used Mar-a-Lago as a main stage. He didn't hide away when he interviewed potential administration officials, but talked with them openly in a potentate-like setting on a gold-flecked sofa beneath a glittery chandelier in the central part of the mansion.

People at Mar-a-Lago had wanted to be around Trump before he was elected. Now it was more intense. You had to dress right to be around the president-elect, and that meant at times wearing clothes that said TRUMP or MAR-A-LAGO. That's one of the reasons the clothes were flying out of the Mar-a-Lago shop.

You had to look right. This kept the spa busy. There were charity and public affairs events in the two ballrooms—more moneymakers—and on occasion Trump showed up to glad-hand for a few minutes, just as he always had done. Every evening the club was full for dinner, with some members booking tables for eight or ten so their friends could be a part of the scene at Mar-a-Lago. That was all money in Trump's kitty. And that was nothing compared to what was going on at Trump International Golf Club, where Trump was making even more money.

On the Friday two days before Christmas, as Trump rode from hole to hole in a golf cart with Tiger Woods, the president-elect looked out and knew that every member playing the course had paid a couple of hundred thousand dollars for the honor, plus the annual fees, all of it going into his heavy pockets. And on Christmas Eve, for the buffet in the Donald J. Trump Ballroom, it was the same story. Each one of the four hundred guests had coughed up a heavy amount just to be there that evening, forget what they had paid to join and all the other fees. Everywhere Trump looked, the money was rolling in. It was better than his take on the slot machines in his casinos in Atlantic City had been in the old days, and he didn't have to worry about anybody hitting the jackpot.

For the Christmas Eve buffet in the ballroom, a giant Christmas tree and poinsettias were set around the fireplace and everything was done with a marvelous sense of panache. The band played one Christmas carol after another and then switched seamlessly to the national anthem as the Trumps entered. It would not be long before taking photos was banned at Mar-a-Lago—though many disregarded the edict—but this evening everyone wanted a selfie with the president-elect, and he did not deny them, smiling at each encounter as if to make sure not to have any bad photos out there. Then he sat down alone with Melania for their Christmas dinner.

Later that evening the Secret Service drove the Trumps to the Church of Bethesda-by-the-Sea for the 10:30 P.M. services. Instead of entering through the central vestibule, across from where the photographers and reporters were lined up, the president-elect chose to enter unobtrusively through a door on the other end of the church. Yet as soon as he entered, most of the five hundred worshippers rose and applauded. "Hear, hear!" some shouted. "Congratulations!"

When President John F. Kennedy attended services at St. Edward's in the early 1960s, he entered quietly, sliding into a pew. The Catholic worshippers were overwhelmingly supportive of the president, but no one applauded or shouted out. After mass, he stood on the front steps greeting worshippers before stepping into the presidential limousine. Unlike the hundreds of agents protecting Trump in Palm Beach, thirty-four Secret Service officers guarded Kennedy in three eight-hour shifts.

Early on the morning of December 31, Trump sent out his New Year's tweet: "Happy New Year to all, including to my many enemies and those who have fought me and lost so badly they just don't know what to do. Love."

If that was love, it was tough love.

New Year's Eve was especially celebratory in Mar-a-Lago's grand ballroom as the president-elect and Melania walked into the gala. He was vigorously applauded. Then there was silence as Trump spoke for almost ten minutes. Among the crowd Trump saw new members he did not know. After the election, the club announced that on January 1, the membership fee would be going up to two hundred thousand dollars. The new members this evening were delighted they had gotten in before the increase.

Trump distinguished between the people who were with him back when things were tough and the ones here now that he'd been elected president. "I want to thank my members," the president-elect said that night in his remarks. "I don't really care too much about their guests, because the ones I really care about are the members. I don't give a shit about their guests. I just love my members."

Trump's media operation had allowed in a number of journalists, and they were gathered in the back of the room. Throughout the campaign, Trump had called them despicable liars, and here was another chance to slam these hacks and their role in the campaign.

"It was dishonest media," he told the exhilarated crowd. "In fact, a lot of them are back there . . . the dishonest media. The dishonest media, right? Are they dishonest? They are the world's most dishonest people. . . . They are really garbage."

The club members were used to top entertainment stars performing and hanging out around the pool. Fabio and Sylvester Stallone were the only notable celebrities present this evening, and their A-list days were in the past century. Hollywood and the music industry almost universally opposed Trump. No major star or performer would come to Mar-a-Lago and risk being seen publicly with Trump that night or any other night.

Security had been tight for President-Elect Trump during the Christmas holidays, but the next time he returned to Mar-a-Lago, in early February, he was now the forty-fifth president of the United States and protection was at a whole different level. He and his entourage danced through security that Friday afternoon, but for anyone else who sought to enter, from members to delivery people, it was an onerous procedure.

Anyone hoping to enter the estate during the presidential visit first had to submit their names in plenty of time for the Secret Service to vet them. South Ocean Boulevard, the one thoroughfare running the whole length of the island, was blocked off for half a mile north of Mar-a-Lago. That meant that getting to the estate from midtown, a person had to drive to West Palm Beach and come over the southern bridge, where there was a parking lot just south of Mar-a-Lago that usually was used by Bath and Tennis for its members.

All visitors to Trump's club had to go there first. If their names were on the Secret Service list and their identification checked out, their car was gone over, including inspection by a dog sniffing the open trunk. Only then was the vehicle allowed to drive across Southern Boulevard and enter through Mar-a-Lago's southern gate. After the guests turned over their vehicles to parking valets, their purses were inspected, and they walked through a metal detector before entering the club.

The Secret Service agents were everywhere, yet most of them stayed in the shadows. Confidential records obtained by NBC News said about 920 Secret Service personnel would be assigned to the new president. Roughly a third of them were likely in Palm Beach when the president was in residence. That number included the sharpshooters in the tower and officers hidden away in unexpected places outside the estate, but not the scores of sheriff's deputies who shared the burden.

With hundreds of people flitting in and out of the estate, the Secret Service could not assume that just because they had protected the perimeter, they had also protected the president. The officers treated the entire club like public space. As many as thirty tiny cameras with sensors were set up all around the mansion, and a central station monitored all of them.

Members learned never to walk on the grass, and if they did, they would be warned to get back on the pathway. Almost no one was foolish enough to walk up to the president unless he'd given them his nod. If someone tried to approach uninvited, a Secret Service agent subtly and politely made them back off. To increase security even further, the resident Secret Service officers varied the procedures each week and met, generally on Tuesday, to discuss how they would handle Trump's weekend visit.

Despite his mercurial nature, Trump was a man of studied habits. His routine rarely varied from that first weekend visit to the island as president. Unless he had to jet off to give a speech somewhere, he played eighteen holes of golf on Saturday and another eighteen on Sunday. Friday and Saturday evening, he usually had dinner on the verandah or in the living room, sometimes alone with Melania, other times with friends or political associates. On Sunday evening, he liked to go over to his golf club, where he and his personal guests were served dinner while everyone else helped themselves at the weekly buffet. He never went out to restaurants, and he almost never accepted invitations to other people's homes. He slept little, and he tweeted at the strangest times.

Melania had figured out how to live the most private of lives in this most public of homes. Accompanied by Secret Service, she might be seen walking toward the club spa early in the morning to have her hair done, but she said little and had almost no personal relationships with members. Unfailingly polite and the best-dressed First Lady since Jackie Kennedy, she was largely an enigma. Melania's parents, Viktor and Amalija Knavs, held green cards giving them permanent residency in the United States, thanks to a legal procedure that Trump railed against in public as "chain migration." The couple spend much of the winter at Mar-a-Lago and were as private as their daughter and kept largely to themselves.

✧

Trump's next trip down to Palm Beach was on Friday afternoon, February 10, with Japanese prime minister Shinzo Abe. Ivanka Trump and Jared Kushner accompanied the president on Air Force One. They were family first and aides second entering the plane at Andrews Air Force Base from the front door behind the president and First Lady. Meanwhile chief strategist Steve Bannon, national security adviser General Mike Flynn, and deputy chief of staff Katie Walsh entered from the back door.

Critics worried that when Trump was in Palm Beach, members of the club would have access to him and could lobby him and attempt to cut all kinds of unseemly deals. *The New York Times* described the fear succinctly in their headline: "FOR $200,000, A CHANCE TO WHISPER IN TRUMP'S EAR."

For some people, it didn't take two hundred thousand dollars, only a treasure in humiliation. Governor Chris Christie had been head of the transition team. But right after the election, Trump dismissed Christie. The New Jersey governor had once been a U.S. attorney, and he had put Jared Kushner's father in prison. Christie sensed the fine hand of Trump's son-in-law behind this unexpected move. Trump rarely performed the bloody act of firing himself, no matter how long the person had been with him or how unusual the circumstance. In this instance, Steve Bannon did the job, and the two men went at each other like raging bulls.

Despite all the affronts, Christie was so obsessed with getting a place in the administration that he kept as close to Trump as he could by coming down to Mar-a-Lago. He even came when Trump was not there. During the primaries, Trump had lambasted Christie for being as fat as a Polish sausage. The governor and his wife wore shorts and walked up and down the stairs and around the estate in an effort to lose weight. Whether by chance or caution, Christie managed to leave just before Kushner arrived.

Trump was used to people hitting him up for all kinds of ventures, and he was not easily bamboozled. But membership at Mar-a-Lago did unquestionably bring with it proximity to the most powerful man in the world. And the new administration already had a casualness to it that led to all kinds of strange, potentially troubling encounters.

On this early February weekend, Trump talked to one longtime Mar-a-Lago member, the New York developer Richard LeFrak, about a business deal. This wasn't LeFrak hitting up his old friend for government business, but instead the president asking LeFrak to build the Mexican-border wall for which the administration was quoting a price of twenty billion dollars. This was beyond LeFrak's ambitions. "I thought you were going to have Homeland Security deal with this," he remembers saying.

"Yes, maybe General Kelly will call you," Trump said.

That Friday evening of Abe's visit, the president was in a particularly congenial mood. Before he sat down for dinner with the Japanese leader and a small group that included club member Robert Kraft, the owner of the New England Patriots, he spent a good forty-five minutes talking with various members and their guests. The president was happy to shoot selfies and discuss possible golf dates or anything else people wanted to ask him. He usually was far more forthcoming to members than guests, but this evening he was open to a word or two with practically anyone.

Nicholas Papanicolaou was a guest at Mar-a-Lago that evening. The scion of a leading Greek family, he had never met Trump, and he worked his way around the room until he was standing beside the president. Papanicolaou thought Trump was getting too much flak for his executive order suspending visas for visitors from seven largely Muslim countries.

"Mr. President," Papanicolaou said solemnly, "if you want to mitigate opposition to your executive order, you should remind corporate chiefs and university presidents that if ever there is an act of terrorism on their premises and people are hurt and they are on record as opposing these legitimate limitations, they will have an enormous liability both on their institutions and personally for criminal negligence."

"That's a good idea," Trump said and moved on to the next person. A week or so later, people in the White House started talking about liability in a remarkably similar way to what Papanicolaou had described that evening.

The next day Trump and Prime Minister Abe played eighteen holes at Trump National Golf Club in Jupiter, followed by nine more holes at Trump International Golf Club in West Palm Beach. After their twenty-seven holes of golf and a change of clothes, Trump and Abe posed for a photo op at the entrance to Mar-a-Lago, the moment handled by Trump's beleaguered press secretary, Sean Spicer. All presidents learn to sidle away from questions they do not want to answer, but Trump seemed to take special pleasure in ignoring reporters shouting queries.

The two leaders, with their wives and entourages, then walked out on the verandah for dinner, where they were greeted by a standing ovation. It was a warm Saturday night, and at the other tables sat members who had booked them early enough to get reservations. Since some members invited so many guests, it was even more difficult than usual to get a table on the weekends when the president was there.

One of the newest members, Richard DeAgazio, a retired investor from Boston, was having his day of days seated just a few tables away from the most powerful leader in the world and his important guest. DeAgazio had gone out to Trump International Golf Club earlier in the day and snapped photos of the two leaders. That wasn't all. During the day, the not-always-convivial Steve Bannon had stood still for a picture. That evening was most amazing of all, because DeAgazio met an officer who said he carried the black bag that contained the codes that would allow the president to launch nuclear weapons. He wore a simple blue outfit with a braided cord on his right shoulder signifying he was an aide-de-camp. This young man, who said his name was Rick, was willing to be photographed, too. "Rick" smiled genially when DeAgazio had someone take their picture.

The waiters and waitresses serving the members and guests that evening were mainly eastern Europeans who were in Palm Beach for the season on H-2B visas. Trump had to prove by law that he truly needed these foreign workers. Each year Mar-a-Lago first had to make an effort to find American employees. The club had met this requirement in a one-day, small-print ad in the *Palm Beach Post* the previous July. The ad said the waiters and waitresses had to work "35 hrs/wk, Mon-Sun 7a-11p. Serve food & bev. Take orders. Complete side work, clear & carry dishes, keep stations clean. May do other job related duties." They must "work split shifts nights, w/ends & holidays; carry min 25 lbs; walk/stand for long time." For this they were to be paid "$11.88/hr min, no tips."

The upscale Mar-a-Lago restaurant added a 20 percent service charge and a line for added tips, enough to provide a good living if the waiters and waitresses had kept their gratuities. But the tips were added to Trump's coffers. The only people who would take the jobs were foreigners willing to work in America under such circumstances.

On the crowded verandah, an electric keyboard player was performing songs one would hear in a bar in a suburban shopping mall. It was not every day that the musician got to play before world leaders, and during the meal he ratcheted up the sound so dinner guests near the speakers had to speak loudly to be heard.

The president and his guests were eating their "Mr. Trump wedge salad," a thick tranche of iceberg lettuce swimming in a glutinous blue cheese salad dressing, when aides rushed to the table and both leaders put down their forks. North Korea had launched a test missile.

A laptop was opened and papers were spread out. National security adviser Michael Flynn and chief strategist Stephen Bannon jumped from their seats and moved directly behind Trump. Other American and Japanese officials pulled out their cell phones and made calls to their respective capitals. The two world leaders read documents that had been quickly brought to them. But romantic candlelight was not sufficient when the matter at hand was the security of the world. Aides turned their iPhones into flashlights and focused the beams on the freshly printed material.

For DeAgazio, this was a moment beyond his greatest imagination. He boldly took out his cell phone to take pictures of the scrambling officials, and he immediately put them on Facebook. "HOLY MOLY!!!" DeAgazio posted later in the night. "Wow . . . the center of the action!!!"

Jay Weitzman sat four or five tables away from the presidential party. Years earlier, Trump had let Weitzman stay in one of the Mar-a-Lago suites for free all season long, and the parking garage magnate knew the club better than most members. Over the years, he had seen his full share of strange things at the club, but whatever they were, he thought that his old tennis-playing buddy handled them with aplomb. What was the big deal if Trump wanted to do a little business over dinner? He could improvise anything anywhere.

Trump and Abe moved inside the mansion, where they stood in front of American and Japanese flags that had been quickly set up for the occasion. As reporters hurriedly assembled, the distinct sound of music wafted into the room. It was unclear whether it came from the inspired keyboard player or from the band playing exuberantly in the ballroom. The sound was no louder than that played in elevators, but it was unusual to have a press conference with background music. The two leaders made short statements that together took no more than three minutes. They each condemned the action but took no questions.

Trump wasn't going to let the launch of a missile by America's most implacable enemy ruin his evening. Two of his members were getting married in the grand ballroom, and the newlyweds deserved a greeting from the president of the United States. This wasn't just any couple hitching up. The marriage of Carl Lindner IV to Vanessa Falk brought together two major midwestern families, part of the new-money royalty that Trump considered his natural constituency. The groom's father, Carl Lindner III, the co-CEO of American Financial Group, had contributed one hundred thousand dollars to super PACs supporting Trump during the campaign. The bride's father, Bob Falk, was the CEO of Healthcare Corporation of Tennessee.

Trump entered the reception and received a fervent welcome. After having his picture taken with the bride and her bridesmaids, not squandering any time with the groom and his friends, the president took the microphone and talked to the wedding guests. "I saw them out on the lawn today," Trump said, motioning toward the newlyweds. "I said to the prime minister of Japan, I said, 'C'mon, Shinzo, let's go over and say hello.'"

Trump looked over at the happy couple and said, "They've been members of this club for a long time. They've paid me a fortune."

Trump's dinner with Prime Minister Abe wasn't the only big event that evening in Palm Beach. Just down the road from Mar-a-Lago at his oceanfront estate, Stephen Schwarzman was celebrating his seventieth birthday. Schwarzman was CEO and chairman of the Blackstone Group private equity firm, and the extravaganza had everything but North Korean missiles.

The president had known Schwarzman for decades and had been invited to the bash. Trump had attended Schwarzman's infamous sixtieth-birthday bash, in February 2007, at New York's Park Avenue Armory, an event extravagant enough even to impress Trump. The three-million-dollar extravaganza featured Patti LaBelle leading the fifty-member Abyssinian Baptist Church choir belting out a song about the birthday boy, "He's Got the Whole World in His Hands," an anthem that the uninitiated might have thought was about Jesus Christ.

The party at the Armory had become one of the defining moments of that giddy time before the '08 crash. Schwarzman even admitted that he had gone too far, and said it would never happen again. But the Trump presidency was already making the previous era seem a decade of monklike frugality, and Schwarzman was at it again.

The four hundred guests entered an all-enveloping desert setting with camels, Mongolian herders, and Japanese geishas set along a rendering of the ancient Silk Road linking East and West. From there, guests entered a stadium for a stunning display of fireworks, after which they moved on to a three-tiered temple, where they sat down for dinner while acrobats dangled above them and Chinese dancers performed. After that, the guests passed through a tunnel that opened out into a second Asian temple, where Gwen Stefani sang and the leads of the musical *Jersey Boys* also performed. It was all a curious juxtaposition of cultures, but this was America, and anything was possible.

Ivanka Trump, Jared Kushner, Donatella Versace, and Jordan's Princess Firyal were among those who wended their way up the pathway that evening. Some tallied that the party had cost Schwarzman up to twenty million dollars, but *The New York Times* said the evening set the billionaire back a mere "$7 million to $9 million." Critics slammed the spectacular event as a profligate act of gross excess, but considering Schwarzman's eleven-billion-dollar net worth, he was hardly going to celebrate his birthday with cheese spread and jug wine.

Schwarzman was famously disgruntled. Wherever he went, he found peas under his mattress, minute distractions that ruined his tranquility. For much of Barack Obama's eight years in office, the president had tried to close the "carried interest" loophole that allowed equity fund managers to pay a 15 percent personal income tax rate, not the 35 percent other wealthy individuals paid. Schwarzman and his friends had fought successfully against Obama over this during those years, in what they considered a life-and-death struggle to hold on to their unique tax break.

"It's like when Hitler invaded Poland in 1939," Schwarzman once said. Trump had promised that once he was in the White House, that war would be over. The emperors of new wealth felt freed.

A Jeb Bush supporter, Schwarzman had not contributed a cent to Trump's campaign, but once Trump won, Schwarzman phoned to offer his services to the man he had once called "the P. T. Barnum of America," perhaps forgetting that P. T. Barnum was American. It didn't matter that Trump had declared that certain trade deals that were royally enriching men like Schwarzman were cheating America. Trump knew few people in the financial establishment, and Schwarzman had the ability to foster Trump's relationship with them. Trump asked Schwarzman to be the leader of his Strategic and Policy Forum of business leaders.

Schwarzman and most of his Palm Beach neighbors believed that patriotism and politics were about paying lower taxes and fostering free trade. As they saw it, what was good for them was good for America, and the more money they had, the better for everybody else. Trump respected Schwarzman and his fellow billionaires more than anyone, and he was going to give them free rein to build fortunes beyond the human imagination. In Trump's America, everywhere you looked there'd be a billionaire.

The president read the *Palm Beach Daily News* when he was in town, and he took particular interest that Sunday in Shannon Donnelly's front-page story about Patrick Park's impending appointment as ambassador to Austria. As much as possible, the president was trying to name people he knew to positions in his administration, and Trump knew Park because he had staged scores of charity events at Mar-a-Lago. Park loved music and was often on the arm of a beautiful young pianist. The president had sent Park a handwritten letter that said, "On to your next chapter, Ambassador!"

Park's billionaire father, Raymond P. Park, had made his fortune recycling industrial waste from his Cleveland headquarters. Patrick's two brothers stayed in the North, working in the family business, but their father deputized Patrick to come south and spend much of his time giving away part of their fortune. Park was one of the few men who regularly chaired charity events on the island. Inevitably, he enhanced the charities' bottom line with his own money.

Park was almost universally liked in Palm Beach, but some people found him strangely distanced and disconcertingly naïve. Being ambassador to Austria would be the most important thing Park did in his life. He had given Donnelly an enthusiastic interview, focusing on the glories of *The Sound of Music,* the classic movie set in Salzburg about the von Trapp family. Christopher Plummer, who played Captain von Trapp in the immensely popular film, was himself a Palm Beach winter resident. Plummer did not consider the role a high point of his career and once called the sentimental film *The Sound of Mucus.*

Park told Donnelly he'd "seen it like 75 times. I know every single word and song by heart. I've always wanted to live in the Von Trapp house." When he flew to Vienna as ambassador, he intended to go to Salzburg to see if the "Von Trapp house is for rent."

Perhaps Trump could appoint as ambassador to Morocco someone who loved *Casablanca* and to Germany a fan of *Cabaret.* At some point, the president decided Park was not right for diplomacy. He liked Park, and he didn't do anything about the appointment until Park announced he was turning down the honor for personal reasons.

15

Games of Chaos

As reports surfaced that operations at the White House were becoming increasingly chaotic, Chris Ruddy went on CNN's *Reliable Sources* to express his worries. "I think there's a lot of weakness coming out of the chief of staff," Ruddy told host Brian Stelter on February 12. "I think Reince Priebus, good guy, well intentioned, but he clearly doesn't know how the federal agencies work. He doesn't have a really good system."

Priebus called Ruddy almost immediately, asking the Newsmax CEO to "keep an open mind." But the damage had been done and a measure of truth had been spoken. Although Priebus was an ineffective administrator, Trump thrived in a systemless system where he flitted into the conflict and chaos, left his marks, and then flitted away. "I like conflict," Trump said in a press conference a year later, in February 2018. "I like watching it. I like seeing it, and I think it's the best way to go."

Ruddy had played an important role in Trump's victory in the general election, and he was listened to by conservative voters. Trump needed Ruddy on board, and he asked him to meet with Priebus and Bannon and get to know them face-to-face. As Trump saw things, no insult was extreme enough to end a relationship, and he thought Ruddy might end up as one of Priebus's biggest cheerleaders.

The Sunday of Presidents' Day weekend, when the president was once again in town, Ruddy took Priebus and Bannon to dinner. As much as Ruddy dissed the job Priebus was doing as chief of staff, the Newsmax CEO was no fan of Bannon's either, considering him "a bomb thrower, not a political strategist, just a guy with a political view." Mar-a-Lago was closed on Sunday evening, and Ruddy booked a table at Buccan, a hot midtown restaurant frequented by a far younger crowd than most other places on the island.

It was Priebus's wedding anniversary, and his wife, Sally, joined the group. Ruddy had brought along a friend, Jacqueline "Jackie" Robinson, a West Palm Beach jewelry designer. She was one of Ruddy's frequent escorts, and she had worked in the Obama White House. Ruddy could talk to Robinson about politics, and he discussed with her his relationship with Trump.

The restaurant roared with the boisterous conversation of its millennial clientele. The only chance at a conversation was for Ruddy and his guests to huddle together, their heads down as they talked. The discussion focused on a concern shared by most White House aides: how to get the president under control.

Robinson said little as the three men talked, but she was stunned at what she was hearing. Never during her time in the Obama White House had the staff discussed how they could manipulate an out-of-control president. Priebus and Bannon were united in their belief that Trump's success as president depended on dramatically changing the way he went about his job. Whatever it took for them to get him to do that was worth it.

The men discussed how to get Trump to stop watching *Morning Joe*. The litany of complaints continued until Priebus said, "You know, we always say he's screwing up here, he's screwing up there, but at the end of the day, he makes his own decisions, and often he turns out right in the end."

Ruddy had been invited after dinner for drinks at the home of heiress and Broadway producer Terry Allen Kramer. He asked Priebus and Bannon to join him. Ruddy also spotted the right-wing firebrand author Ann Coulter in the restaurant and invited her to come along as well.

As White House chief of staff, Priebus was given Secret Service protection, and a shiny black government SUV was waiting outside to take him and Bannon wherever they wanted to go. Robinson joined them, as did Sally Priebus, and Coulter jumped in the last empty seat. When Ruddy saw that, he said Robinson should stay there and he would follow in his car to the Kramer mansion, south of Mar-a-Lago.

Ruddy didn't mind driving his own automobile, but when he reached a security barrier a half mile north of Mar-a-Lago, his car was not on the official list and the police refused to let him through. Ruddy called Robinson and asked her to have the SUV turn around and pick him up before it reached Kramer's. He would squeeze in some way. After all, it was only a mile.

"Chris is stranded at the barrier," Robinson said urgently. "We gotta go back and get him."

"Well, I don't think we can do that," Priebus said.

"What do you mean you can't do that?" Robinson said.

"Well, I think it's against procedures."

Robinson could not believe these people were running America. The more she saw of them, the more she felt the nation had been kidnapped by the Gang That Couldn't Shoot Straight.

"Don't you understand, Reince?" Robinson said. "You're the chief of staff. You just order the driver around. Turn the damn car around."

Priebus wasn't buying. He did agree that after the driver dropped off the group at the home of a person no one in the car knew, he could go back and possibly bring back their host for the evening. As Robinson continued arguing with Priebus, Coulter jabbered away at Bannon, who diddled with his BlackBerry, oblivious to everything.

After dropping off his passengers, the driver of the SUV headed back to pick up Ruddy, who had parked his car at the barricade. When he finally arrived at Kramer's forty-four-thousand-square-foot oceanfront home, the group was at the bar. At the far end, Coulter had corralled Bannon into a corner. "I have control of Steve, and I'm discussing the issues with him," she said, warning everyone back. "I'm not going to let anyone here talk to him until I'm finished with him."

As Coulter maintained a *cordon sanitaire* between the chief strategist and the rest of the guests, Bannon looked more dazed than accommodating. Ruddy was appalled by Coulter, but he couldn't do anything. Trump had wanted him to get together with his two top aides to try to find things in common. It had happened, but not quite the way the president anticipated. The three men agreed that less than a month into the Trump presidency the administration was in deep trouble. Things had to change and soon.

At about 9:00 P.M., Ruddy received a call saying that Trump wanted to see him. He quickly said good-bye. When he arrived at Mar-a-Lago, the president was walking on the verandah.

Ruddy never knew how the president would respond when they saw each other. That was true of everybody who had even vaguely personal moments with Trump. He could turn against almost anyone around him. "Trump has a love/hate relationship with everybody and everything," says one close friend.

"Chris! I thought I was going to see you earlier," Trump fumed. "Oh, just come here a second. I need to talk to you."

Ruddy would have liked to tell Trump what his two top aides had been saying about his administration's early weeks, but a couple of Trump's golfing buddies were sitting at the same table where the president sat down. Ruddy was also well aware that Trump didn't like the idea of advisers, or anybody who thought they knew more he did, telling him what to do. Often if he didn't like someone's opinion, he simply kept asking other people until he got the answer he wanted.

Ruddy had to work his way at this gingerly if he wanted to maintain his relationship with the president. He talked about problems with several of the White House aides, but in a way that was nothing less than judicious and endlessly careful.

The one newly appointed member of Trump's cabinet who lived in Palm Beach, Secretary of Commerce Wilbur Ross, had to be careful around the president, too. Ross belonged to the Everglades and the Bath and Tennis, but he also fit in with the new Palm Beach. All it took to be an aristocrat in that world was people thinking you were worth a billion dollars—whether you were or not. Years before, Trump had learned that lesson.

Ross and his third wife, Hilary Geary Ross, were equally obsessed with money. Hilary was a stylish society reporter who was twelve years Wilbur's junior. "She wants her husband to be on the Forbes 400," one contemporary told that magazine.

Ross had pretended for years that he was a billionaire two times over when he wasn't even close. But with that title affixed to his name, the Rosses rose to the top of the Palm Beach social world. This "billionaire status" also brought business his way that he probably wouldn't have gotten, and his fortune increased ever closer to the magical billion dollars. If the seventy-eight-year-old Ross had never become a cabinet secretary, which meant he had to submit his financial documents, no one would have ever known he was worth seven hundred million dollars or maybe even a little less.

Ross made his money by buying distressed companies, spiffing them up a little, and selling them for a profit. Like most of Palm Beach's new generation of businessmen, he had little real relationship with the people who worked for his companies.

When coal prices started shooting up, Ross didn't let his lack of knowledge about coal mining stop him from forming International Coal Group Inc. and buying the nonunion Sago mine in Sago, West Virginia. He and his associates did little about the mine's 208 safety violations in 2005, and the next year twelve miners were killed in an explosion. Ross didn't go down to West Virginia to visit the victims' families. He made a financial contribution and his lawyers handled the lawsuits against his company, while he and his wife partied almost every night in Palm Beach, often wearing color-coordinated outfits.

In 2014 Ross was accused of insider trading involving the sale of shares of the Bank of Ireland. Luke "Ming" Flanagan, a member of the European Parliament, talked of "money . . . lost to the Irish people." Nothing was proved, and when Trump nominated Ross as commerce secretary, he neatly finessed his way through his Senate confirmation hearings. He did not have the unblemished record usually expected of a high-level government official. But Ross was Trump's kind of guy.

Whenever Trump was in residence, White House aides and other officials stayed in the suites and had many of their meals at Mar-a-Lago. Freedom of Information Act (FOIA) records obtained by the advocacy group Property of the People show that during the president's first six months in office, the Department of Defense spent $58,875.69 on food and lodging at the estate for its own personnel. The White House itself is not legally obligated to reply to FOIA requests. Both the administration and Mar-a-Lago refuse to say whether the government pays Mar-a-Lago for the rooms and food, but it is highly likely that it does, and the figures are probably far higher than those from the Department of Defense.

Trump was increasingly being criticized for golfing while Washington burned. That weekend in Palm Beach, as Trump headed out Saturday morning to his golf club, his press office said he was going there to do business. A little later, Chris Ruddy tweeted a photo of Trump in golf clothes standing with political operative Peter Flaherty and chef Max Kramer. They looked like a threesome ready for tee time.

When Trump walked out of the family quarters before dinner, he saw Ruddy having dinner with retired Harvard law professor Alan Dershowitz, a lifelong Democrat. "If I can get you to vote for me in 2020, that'll be the real accomplishment, because you've probably never voted for a Republican," Trump said to Dershowitz. The president was dining at a nearby table with Ike Perlmutter and Wilbur Ross. They were joined for dessert by Vice President Mike Pence, who was in town to give a speech to the conservative Club for Growth at the Breakers.

Soon into the dinner, Trump left his own table, returning to Ruddy and Dershowitz's table for a long conversation. It was time well spent and yet another example of the unexpected services Ruddy did for the president. Dershowitz became the president's least likely proponent, developing a new public life for himself going on cable defending many of the administration's legal positions and getting a book deal as well.

Now that Trump was president, club members were witnessing Trump camped out in the library, while in the living room supplicants waited to be called, including Howard Lorber, the billionaire chairman of Douglas Elliman Real Estate. "They're waiting there for him like in a barbershop," said one member. "They're just sitting there, eying each other, not saying a word. He must have kept Lorber—and he's a friend—waiting two hours."

When the weekend was ending, everyone who was flying back on Air Force One gathered in the small ballroom surrounded by Secret Service. As soon as the group assembled, Trump walked into the room. "Okay, are we ready," he said, an answer more than a question, and clapped his hands. "Let's go." Everyone piled into the vehicles and no more than half an hour later, Air Force One flew over the Mar-a-Lago tower heading back to Washington.

Trump loved to show off the splendors of Mar-a-Lago. Early in April he invited Chinese President Xi Jinping to fly to Palm Beach for their summit meeting. Xi was staying at the Eau Palm Beach Resort and Spa in Manalapan, seven miles south of Mar-a-Lago.

The security for this first meeting of the world's two most powerful leaders needed to be extraordinary. Authorities closed the public beaches, tennis courts, and parking lots in the south end of Palm Beach, and Mar-a-Lago Club members were severely limited in their access as well. Only those who called early or knew best how to schmooze manager Lembcke were able to book dinner reservations on the verandah for the first evening of the two-day summit while Trump and Xi and their aides dined at elegantly appointed settings in the ornate dining room.

For most summit meetings, the principals' staffs have worked out the agenda and much of the intended results beforehand. The leaders have little to do but to stay close to the script. That wasn't Trump's style. He believed in the transcendent importance of human personality.

On Air Force One, flying down to Florida earlier in the day, Trump brought with him Secretary of the Treasury Steven Mnuchin, Secretary of Commerce Ross, National Security Adviser Lieutenant General H. R. McMaster, Bannon, and Priebus. While the jet bounced up and down through rough pockets of air, the president met with his National Security Council team.

Earlier in the week Syrian president Bashar al-Assad had bombed the rebel-held town of Khan Sheikhoun with chemical weapons. Trump had seen photos of suffering children that were so horrifying, they had not been shown on television. Perhaps no one could view those pictures without feeling anger and anguish and a desire to seek some measure of justice.

Trump's generals proposed sending Tomahawk cruise missiles to bomb the Syrian air force base where the planes carrying the chemical weapons had originated. Only a few people at the base might die, and the action was far from eye-for-an-eye biblical revenge. Trump ordered the missiles sent skyward as soon as possible.

As Trump sat with Xi over a dinner of pan-seared Dover sole with champagne sauce or dry-aged prime New York strip, the missiles were being readied for launch from navy ships in the Mediterranean. As the two men ate, Trump sought to connect emotionally with the Chinese leader. That's how Trump had always made deals. If he could make an empathetic connection, he felt he could get what he wanted.

This was by far President Trump's most important dinner so far, and the guest list reflected that. The president's daughter Ivanka was there alongside Jared Kushner. Priebus and Bannon were there, each one of them scrambling to be closest to the president. Commerce Secretary Ross, who spent many weekends at his Palm Beach home, was also at the elegantly appointed long table.

Trump watched as Xi took apparent delight in eating what the president called "the most beautiful piece of chocolate cake that you've ever seen." It was overly large and overly sweet, just the way Trump liked it.

As Xi continued with the cake, Trump was given the message he had been anticipating. "Mr. President, let me explain something to you," Trump told the Chinese leader. "We've just fired fifty-nine missiles, all of which hit, by the way, unbelievable, from, you know, hundreds of miles away, all of which hit, amazing."

In an instant, Trump had upstaged Xi's plans for the summit and put the Chinese leader in the unenviable choice of either criticizing his host for his action or seemingly condoning his behavior by being largely silent on the subject, which is what Xi chose to do. During the two-day visit, Trump reached out and embraced the Chinese leader, but Xi made no major concessions to Trump; if this supposed friendship were to reap any important benefits, they would happen in the future. The meeting's most intriguing moment, and one that spoke to how much the cultural relationship between the two nations has changed, came when Trump showed the Chinese leader a video of his six-year-old granddaughter, Arabella Kushner, singing a song in Mandarin.

On Saturday evening, after the Chinese delegation had departed, Trump had dinner at a round table for four that was his favorite place on the patio. Rumors circulated that some members were tipping thousands of dollars to have dinner near the president. That may not have been true, but no one thought it was an unseemly amount, considering what might be gained.

Chris Ruddy was there that evening, hosting a dinner with two billionaire brothers, David and William Koch. For decades, the Koch brothers had been famously estranged, and it was almost a miracle that they were dining together. Their father had built Koch Industries into one of the two largest private companies in America. William believed that David, along with another brother, Charles, had cheated him when he sold them his part of the family business in 1983. The $470 million William received at the time was hardly a pittance, but to him, it was not enough. He had sued his brothers and fought with them for decades before the three men arrived at a measure of accommodation.

David and William each had homes in Palm Beach. One only had to visit the two residences to understand why the brothers might have once despised each other. David, who, like his brother, was a member of the Everglades, lived in one of the island's most traditional homes, which was furnished with antiques and the predictable artwork of a conservative man. Along with Charles Koch, he was a leading funder of America's far right. David and Charles tried to affect change as surreptitiously as possible.

Bill Koch lived in a gigantic man cave set on a massive property south of Mar-a-Lago that ran from the ocean to the Intracoastal Waterway. The sweeping lawns featured dramatic sculptures, including enormous Boteros. Koch's thirty-five-thousand-square-foot mansion housed masterworks by Renoir and Monet, a collection heavy on breasts and bottoms. The basement contained one of the world's finest private wine cellars; a replica of a western frontier bar; a copy of Lord Nelson's stateroom, with lanterns swaying back and forth as if the admiral was on the high seas; and a bowling alley.

As with Trump, women were drawn to Bill Koch as much for the money as the man. Before the billionaire married his second wife, Angela Browder Gauntt, he presented her with a forty-five-page prenuptial agreement (they were divorced in 2000). Bill Koch was a member of Mar-a-Lago, and he was Trump's kind of billionaire. In August 2016, he hosted a fund-raiser for Trump at his Cape Cod estate. His more traditionally conservative brother David had used his money throughout the primaries to oppose Trump, then sat out the general election. Charles Koch said that picking between Trump and Clinton was like choosing cancer or a heart attack. Trump dismissed David and Charles Koch, tweeting in July 2015, "I really like the Koch Brothers (members of my P.B. Club), but I don't want their money or anything else from them. Cannot influence Trump!"

There was another reason why it was startling that David Koch had shown up at Mar-a-Lago this evening. A member of the Trump International Golf Club, he had arrived one Friday in December 2016, with three companions, ready to play eighteen holes of golf. One of his guests was Harry Hurt III, who had written *Lost Tycoon: The Many Lives of Donald J. Trump*, a 1993 biography Trump considered little but sordid lies. When President-Elect Trump saw Hurt planning to play golf on *his* course, he kicked him off. Koch wasn't about to let his guest leave alone, and the four men departed without playing.

Koch had to know Trump would be here this evening, and considering what had happened, his acceptance of Ruddy's invitation was an extraordinary gesture. Trump got the significance of this, and he came over to the table and had a polite conversation with the brothers.

The two brothers returned to the club for another dinner, and it was a scene few would have expected only a few months before. "The Koch brothers came up to Trump at his favorite table that evening," recalled a member who was there. "They're yapping away at Donald. Bill Koch, I swear, was almost bowing, sort of a Japanese knee bow. They were both like that. I'm thinking, 'This is really weird.' They're billionaires. Maybe they don't even like Trump, but they're paying tribute to him like the Godfather. Very strange."

On August 12, 2017, at a "Unite the Right Rally" in Charlottesville, Virginia, armed neo-Nazis and ultra-rightists faced off against counterprotesters over a looming legal battle about tearing down Confederate statues in the town. Before the day was over, one cryptofascist protester drove his car into a crowd, killing a young woman and injuring nineteen others.

President Trump was in New York, and when he was asked about the conflict in Charlottesville at an impromptu press conference, he remarked, "I think there is blame on both sides. You had a group on one side that was bad. You had a group on the other side that was also very violent." The president also said, "You also had people that were very fine people on both sides."

Steve Schwarzman had much to gain from leading the council of top executives who made up Trump's Strategic & Policy Forum, but he was distressed by Trump's remarks. Two days after the president's statements, Schwarzman led a conference call with members of the council, all of whom were upset at Trump's remarks. Two retired executives, Boeing's Jim McNerney and General Electric's Jack Welch, wanted the group to condemn the president publicly and then continue their efforts. IBM CEO Virginia M. Rometty said it was too late, and they should simply disband. Schwarzman did little but listen and agree with the consensus to end things.

After Schwarzman hung up, he called the White House to say the forum was terminating. He was asked to let the president save face by saying it was his decision to end the group. Most of the executives wanted no more to do with Trump, but Schwarzman agreed to the request, allowing him to maintain his personal relationship with the president.

After Trump's Charlottesville remarks, several members left Mar-a-Lago and their substantial deposits. But no one would say publicly that their departure had anything to do with Trump. Others actively contemplated leaving. As a big-time Hillary Democrat, Cynthia Friedman wondered if she had any business belonging any longer. But if she left, she would lose her membership fee. She rationalized that if she left she would no longer be able to observe Trump's actions. She hemmed and hawed for months before deciding to pay her dues for another year.

One by one, almost all the charities that had recently held their events at Mar-a-Lago began canceling for the next season: the American Red Cross, the Palm Beach Zoo, the Salvation Army, the American Cancer Society, American Friends of Magen David Adom, the Preservation Foundation of Palm Beach, the Palm Beach Symphony, more than twenty groups in all. These organizations did not want their decisions to be seen as political statements, though that's precisely what they were. Even so, they couldn't afford to rile the Trump supporters among their donors, and they left Mar-a-Lago as quietly as possible.

Lois Pope, on the other hand, made a powerful public statement as she quite loudly took her LIFE Foundation gala to the Breakers and herself walked away from her Mar-a-Lago membership. It was a daring thing to do that cost her friends and donors and left her isolated.

Pope laid out her reasons for leaving in an essay for *Time* magazine: "Anyone, including the President, who would demonstrate even a modicum of support for [neo-fascist protesters] by insisting that there are 'very fine people' among them is not deserving of patronage in any form, from any person or foundation. When you march wearing the very same swastikas and shouting the very same mantras championed by Hitler, you are not a 'fine' person by any definition."

Toni Holt Kramer believed Pope had betrayed Trump. The Trumpette founder showed her displeasure by leaving Pope's LIFE Foundation board. "Half the town was alienated from her," says another board member who also resigned. "In Palm Beach, you're only as good as your last donation. So she started giving away big bucks to win her way into everyone's favor. Tops was twelve million dollars to Bascom Palmer Eye Institute. And, voilà, some people decided Lois was okay."

Pope gave the money to the eye institute with the stipulation that it be used to create the Lois Pope Center for Retinal and Macular Degeneration Research.

She also set out to prove she was still relevant in Palm Beach by throwing the most spectacular Lady in Red Ball ever in January 2018. She had a hard time filling the Breakers ballroom, but she did what was necessary to make the event look like a sellout. The evening began with selections by the Palm Beach Symphony, followed by performances by Jay Leno and the Fab Four Beatles clones, and dancing to the strains of the Soul Survivors Band. One guest said, "I don't think she cared what it cost. It was her way of getting even."

Laurel Baker, the executive director of the Palm Beach Chamber of Commerce, also took a strong public stance against Trump after his Charlottesville statement. "If you're looking at your mission statement, can you honestly say having an event at Mar-a-Lago, given all that has transpired, is the best stewardship of your efforts?" she asked in *The Washington Post* in mid-August. "The darkest places in hell are reserved for those who maintain their neutrality in times of moral crisis. Especially for nonprofits. Especially for groups who help people who can't help themselves."

Most in Palm Beach preferred to have its truths whispered about privately, not delivered openly in a fierce broadside, and the chamber of commerce immediately apologized for Baker's utterance. Baker was unhappy about more than Charlottesville. She had devoted most of her professional life to the island. She believed that Palm Beach's small-town quality was disappearing and was being taken over by restless acquisitiveness. "It's just not the same place," Baker says. "I've been a witness to all the changes."

Until the 1980s, Palm Beach had local banks that knew their customers and the community. That had given way to national banks and to financial institutions along Royal Poinciana Way that were charged with maintaining the wealth of the 1 percent and their kin. Worth Avenue had been a street of local stores, but the glittery names of luxury arrived, and the street became as celebrated and as familiar as Beverly Hills's Rodeo Drive.

The *Palm Beach Daily News* had changed too and no longer liked to deal with unpleasantness. One evening in November 2016, a wealthy couple came home to discover that burglars had broken into their home, ripped their safe containing $1.5 million in jewelry out of the wall, and carried it off. It was the island's most lucrative theft in years and one of a series of burglaries that did not appear in the Shiny Sheet, where it would have upset the island's image as a bucolic paradise free from danger.

Trump alone had not created this world, but he was the most glaring symbol of it, and Laurel Baker thought he had harmed the island she loved so much. He had commandeered the evolution of Palm Beach into a place where an obsession with wealth no longer condemned one as a vulgar arriviste but instead represented the highest expression of human endeavor.

It was peculiar what wealth did to people sometimes. One day Paul Trupia, who ran the Mar-a-Lago tennis shop, noticed an empty hanger where he was sure there had been a shirt. He looked at the store's video record and identified a member who had taken the clothing. The man was one of the club's most disliked tennis players, a constant complainer. Trupia took the matter to Eric Trump, who was overseeing Mar-a-Lago for his father. Eric banned the man from the club premises until January 2019.

After Trump's Charlottesville remarks, someone had started a website that posted the names of Mar-a-Lago members, which was profoundly unsettling to some of them. "Now they can find our addresses and come after us," says one member. "These people are so angry at Trump. They really hate him. I don't go to Mar-a-Lago Friday and Saturday evenings, when it may be more dangerous. I don't go to the pool on Sunday, either. And I'm careful when I'm pulling out of there that nobody is following me home."

Trump had not changed his Palm Beach routine, and he had Thanksgiving dinner in 2017 with Melania, surrounded by scores of club members. When they went to late Christmas Eve services the next month, the worshippers again stood and applauded his arrival.

Three mornings later, the president headed out to his golf club with his son Eric and the professional golfer Jim Herman. Trump was a competitor, and playing with someone like Herman elevated Trump's game. Beyond that there was no intrusion of politics or business, just manly chat. When the men finished their rounds, Trump walked into the grill room with his golf buddies, sat down at a table, took off his cap with "45" on the sides, and ordered salad for lunch.

The man the *Atlantic* called "the Zelig of the Trump administration" sat at a table near the president's, close by yet apart. Chris Ruddy talked to Trump often and had become arguably the administration's most effective outside defender. For all the high public posture that Ruddy's relationship with Trump had given him, it hadn't helped Newsmax much. Newsmax TV still had not taken off, and the company's new high-tech offices in Boca Raton sat half empty. Ruddy was talking about turning things around by signing up Bill O'Reilly, who had recently been fired from Fox News for sexual transgressions, to do a prime-time show, but as of then, that was just talk.

Sitting with Ruddy was Michael S. Schmidt of *The New York Times*. Ruddy almost always had a guest with him, and he made sure it was someone who would not offend Trump's sensibilities. Some journalists riled Trump up to nearly murderous intent, but others were okay.

Ruddy went over to speak to Trump, and Schmidt followed closely behind. The journalist was not a regular on the Trump beat, but he was a rising star at the newspaper, and he was there that day because his colleagues were on a holiday break.

Schmidt knelt down beside the president and started making polite, carefully calibrated small talk. He sensed that Trump "was bored by vacation and wanted to engage with the news media." That was probably true and likely part of the reason Trump agreed to an interview after he finished lunch.

Things weren't done this way, especially not with the paper Trump called "the failing *New York Times*," the most notorious enemy of the people of them all. Although the president talked to *Times* reporters far more than he admitted, for Schmidt to get this on-the-record interview in this unorthodox manner was a major coup. This was also a high-stakes risk for Ruddy: If the interview worked to Trump's advantage, he would be praised. But if Trump said too many controversial things, Ruddy would be blamed for bringing this scheming ingrate into the sacred circle.

During the half-hour recorded interview, the president often spoke in a startling stream of consciousness, moving from subject to subject without transition. It was like a quilt made out of scores of little pieces, but nobody had sewn them into a whole, and they were all muddled together.

Trump dismissed the idea that his campaign colluded with the Russians. "But there is tremendous collusion with the Russians and with the Democratic Party," he said. "Including all of the stuff with the—and then whatever happened to the Pakistani guy, that had the two, you know, whatever happened to this Pakistani guy who worked with the D.N.C.? Whatever happened to them? With the two servers they broke up into a million pieces? Whatever happened to him? That was a big story. . . . So I know *The New York Times* is going to— because those are real stories. Whatever happened to the Hillary Clinton deleted 33,000 emails after she got [inaudible]—which you guys wrote, but then you dropped—was that you?"

Schmidt's story ran on the front page of the next day's *Times*. In his article, the reporter used quotes that made Trump sound largely focused and articulate. The president had reasons to be happy, but that didn't end his feuding with the media. On New Year's Eve, Trump tweeted holiday wishes to "friends, supporters, enemies, haters, and even the very dishonest Fake News Media, a Happy and Healthy New Year."

At the end of the year, within Mar-a-Lago there was increasing paranoia about the Secret Service that had once not been there. "All around the property, everywhere I saw there was somebody with a gun," said one member. "And it made me so uneasy. It felt that if there ever were anyone there seeking to do harm, there would be lots of blood. My husband and I always spent New Year's Eve at Mar-a-Lago, but there were so many guns that we decided to go elsewhere."

It wasn't just the massive security that bothered club members. It was a different place since Trump became president. "All kinds of people used to come here just to relax, L.A. people, movie stars, musical artists, famous tennis players when there'd be a tournament, and now there's nobody like that," says one charter member. "You won't believe the people that came here. Whitney Houston. Mary Tyler Moore. Paul Anka. Regis Philbin was always here, and even he doesn't come any longer. Instead, you see all these political types, senior Republicans. Either they're involved with the administration or they're just major politicians."

As the members observed the changes in the club, Trump still had his supporters, but others abhorred the president Trump had become. Those sentiments they dared whisper only to the few they trusted. No matter what they felt, like everyone else, they rose and applauded when the president entered and reached out to offer him their tributes.

16

"The President!!! The Great President!!!"

Mar-a-Lago had always been an abode of peace and security for Trump that was away from the endless drama of his life, but the world was intruding even here. On January 12, 2018, when he flew down, he was not in a good mood.

The problem that overshadowed everything was special counsel Robert S. Mueller III's investigation into Russian involvement in the presidential election. Trump averred again and again that he had not colluded with Moscow and condemned the investigation as a partisan witch hunt. Although the president had been talked out of firing the much-respected former head of the FBI, Trump continued to fume and wait with foreboding the final report.

That was far from Trump's only irritation. The previous week in Washington, during a meeting with congressional leaders of both parties to discuss an immigration-reform deal that would protect the rights of immigrants from El Salvador, Haiti, and Africa, Trump said, "Why are we having all these people from shithole countries come here?" The president used the offensive word a number of times, as if for emphasis. He may have been playing to his supporters, but the foul language set off a fierce wave of criticism from Democrats and Republicans.

Trump was shaken by the onslaught, and throughout the weekend at Mar-a-Lago, he had no interest in chatting with an endless array of members. On Sunday evening Trump drove over to his golf club to have dinner with House Majority Leader Kevin McCarthy. Just a few weeks earlier, he would have walked slowly through the crowd, bathing in the praise he received. This time he moved briskly, shouting out a few greetings before sitting down at a table in the middle of the room, isolated from the other diners and surrounded by Secret Service.

On the next Thursday, the country was on the verge of a government shutdown. If it hadn't been, Trump might well have flown down to Palm Beach for the Red, White and Blue Celebration for We the People, which was being held at Mar-a-Lago to honor Trump's first year in office. It was a mouthful of a title and a mouthful of an event.

Toni Holt Kramer had thought the Trumpettes should stage a gala to counter all the charities boycotting Mar-a-Lago. The group priced the tickets at three hundred dollars per person, less than half what most charities charged. Kramer kept the price low so the event would draw people who were less well-off, but of course three hundred dollars a person for an evening out was a lot of money to most Americans. Among the 813 people who signed up for the evening from across the nation were many to whom this evening was a very big deal, not to mention a financial sacrifice. Still, the ballroom was primarily full with, if not the 1 percent, the 10 percent.

Patriotism was the color of the day. There were red-white-and-blue ties and shawls and a star-spangled band playing songs of American triumph. Even the apple pie dessert had an American flag on it. It was a wildly enthusiastic gathering of people who were happy to know that wherever they looked they were surrounded by others of a like mind.

Judge Jeanine Pirro was the main speaker. Her weekly program on Fox News was the shrillest pro-Trump hour on television, all praise to the great man and slow death and dismemberment to his enemies. Pirro's total devotion to Trump had brought her a prominence she had never known before, and she owed the president big-time. But like so many of those around Trump, she saw this as an opportunity to make money. Pirro wasn't about to speak for free. She insisted on a twenty-five-thousand-dollar payment.

"Welcome to Mar-a-Lago," Pirro half shouted as she began her speech. "A magnificent place. It sure ain't no shithole!" The audience roared its approval at her vulgarity.

"Barack Obama wanted to give our enemy [Iran] $150 billion so that they are in a position to create a nuclear bomb," the TV personality half shrieked. "And don't you believe anything else." That this was untrue was irrelevant. The audience hooted its approval.

Pirro revved up fears and prejudices from somewhere deep in the American psyche, and the partygoers went wild. Then Pirro went on to talk about realities that none of the eight-hundred-plus people listening had ever seen and were equally false. Pirro described an America with "record numbers of illegal aliens, crossing our borders, taking jobs, bringing with them family members, and a lawyer and translator just in case they decide to hurt or kill us."

The judge stopped just long enough to look out and appreciate the ecstatic fears she had evoked. "Do you want America overrun by people who despise us and burn our flag?" she asked, with shouts of "NO!!!!" sounding across the grand ballroom. "Then you can say I am damn proud to point to God, my guns, and the United States of America." Left-wing Neanderthals were ready to break into their homes to take their weapons, and they must "cling to guns, God, and the United States of America."

Until Pirro stood up, the crowd had been like most any gala in the ballroom, the people at each table amiable, chattering away, enjoying their common beliefs. They were an educated crowd, and by any measure they knew better, but they didn't care. They loved to hear their enemies beaten up and stomped upon, and they cheered Pirro on. Kramer was so ecstatic that afterward she invited Pirro to be the headliner again the next year.

The president wasn't there, but he was in spirit. Pirro gave the kind of ugly, unforgiving speech that had been so common during the Trump campaign, and now it had come home to Mar-a-Lago.

With Trump in office for a year now, politics inserted itself everywhere at Mar-a-Lago—even into a talk being given by Lama Migmar Tseten, a Buddhist chaplain at Harvard and the founder of the Sakya Institute for Buddhist Studies.

Sixty people sat in the small ballroom in February 2018 to listen to the Tibetan-born monk talk about Buddhism. When the soft-spoken intellectual completed his talk, Lama Migmar said, "Before we begin meditation, are there any questions?"

One woman shouted from one side of the room, "What are we going to do about Trump and North Korea?"

Someone from the other side of the room yelled, "Yeah, and what about fake news?" The whole internecine political debate erupted in the middle of the monk's decidedly nonpolitical talk. On and on the members yelled, voices erupting on top of each other, one uncompromising statement after another.

Through it all, Lama Migmar stood in silent contemplation. Finally, when the uproar began to die down, he said, "Let us meditate."

Everyone in the room sat quietly, and when the meditation was over, there was peace and tranquility that lasted at least as long as Lama Migmar was in the room.

By this time, any organization coming to Mar-a-Lago was doing so in part because it wanted to make political statements. A group called The Truth About Israel was run by Steven Alembik, who was delighted to pull his event out of the Boca Raton Resort & Club and bring it to Palm Beach. "Somebody needs to take a stand here and do something," he said. "My president is my president. He's got Israel's back."

That evening about a third of the guests were Chinese. They had paid $750 to attend, but they weren't there because they were interested in watching Israel's back. They paid to see the glorious home of the president of the United States. "The Chinese are infatuated with Trump and Mar-a-Lago," Alembik said. "As soon as we announced the event, they were lining up. They would have paid anything." Most of them didn't speak English, and they continued their conversations in Mandarin as the evening's speakers extolled American-Israeli relations.

Politics had become everything. Even Ike Perlmutter got involved. Almost as reclusive as Howard Hughes, the Marvel billionaire was an unlikely person to have much to do with the public profession of politics. Yet there he was not only whispering into the president's ear but deputized by Trump to work to reform the Veterans Administration. Perlmutter brought in another Mar-a-Lago member, his personal physician, Bruce Moskowitz, who added his Palm Beach squash partner, lawyer Marc Sherman. The threesome, known in Washington as "the Mar-a-Lago crowd," called the agency almost every day. Top VA officials flew down to Mar-a-Lago to meet with the troika, none of whom were veterans. "Everyone has to go down and kiss the ring," one former administrator told ProPublica.

Perlmutter and his colleagues say they were only offering suggestions. "To the extent anyone thought our role was anything other than that, we don't believe it was the result of anything we said or did," they asserted, feigning innocence of their unprecedented clout. If that's what they thought, it shows how ignorant they were of the way government works. When a call comes to a top official at the VA from an individual who has the president's ear, it is not a suggestion but an order. The three men may have had the best of intentions in skirting the ponderous rituals of government, but those are there to protect democracy. In the end, after ProPublica exposed "the Mar-a-Lago gang," they retreated to the privileged precincts of Palm Beach.

Perlmutter's neighbor Secretary of Commerce Wilbur Ross was a legitimate figure of government, which Perlmutter was not. Ross's problem was that he was a pure creature of the new class of wealth in Palm Beach. As more and more of his past activities became public, thanks largely to *Forbes*, his reputation radically diminished, though not in the eyes of some members of the golden elite, who admired the way good old Wilbur had pulled things off.

Ross had lied again and again to get on the Forbes 400 as a billionaire. This was a man who, according to those who knew him, would fill his pockets with packets of Sweet'N Low at restaurants so he wouldn't have to buy the sweetener. A Commerce official labeled the claim "petty nonsense," but *Forbes* made far more serious charges.

"Many of those who worked directly with him claim that Ross wrongly siphoned or outright stole a few million here and a few million there, huge amounts for most but not necessarily for the commerce secretary," *Forbes* wrote. "All told, these allegations—which sparked lawsuits, reimbursements and an SEC fine—come to more than $120 million. If even half of the accusations are legitimate, the current United States secretary of commerce could rank among the biggest grifters in American history."

This is the man Trump called a "legendary Wall Street genius," just the kind of person he wanted in his cabinet. "In these particular positions, I just don't want a poor person," Trump said.

Trump came down to Palm Beach almost every winter weekend in early 2018. He was planning yet another regular visit when, on a Wednesday morning in mid-February, a nineteen-year-old former high school student walked into the Marjory Stoneman Douglas High School in Parkland, Florida, and began shooting an AR-15-style semiautomatic weapon. He killed fourteen students and three staff members, and wounded seventeen others.

The next day Trump spoke by phone to Florida governor Rick Scott, who was visiting survivors at Broward Health North hospital. The governor said one of the surviving victims had expressed a desire to talk to Trump, and the president said he would call. Scott went back into eighteen-year-old Samantha Fuentes's room and told the teenager that the president would be phoning her.

The senior had been in her class, listening to her history teacher discuss the Holocaust, when the shooting began. Two of her friends in the class, Nicholas

Dworet and Helena Ramsay, were dead. Fuentes's leg wounds turned out to be minor, but her face would require plastic surgery, and the shrapnel behind her eyes would stay there for the rest of her life.

Fuentes couldn't remember why she told Governor Scott she would like for President Trump to call her. And then the phone rang.

"Are you okay?" Trump asked.

"Yeah, I'm okay," Fuentes said. As she spoke, her family and friends huddled around her cell phone listening intensely.

"Good, because I spoke to your governor, and he said you're a fan, but I'm a fan of yours."

One of Fuentes's friends began to giggle, pumping her arms up and down. This was the president of the United States on the phone, but it was just funny.

"So, were you, uh, very seriously hurt?" Trump asked. "Are you . . . what happened?"

"I got shot in both of my legs," Fuentes said. "Like, I got shrapnel in the back of my eye. I was so close to losing my legs and my eyes, but it's a miracle."

"Unbelievable! You saw him, right?"

"Yeah, I saw the shooter," Fuentes said. "He was aiming through the window and everything."

"Boy oh boy, oh boy," Trump said. "Did you see, like, a rage in his eyes or something?"

"It's like he had absolutely no emotion at all," Fuentes said.

"No emotion. Boy oh boy. What a sick puppy that was. What a disgusting person."

After Trump hung up, Fuentes tried to make sense of the phone call. "When I compare my conversation with him with that of everyone else who called after the shooting, unlike those others, I didn't get that initial empathy or sympathy," she says. "It's clear he's never had to deal with something traumatic like this. He's not comfortable going through these painful emotions."

Trump and Melania stopped at Broward Health North hospital to visit shooting victims on their way to Palm Beach that weekend. When the president got back to Mar-a-Lago, he didn't golf. It wouldn't look good for him to be seen amusing himself on the links after the tragedy. With the extra time he had that weekend, President Trump tweeted twenty times, attacking everyone from his soon-to-be-fired national security adviser McMaster to Oprah Winfrey, and CNN to "Crooked Hillary Clinton."

Perhaps Twitter was where he was most comfortable, but if there was a place on earth Trump belonged, it was Palm Beach. Everywhere he looked on the island, there were people like him of wealth, power, and privilege who wanted to live among their kind. Trump exulted in the public display of wealth, in planes, opulent residences, luxury cars, beautiful women, and privilege beyond measure. He and his contemporaries resided in an enclave of privilege, almost totally unaware of their own isolation. By the looks of the parking lot, almost no one at Mar-a-Lago took seriously the pledge to buy American. There were the ubiquitous Bentleys, the people's car in Palm Beach, plus Rolls-Royces, Ferraris, Maseratis, Mercedes-Benzes, Audis, BMWs, Land Rovers, Jaguars, a Tesla or two, and one lone refugee from Detroit, the once glorious Cadillac.

Trump arrived in Palm Beach on the first Friday in March, after attending the funeral for Reverend Billy Graham in Charlotte, North Carolina. An influential piece in *The New York Times* by White House reporters Mark Landler and Maggie Haberman had just appeared, arguing, as the headline expressed it, that "TRUMP'S CHAOS THEORY FOR THE OVAL OFFICE IS TAKING ITS TOLL."

The president was portrayed as a brooding King Lear, roaming the ramparts, spewing out invective while beneath him played out a hapless scene of endless infighting and finger-pointing. By this point, Bannon and Priebus were long since gone, along with any number of other aides and officials. All that remained was the turmoil.

As always, the president's knight Chris Ruddy came riding in to defend his liege, his lance at the ready. "I always said that it was going to take a while for Donald Trump to adjust as president," Ruddy told the *Times*, ignoring the fact that Trump had been president for more than a year. But as Ruddy explained it, that was just the way it had been in Trump's business life. He had survived in a Darwinian world of "trial and error—the strongest survived, the weak died."

Ruddy believed that Trump's internal angst stemmed in part from the recent shooting. "He had just come off Parkland," Ruddy says. "He's a John Wayne type, and you're not supposed to show your emotions on your shirtsleeve. But when you see something like those deaths, you internalize it, and it comes out other ways."

Trump flew down to Palm Beach on Friday afternoon for the weekend of March 24–25 and did what he always did. He went out Saturday morning to the Trump International Golf Club. But this morning, as he was playing a round of golf, surrounded by as many as twenty-five other golf carts, people gathered at Dreher Park, two miles away, to take part in the March for Our Lives, a worldwide event for gun control that was spurred by a group of the surviving Stoneman Douglas students.

Arriving at the park were working people and professionals; large families and singles; teenagers and seniors; children barely old enough to walk and people in wheelchairs and walkers; whites, blacks, Latinos, Indian Americans, and other Asian Americans. By the looks of it, representatives of all of America had shown up to march.

In the shooting's aftermath, Trump had called for strong gun control measures, but as had happened before, a talk with the National Rifle Association changed his mind. For his return, Trump managed to avoid the Dreher Park marchers by taking a circuitous route back to Mar-a-Lago over the middle bridge. By the time the thousands set off down Southern Boulevard, Trump was back at his estate.

One of the marchers carried a sign, GRANDMAS FOR GUN CONTROL. A student hoisted a sign, BOOKS NOT BULLETS. The multitudes walked a mile east on the broad street until they reached the Intracoastal Waterway and stood on Flagler Drive looking across the water, where Mar-a-Lago's pink tower rose high into the blue sky. Someone had placed seventeen signs along the road, each one with a picture of one of the victims.

When the marchers had gathered together, they began to shout their slogans. They yelled in the many accents of America. The sounds rose high into the sky, but they did not carry over as far as inside Mar-a-Lago, and Trump could not have heard them.

On the last Thursday in March, Trump flew down for the Easter weekend. As Trump and Melania walked from the family quarters to dinner that evening on the verandah, he nodded a greeting to Toni Holt Kramer and her husband, Bob, before he sat down at his favorite table for four.

As much as Trump attempted to run from the issue, allegations of sexual misconduct continued to haunt his presidency. *Playboy*'s 1998 Playmate of the Year, Karen McDougal, had just come forward claiming a ten-month affair with Trump when he was newly married to Melania. And on the previous Sunday, CBS's *60 Minutes* had aired its interview with porn star Stormy Daniels, who said she had a one-night stand with Trump while Melania was home with their newborn. As Trump drove in from the airport, his vehicle passed a protester wearing a giant papier-mâché head of the porn star and hoisting a sign that read, STORMY DANIELS SAYS HI.

Trump's lawyer Cohen had paid both these women off and they hadn't stayed bought. As Trump viewed the world, that was the real betrayal. No matter what evidence was brought forward, he denied everything. What was an untruth told to people who might one day turn against you? And that was everybody. That wasn't paranoia. That was the lesson of this life of his making.

These stories of Trump's affairs led many to ask how Melania could stay with her husband. Had she no pride and honor? How could she remain with a husband whose supposed acts of unfaithfulness had begun when she was a young wife and mother? What must she be receiving to stand beside him and accept this endless humiliation?

Melania said nothing, but surely whatever she still felt for her husband was wrapped up in how she thought best to take care of her son as well as her parents, who spent much of the winter at Mar-a-Lago in a life beyond anything they might have imagined in Slovenia. But that was all speculation. On that evening, she stayed with her husband at dinner for three hours, conversing with him amiably and sometimes even laughing.

Another mark of the Trump family's complications was on view that evening. Donald Jr., his wife, Vanessa, and their five children were seated near the president. After multiple reports of her husband's infidelity, the news had gotten out that Vanessa was seeking a divorce, but this evening they appeared as cooing as newlyweds. At one point, the couple sat with the president at his table. Eric Trump and his wife, Lara, also took their turn coming up to sit with Trump, and some of his grandchildren came forward, too. For this moment, the president appeared the patriarch of a great united family.

Yet even in this room full of family and friends, Trump was alone. On an evening like this it was impossible not to think of Trump's favorite movie, Orson Welles's *Citizen Kane*, the 1941 masterpiece based in part on the life of press magnate William Randolph Hearst. This story of the all-powerful Charles Foster Kane, who ends up isolated and alone, stumbling around his haunted mansion, Xanadu, on Florida's Gulf Coast, had long resonated with the president.

In the film, after Kane's death, the journalist Jerry Thompson goes around the country learning what he can about the newspaper mogul. It is not easy for him to find people who truly knew the man and are willing to talk. But even so, Thompson returns with this assessment: "He was the most honest man who ever lived, with a streak of crookedness a yard wide. He was a liberal and a reactionary; he was tolerant—'Live and Let Live,' that was his motto. But he had no use for anybody who disagreed with him on any point, no matter how small it was. He was a loving husband and a good father—and both his wives left him. . . . He had a gift for friendship such as few men have—he broke his oldest friend's heart like you'd throw away a cigarette you were through with."

Trump had his own insights into the film. "*Citizen Kane* was really about accumulation, and at the end, you see what happens, and it's not necessarily all positive," he reflected in a video interview with documentary maker Errol Morris in 2002. "He had the wealth, but he didn't have the happiness. The table getting larger and larger and larger with he and his wife getting further and further apart as he got wealthier and wealthier. Perhaps I can understand that. In real life, I believe that wealth does in fact isolate you from other people . . .

it's a protective mechanism. You have your guard up much more so than if you didn't have wealth."

Sitting as he did at his favorite table for four, the president may have been attempting to avoid Kane's fate. Trump didn't like big tables. He preferred a setting like this evening, with people crunched close together, yet with him in control of anyone who sought his company.

Trump needed to be the center of things, and with the powerful media and social media of the twenty-first century, he dominated the American consciousness the way nobody ever had. There was hardly any news any longer. There was just Trump. When the president got up early in the morning and turned on the TV, he didn't have to switch channels to hear about himself.

Palm Beach had been Trump's training ground. The president had studied hard and learned well. In the same way that he had divided the island into pro- and anti-Trump camps, he had largely transformed America into two nations, those who admired him for what they thought he was doing and those who loathed him for what they believed he was.

In Palm Beach, Trump had helped banish to the hinterlands the old elite who fancied that without class and manners, wealth was meaningless. Since time immemorial, philosophers and religious savants have said money does not bring happiness, but they had not met Donald J. Trump. Money is everything, and don't you forget it.

As president, Trump was seeking to educate the whole country in his university of wealth. By the time he left the White House, if things worked out the way he planned them, there would be Palm Beaches all across America where the royalty of new wealth lived together.

Other men would not have felt comfortable in the grand, overwrought surroundings of Mar-a-Lago, but the estate and its style were long familiar to Trump. He belonged here. He controlled everything within his purview. Most of the people in the room were his, too. Many of them had joined just so they could be close to him.

Trump focused on the conversation at his table, but he missed nothing on the verandah. As he looked beyond his table, he saw Kramer. He knew she would do anything to advance his presidency and ask nothing in return. As much as she revered Trump, she felt he was too focused on advancing his fellow billionaires and not enough on the rest of us, but that was nothing she was going to tell the president.

Behind Kramer sat Chris Ruddy with his guest. The Newsmax CEO had a far more nuanced take on Trump than would ever find its way into his public utterances. Ruddy asked little, either, and continued to defend the administration publicly. He kept to a narrow, twisting pathway, rarely veering off, but Ruddy could never be sure where he stood.

Trump enjoyed his pleasures, and so far he didn't appear to have given them up or even cut them down. Despite the burdens of the presidency, he lingered at the table. Mar-a-Lago had no royal edict that guests could not depart until the president got up to go, and most of the other diners had already left while the Trump party was still sitting there.

The evening might have ended earlier, but well after dessert, boxing promoter Don King appeared on the verandah, dressed as Uncle Sam. Often wearing a flamboyant outfit, King had been coming to Mar-a-Lago for years, but he had only joined a few months earlier and was the one black member of the club.

Years before, King had murdered two men. One of the killings was declared a "justifiable homicide," but the other was second-degree murder for beating one of his employees to death. He served almost four years in prison, a crime for which Governor Jim Rhodes of Ohio pardoned him. These were mistakes, glitches, and the world had long since moved on. During the campaign, while wearing a coat of many colors and a red-white-and-blue tie, King introduced candidate Trump in a church and let fly with the n-word. It was a mistake, a mere glitch, and the only thing the campaign could do was ignore it and move on.

King was the court jester always ready to tout the miracle of the reign of King Donald. He sat down at the Trump table and leaned forward to have an intimate conversation with the president of the United States. After a while, Trump had enough and gestured that he was leaving, causing everyone else in his party to get up.

Trump and Melania walked back to the family quarters past Kramer and Ruddy. King followed behind, shouting at the top of his lungs, "THE PRESIDENT!!! THE GREAT PRESIDENT!!!" In all of Mar-a-Lago's history, it's doubtful that anyone had ever yelled in such a loud voice. "THE PRESIDENT!!! THE GREAT PRESIDENT!!!"

As Trump and Melania turned and walked up the steps to the family quarters, King kept yelling, the sounds reverberating down the empty corridor.

Acknowledgments

My wife, Vesna Obradovic Leamer, made astute comments on several drafts of this book and took care of everything else in our lives so I could work more than full-time on this project. Beyond Vesna, I am blessed with a group of wonderful friends. Raleigh Robinson read so many versions of the manuscript, I would be embarrassed to list the number here if I even remembered. The historian Nigel Hamilton had many useful suggestions. My dear friend Father Hugh Duffy was always ready to discuss Trump, as was another close friend, the psychoanalyst Dr. Heath King, who earlier than almost anyone publicly predicted Trump would win the presidency. The late ambassador Faith Whittlesey was full of intriguing insights culled from her long career in Republican politics. At the end of the process another one of my longtime friends, the novelist Diane Leslie, gave the manuscript a last careful reading.

The Library of Congress, the Palm Beach County Library, and the District of Columbia Library all had useful information, as did the website newspapers.com. The Palm Beach Town Clerk's office dealt expeditiously with my requests, as did the public information officer at the Palm Beach Police Department. Nick Golubov, research director of the Historical Society of Palm Beach County, was helpful.

Among those who granted me on-the-record interviews or helped in other ways were: Earl Hollis, Toni Hollis, Patrick Park, Ronni Fingold, David

Fingold, Thom Smith, Daryl Davidoff, Ken Davidoff, Jo Ella Manalan, Melissa Legare, Judy Schrafft, Page Lee Hufty, Elaine De Bothuri, Alexandre De Bothuri, Brownie McLean, Gunita Singh, Eric Schultz, Bernie Schultz, David Schumacher, David A. Fahrenthold, Dan Moldea, Bob Kramer, Toni Holt Kramer, the late Howard Reed, the late Cecilia Farris Lipton, Bill Thomas, Bruce Bobbins, Moira Fiore, Jose Lambiet, Lois Romano, Frank Cerabino, the late Stanley Rumbough Jr., Paul Rampell, Barbara Marshall, Liz McNeil, Shannon Donnelly, Richard Haynes, Paul Onish, Judith Thibaut, Richard Cowell, Buffy Donlon, the late Liz Smith, William Martin, Richard René Silvin, Chris Ruddy, Laurel Baker, Ronald Jones, Gus Russo, Don Mendyk, the late Simon Fireman, Sean Bianca Lee, Nicholas Papanicolaou, Mike Morgan, Nick Leone, Nadine Epstein, Paulette Noble, Eva Weiss, Wes Blackman, Terry Vaccaro, Richard Rampell, James Oelsner, the late Robert Moore, Wayne Grover, Tony Senecal, Richard Grigonis, Etonella Christlieb, David Patrick Columbia, Dale Coudert, Steven Alembik, Bernard Goupy, Herb Gray, Mindy McGillivray, James Patterson, John Connolly, Torrance Harder, Samantha Fuentes, Carmen Cruz, Jack McDonald, Joan Parker, Alvin S. Felzenberg, Agnes Ash, Faustina Pace, Bruce Zeidel, Mark Hollingsworth, Nancy Lubin, Jack Blum.

My longtime agent, Joy Harris, was her usual indispensable self. One of the many things she did for this project was to bring in Henry A. Ferris Jr. to help shepherd the manuscript along. At Flatiron, editorial director Noah Eaker and editor James Melia took the manuscript through the editorial process with aplomb. I have been writing books for many years, and I have never been in better hands—and four of them at that. That said, I have little choice but to say that any weaknesses in this book are mine alone. I would like to say the cover was my idea, but the credit goes to art director Keith Hayes. Flatiron publicists Marlena Bittner and Amelia Possanza sail confidently through even the most treacherous media seas, and I am glad to be on board.

Notes

1. TRUMP'S PALM BEACH

1 The forty or so billionaires who winter: *Palm Beach Daily News*, March 6, 2018.

2 A parade of thirty-one vehicles sat: *Palm Beach Post*, February 4, 2017.

2 traffic on the state's: *Palm Beach Post*, February 4, 2017.

4 run around $130 million: *Washington Post*, March 17, 2017.

4 "I'm the king of Palm Beach": Timothy L. O'Brien, *TrumpNation: The Art of Being The Donald*, (2005), p. 181.

5 "the feel and look of Louis XIV": *Palm Beach Post*, January 2, 2005.

6 The waiters wore powdered wigs: *Palm Beach Daily News*, February 6, 2017.

6 three hundred protesters: Associated Press State Wire Florida, February 5, 2017.

6 a convicted felon who in 2001: *Akron Beacon Journal*, August 14, 2001; *Miami Herald*, February 6, 2017.

6 "fantastic man": *HuffPost*: January 29, 2016.

6 Seated next to Trump at his table: *Washington Post*, February 6, 2017.

7 "I don't think I've ever seen": Ibid.

7 The Red Cross spent $436,125: Town of Palm Beach Charitable Solicitation Permit No. T-16-00964, January 20, 2017. The Palm Beach County Red Cross refused to break down this figure, saying they were under no obligation to do so.

7 danced to "Old Time Rock and Roll": *New York Times*, February 6, 2017.

2. FANTASY ISLAND

8   Donald and Ivana Trump decided: "The Palm Beach Story" by Susan Goldberger, *House and Garden*, December 1989, pp. 110–119, and Donald J. Trump with Tony Schwartz, *Trump: The Art of the Deal* (1987), p. 25.

9   the palm-tree-bordered pathway: *Palm Beach Life*, April 2, 1907.

9   boarded a trolley car pulled by a mule: Alice DeLamar to Alva Johnson, March 14, 1948, Palm Beach Historical Society.

10   all seventeen hundred guests could sit down to dinner: Ibid.

10   moss-green carpeting and the pale-green tint: *Palm Beach Daily News*, January 17, 1902.

10   Mark Twain strolling: *Palm Beach Daily News*, March 28, 1902.

10   "To stand off and see": Henry James, *The American Scene* (1907), p. 426.

10   "This was the greatest ball": *Boston Post*, February 23, 1911.

11   "more wonderful than any palace": https://www.flaglermuseum.us/history /whitehall.

12   When the wooden Breakers burned down: https://www.thebreakers.com/about -breakers/.

12   in 1960 it became: https://www.flaglermuseum.us/history/whitehall.

12   "artificial life": "The Florida House: Mr. Addison Mizner, the Architect, Recounts the Birth of the new Florida Architecture," *Arts & Decoration*, January 1930, p. 40.

12   "a nunnery, with a chapel built into the lake": Donald W. Curl, *Palm Beach County: An Illustrated History* (1987), p. 61.

12   twenty-two wildly different window treatments: Judy DiEdwardo, "History: The Never-Ending Story," *Worth Avenue*, n.d., Palm Beach County Historical Society.

13   he oversaw eighteen major projects: *Palm Beach Post*, May 23, 1923.

13   "To him what was ugly": Alice DeLamar to Alva Johnson, March 14, 1948, Palm Beach County Historical Society.

13   When the Everglades Club got: "Best Friends: Jewish Society in Old Palm Beach" by Augustus Maynew, http://www.newyorksocialdiary.com/social-history/2008 /best-friends-jewish-society-in-old-palm-beach.

15   Trump's father took him on vacations: Gwenda Blair, *The Trumps* (2000), pp. 208–09.

16   "Well, the best thing by far is Mar-a-Lago": Donald J. Trump with Kate Bohner, *Trump: The Art of the Comeback* (1997), p. 61.

16   thirty-nine-member household staff: *Palm Beach Post*, September 6, 1990.

16   the enormous tax write-off: *Palm Beach Sun*, May 1981.

16   received between forty and fifty million dollars: *Washington Star-News*, September 26, 1973.

17   "providing a reasonable sale price": *Palm Beach Post*, June 18, 1989.

17   403 feet of the 456-foot parcel for $348,321: Ibid.

17   seventy-five-thousand-square-foot main house: Paul Rampell testimony at Town of Palm Beach Special Town Council Meeting, May 13, 1993.

17   to look too large: Nancy Rubin, *American Empress* (1995), p. 154.

18   propped up with a board: *Palm Beach Post*, January 7, 1995, and interview, Richard Haynes

18   fourteenth- and fifteenth-century Spanish tiles: Olympia Devine, *Mar-a-Lago: Ocean to Lake* (2016), p. 66.

18   walls were set ten coats of arms: Ibid., p. 68.

19   In Florence, fifteen artisans: Ibid., p. 89

19   mold had grown around it: *Palm Beach Post*, April 29, 1999.

20   decorated in the ornate, elaborate: Devine, *Mar-a-Lago*, pp. 139–42.

20   door handles shaped like squirrels: *Palm Beach Post*, April 24, 2005.

20   Urban minimized the foreboding: Interview, Rene Silvin.

20   an art deco sitting room: *Palm Beach Times*, March 28, 1985.

20   the Pavilion, built in the early sixties: Devine, *Mar-a-Lago*, p. 171.

21   to hire Ringling Bros.: Rubin, *American Empress*, p. 166.

21   hiding diamonds: *Palm Beach Daily News*, October 13, 1985.

22   invitations specified as "Daytime Dress": Augustus Mayhew, *Palm Beach: A Greater Grandeur* (2016), p. 64.

22   guests join hands and sing: History Sunday, *Palm Beach Post*, December 5 and 12, 1999.

23   sparkling, over-the-top glitz: "The 1990 Playboy Interview with Donald Trump" by Glenn Plaskin, *Playboy*, March 1990.

23   "posh ladies' powder-room décor": *New York Times*, May 6, 1984.

23   "maybe the greatest place": *Palm Beach Post*, May 24, 1987.

23   "I never thought it was": *Palm Beach Life*, July 1986.

23   twenty million dollars: *Miami Herald*, March 1, 1983.

3. ESTATE SALE

25   nine-million-dollar bid: *Palm Beach Daily News*, March 30, 1988.

25   Tax returns and other documents: https://www.washingtonpost.com/wp-stat/graphics/politics/trump-archive/docs/dge-report-to-ccc-oct-16-1981.pdf.

26   *The New York Times* found: *New York Times*, October 2, 2018.

26   already given his son: Ibid.

26   Trump called twenty-five-year-old *Forbes* reporter Jonathan Greenberg: *Washington Post*, April 20, 2018.

27   up to a million dollars: *Palm Beach Daily News*, January 3, 1985.

28   a pink Fabergé diadem: Interview, Judith Thibaut.

28   willing to pay twenty million dollars: *Palm Beach Daily News*, December 4, 1981.

28   purchase the estate for fourteen million dollars: *Palm Beach Daily News*, August 23, 1984.

28   "We have tried—God knows we": *Miami Herald*, November 14, 1984.

29   called his brother's wife: Interview, Judith Thibaut.

29   Scotsman had one serious stipulation: *Palm Beach Post*, June 18, 1989.

29   "Sometimes you play dirty": *Palm Beach Daily News*, March 4, 2001.

30   members of the Bath and Tennis: *Palm Beach Daily News*, October 8, 1989.

30   president of the Palm Beach Civic Association: *Palm Beach Daily News*, April 11, 1984.

30   estimated to be worth: *Palm Beach Daily News*, January 3, 1985.

30   "I was surprised, very surprised": *Palm Beach Daily News*, January 5, 1986.

31   got a commission: *Palm Beach Daily News*, April 17, 1986.

31   first dinner parties: *Palm Beach Daily News*, April 20, 1986.

31   hired Doyle: *Palm Beach Daily News*, June 1, 1986.

31   The remaining five hundred thousand dollars: *Miami Herald*, November 9, 1988.

31   as much as half a billion dollars: Interviews, Earl Hollis and Toni Hollis.

31   planning to construct: *Palm Beach Post*, November 25, 1985.

32   "Who's Who": *Palm Beach Daily News*, November 3, 1986.

32   "you can't respect people": *New York Times*, October 25, 2016.

32   "I generally find them to be": "Trump: The Soap" by John Taylor, *New York*, March 5, 1990.

33   "Will Trump, the parvenu": *Palm Beach Post*, May 18, 1986.

33   "People there are hoping": *Palm Beach Post*, January 27, 1986.

33   dating a Czech skier: Michael D'Antonio, *Never Enough* (2015), p. 171.

33   had been a top model: "That's Why the Lady Is a Trump" by Jonathan Van Meter, *Spy*, May 1989.

34   Their guest list: *Palm Beach Daily News*, February 7, 1986.

34   "It was mind-boggling": *Fort Lauderdale News*, March 8, 1986.

34   honorary chairman: *Palm Beach Daily News*, January 28, 1986.

35   "The Lucky Sperm Club": O'Brien, *TrumpNation*, p. 177.

35   only 350 guests could attend: *Palm Beach Daily News*, March 9, 1986.

35   could not take place: Ibid.

36   E. James Illenye, stood at the entrance: Ibid.

36   He called Ivana "Madame": *Palm Beach Daily News*, January 5, 1986.

36   Saudi Arabia's King Faisal: Ibid.

36   "There were some frowns": *Palm Beach Post*, May 12, 1986.

37   one evening at Le Club: Trump with Schwartz, *Trump: The Art of the Deal*, p. 97.

38   suspected a guest might have the disease: *Palm Beach Post*, July 3, 1990.

38   His partner that evening was Jay Taylor: Nicholas von Hoffman, *Citizen Cohn* (1988), p. 378.

38   guests included Chrysler CEO Lee Iacocca: Ibid.

39   Cuban Americans Alfonso and Tina: *Palm Beach Daily News*, April 20, 1986, and interview, Richard Cowell.

39   After dinner, when the waiters: "After the Gold Rush" by Marie Brenner, *Vanity Fair*, September 1, 1990, and interview, Richard Cowell.

39   "All of the top people": Interview, Richard Cowell.

41   walking with a cane: Interview, Richard Haynes.

41   "There was such beautiful": Ibid.

41   "Before the days": *Palm Beach Post*, January 27, 2002.

42   she sat up there: Interview, Richard Haynes.

42   even before he closed: *Palm Beach Daily News*, February 9, 1986.

42   "I'm a product of my": Interview, Buffy Donlon.

42   discovered nineteen sets of china: *Miami Herald*, February 23, 1986.

42   fifty-eight bedrooms: *Sun Sentinel*, March 8, 1986.

42   fifty-three thousand movable items: *Palm Beach Post*, January 3, 1986.

43   "Well, you just don't do those things": "Pop Goes the Donald" by James S. Kunen, *People*, July 9, 1990.

43   "They wouldn't let us": *Palm Beach Post*, September 6, 1990.

43   "steel rods up her nose": "Pop Goes the Donald" by James S. Kunen, *People*, July 9, 1990.

43   precious lace bedspread: *Austin American Statesman*, July 9, 1990.

43   "He liked to get in bed": Interview, Liz Smith.

43   Mercedes with its IVANA: *Palm Beach Daily News*, January 3, 1986.

43   made a sailor blush: Interviews, Buffy Donlon and Bruce Zeidel.

44   "Do you think if I wanted": "After the Gold Rush" by Marie Brenner, *Vanity Fair*, September 1990.

44   "I thought it would be good": Interview, James Oelsner.

44   Others gave Ivana's husband: Interviews, James Oelsner and Robert Moore.

4. TABLOID PRINCE

46   only a few great dealmakers: *Palm Beach Post*, March 7, 1987.

46   "He's the biggest thing": *Sun Sentinel*, October 20, 1986

46   $272,000 to $1.5 million: *Palm Beach Post*, December 7, 1986.

46   "It was unbelievable": *Miami Herald*, October 7, 1986.

47   this taught him enough: *Palm Beach Post*, December 16, 1990.

47   one-ton brass-and-granite: *Wall Street Journal*, November 7, 1986.

47   "I expect a great many": *Palm Beach Daily News*, October 22, 1986.

47   "Looking down at Palm Beach": *Palm Beach Daily News*, October 27, 1990.

47   "I wish I could" *Palm Beach Post*, May 24, 1987.

47 "Two blocks away they": *Wall Street Journal,* November 17, 1986.

48 "Donald has such a knack": *Palm Beach Post,* December 21, 1986.

48 "unbelievably well": *Palm Beach Daily News,* January 15, 1987.

49 "I will as soon as I get my money": Interview.

49 "unavoidably unavailable for trial": *Palm Beach Post,* September 6, 1987.

49 the judge ruled in Lewis's: *Scott Lewis Gardening and Trimming, Inc. v. Trump Palm Beaches Corp.,* Case No: MS-87-4995-RF, July 9, 1987.

50 wealthy new arrivals included: *Palm Beach Post,* January 8, 1988.

50 "Donald Trump started the trend": Ibid.

51 "A lot of young people": *Palm Beach Post,* November 2, 1987.

51 When Prince Charles flew: *USA Today,* February 16, 1989.

51 "For Christ's sake, Mary": Trump with Schwartz, *Trump: The Art of the Deal,* p. 80.

52 in 1981, there had been: *Palm Beach Daily News,* November 13, 1985.

53 a mere eight million dollars: *New York Times,* April 23, 2016.

54 "I wasn't invited": Interview.

54 landing on the helipad: *Palm Beach Daily News,* January 24, 1989, and *Orlando Sentinel,* January 24, 1989.

54 the thirty-one-person crew: *Palm Beach Post,* July 5, 1998.

54 "something in excess of 400 feet": *Los Angeles Times,* June 28, 1989.

55 "If he had offered $15 million": *Sun Sentinel,* April 1, 1988.

55 "Send him a bill for all": *Palm Beach Post,* June 8, 1989.

56 "That was my first wall": *Washington Post,* November 14, 2015.

57 HE GETS $10 MILLION ESTATE: "He Gets $10 Million Estate and $2 Million—For Just $2,812 in Cash!" by Wayne Grover, *National Enquirer,* November 29, 1988.

57 She gave Grover a quote: Norma I. Foederer to Wayne Grover, June 23, 1989.

57 "professional baseball teams asked him": Ibid.

57 "The most important influence": Trump with Schwartz, *Trump: The Art of the Deal,* p. 65.

58 "In the second grade": Trump with Schwartz, *Trump: The Art of the Deal,* p. 71.

58 remembered by fellow students: Interview, Paul Onish.

58 "I always loved to fight": *New York Times,* October 16, 2016.

58 DONALD TRUMP WAS AN AMAZING SUCCESS: "Donald Trump Was an Amazing Success—Even as a Teen" by Wayne Grover, *National Enquirer,* January 2, 1990.

58 "Palm Beach should riot over": *Palm Beach Post,* February 7, 1988.

59 "The problem was the Donald Trump thing": *Palm Beach Post,* November 10, 1988.

59 "Whenever I hear Palm Beachers": *Miami Herald,* January 29, 1989.

60 a week after the column: *Miami Herald,* March 19, 1989.

5. "IS THAT ALL THERE IS?"

61 "What was to dislike": Interview, Liz Smith.

62 One of his favorite songs: *New York Times*, October 25, 2016.

62 "Is That All There Is?": song written by Jerry Leiber and Mike Stoller.

63 "Instead of having a wife": *Howard Stern Show*, November 4, 1997.

63 "It was so cute, and then": *Howard Stern Show*, November 9, 1999.

63 "I couldn't stand it": *Howard Stern Show*, December 15, 2004.

64 He got a room at one: Interview, Wayne Grover.

64 "a beautiful structure": Donald Trump interview with Howard Stern on *Howard Stern E! Show*, May 8, 1993.

64 "You really have to think of yourself": O'Brien, *TrumpNation*, p. 216.

65 "I saw people taking advantage": "*Playboy* Interview: Donald Trump," *Playboy*, March 1990.

65 She asked herself: D'Antonio, *Never Enough*, p. 203.

66 "TRUMP'S MISTRESS: HE HID HER": "Trump's Mistress: He Hid Her for 3 Years—Then Wife Ivana Found Out!" by Steve Herz, Patricia Towle, Bennet Bolton, and Richard Taylor, *National Enquirer*, February 27, 1990.

66 "You bitch, leave my husband alone": "The Trumps Head for Divorce Court" by Mary H.J. Farrell, *People*, February 26, 1990.

67 "'Marla, it's over—we're breaking'": "'It's Over!'" by Steve Herz, Wayne Grover, and Patricia Towle, *National Enquirer*, March 6, 1990.

67 told Glover he never cried: Interview, Wayne Grover.

67 "the biggest thing that ever": *USA Today*, February 20, 1990.

69 "There's always a chance for reconciliation": *Chicago Tribune*, February 18, 1990.

69 two strolling violinists: *Palm Beach Post*, February 20, 1990.

69 Ivana stayed in Palm Beach: Ivana Trump, *Raising Trump* (2017), ebook.

69 "I always figure every man's": *Palm Beach Post*, February 16, 1990.

70 "Mr. Trump has a home": *USA Today*, February 21, 1990.

70 "Donald Trump's bankers have ordered": "Dump Marla" by Wayne Grover and Steve Herz, *National Enquirer*, June 19, 1990.

71 diminished stipend of $450,000: *New York Times*, June 25, 1990.

71 almost two-thirds of the respondents: *Palm Beach Post*, July 21, 1990.

71 two years behind on paying: *Palm Beach Post*, May 25, 1991.

71 $2.5 million annually: *Sun Sentinel*, July 3, 1990.

71 $100,625 in monthly interest: *Palm Beach Post*, August 24, 1990.

71 $413,000 a month: *Palm Beach Post*, August 24, 1990.

72 During the first five months: *Palm Beach Post*, June 7, 1990.

72 Trump's people jumped: *Palm Beach Post*, Ibid.

72 obligated for fourteen million dollars: *Palm Beach Post*, August 29, 1990.

72   the apartments had concrete walls: *Palm Beach Post*, December 16, 1990.

73   Trump paid five hundred thousand dollars to LFC Real Estate: *Miami Herald*, December 17, 1990.

73   "the worst day of my life": Donald Trump interview with Howard Stern on *Howard Stern E! Show*, May 8, 1993.

73   Rowanne Brewer, the 1989 "Miss Snap-On-Tools": *Palm Beach Daily News*, December 17, 1990.

74   "That is a stunning Trump girl, isn't it?": *New York Times*, May 14, 2016.

74   "Auctions are the wave of the future for real estate": *Palm Beach Post*, December 17, 1990.

74   mid-February only eleven of the thirty-five: *Palm Beach Post*, February 16, 1991.

74   a lawsuit in Palm Beach County: *Palm Beach Post*, April 3, 1991.

74   the more desirable: Donald Trump interview with Howard Stern on *Howard Stern E! Show*, May 8, 1993.

74   Trump invited seventy-five local real estate: *Palm Beach Post*, February 19, 1991.

75   total of $13.56 million: *Palm Beach Post*, April 29, 1991.

75   "I came out fine on everything": *Miami Herald*, April 29, 1991.

75   for him to unload: *Sun Sentinel*, April 30, 1991.

75   One Sunday, Robert Moore, the town: Trump with Bohner, *Trump: The Art of the Comeback*, p. 68, and interview, Robert Moore.

76   "Those of us on the town": Interview, Robert Moore.

77   a large number of people came forward: *Palm Beach Daily News*, May 18, 1991.

77   "If anyone else but Donald Trump": *Washington Post*, August 6, 1991.

77   no one had ever publicly thanked him: Ibid.

77   several gifts, including a picture: Ibid.

77   "Best thing they could do": Ibid.

78   "some interesting people who aren't": *Palm Beach Daily News*, May 23, 1991.

78   estate as a retreat: *Palm Beach Daily News*, May 24, 1991.

78   an outright rejection of Trump's plan: *Palm Beach Post*, May 24, 1991.

78   "absolutely no interest": Ibid.

78   Grover attended meetings: Interviews.

79   "We believe, that if some form": *Palm Beach Daily News*, August 8, 1991.

80   "hocus-pocus, sleight-of-hand": *Palm Beach Post*, August 17, 1991.

80   "ridiculous": Ibid.

80   "All the others": *Palm Beach Daily News*, April 17, 1992.

81   "My only question": *Palm Beach Daily News*, April 17, 1992.

81   belonged to organizations opposed: *Palm Beach Daily News*, July 12, 1992.

6. THE FORBIDDEN CITY

83 "kind of like the forbidden city": Interview, Paul Rampell.

84 "Club members will come": Ibid.

84 "The town of Palm Beach is": Ibid.

85 The group decided that: *Palm Beach Life,* April 1979.

85 the Nazis' Nuremberg Race Laws: https://www.ushmm.org/outreach/en/article .php?ModuleId=10007695.

86 one of the boys: Interview, Paul Onish.

86 often to the Concord: "Growing Up Trump: How Donald Trump's Youthful Encounters with Jews Helped Shape the Man, and President, He Is Today" by Marc Fisher, *Moment Magazine,* June/July 2017.

87 "Think of it like you're": *Palm Beach Daily News,* March 28, 1993.

87 "I don't think anti-Semitism": *Palm Beach Daily News,* May 2, 1993.

88 "What, what, WHAT was *Donald Trump*": *Palm Beach Daily News,* January 31, 1993.

89 He drove an ancient, battered Toyota: Interview, Frank Cerabino.

89 one of the nineteen valets moved: Minutes of Palm Beach Town Council Special Meeting, May 13, 1993.

89 Wayne Grover got out of his car: Interview, Wayne Grover.

90 twenty-second straight time: *Palm Beach Daily News,* February 1, 1993.

90 "Come on, admit it": Ibid.

90 "far too properly deported": Ibid.

90 "Trump's inside the": *Palm Beach Post,* January 31, 1993.

91 "He went nuclear on us": *Palm Beach Post,* February 3, 1993.

91 Trump pushed Franzo's: "Trump Makes a Splash!" by Wayne Grover, *National Enquirer,* February 16, 1993, and Interview, Wayne Grover.

91 driving his Jeep Cherokee: *Palm Beach Post,* February 2, 1993.

92 "bemoaning the lack": *Palm Beach Post,* January 21, 1993.

92 "Are you kidding me?": Interview, Frank Cerabino.

92 "Trump just called me": Ibid.

92 shooting a 3-over-par 75: *Santa Cruz Sentinel,* February 6, 1993.

93 "Wayne, I just scored two holes": Interview, Wayne Grover.

94 charged a heady $125 a person: *Palm Beach Post,* February 19, 1993.

94 "Maybe we'll do this": *Palm Beach Daily News,* February 19, 1993.

94 "It will guarantee": *Palm Beach Daily News,* February 20, 1993.

95 headed out to their cars: Minutes of Palm Beach Town Council Special Meeting, May 13, 1993.

95 "I've heard what you're doing with this school": Interview, Etonella Christlieb.

95 "It may have been my fault": *Palm Beach Daily News,* February 28, 1993.

96 Royal triumphed in the March runoff: *Palm Beach Daily News,* March 10, 1993.

96   when she believed she became pregnant: "Trump to Wed Pregnant Marla" by Wayne Grover, Patricia Towel, and Bennet Bolton, *National Enquirer,* April 27, 1993.

96   ten guest rooms: *Palm Beach Daily News,* May 9, 1993.

96   a storage area: *Palm Beach Daily News,* March 13, 1993.

96   "the wedding of the century": "Trump to Wed Pregnant Marla," by Wayne Grover, Patricia Towel, and Bennet Bolton, *National Enquirer,* April 27, 1993.

96   the marriage was off: *National Enquirer,* May 18, 1993.

96   could be with Marla five days: "Are We Having Fun Yet, Marla?" by Wayne Grover, *National Enquirer,* July 20, 1993.

96   "could leave one legacy to Palm Beach": *Palm Beach Daily News,* May 14, 1993.

97   "Another question that's often": Minutes of Palm Beach Town Council Special Meeting, May 13, 1993.

97   "Mr. Trump's close association": Minutes of Palm Beach Town Council Special Meeting, May 13, 1993.

97   he began by saying: Minutes of Palm Beach Town Council Special Meeting, May 13, 1993.

98   "Mar-a-Lago was Trump's": Interview.

99   "If the preservation easements are": Minutes of Palm Beach Town Council Special Meeting, August 12, 1993.

99   worth more than one hundred million dollars: *Palm Beach Post,* December 21, 2017.

99   more than two hundred million dollars: In the last three years alone, the Mar-a-Lago Club profits were $82.6 million. http://www.businessinsider.com/how-much-does -trump-make-on-maralago-financial-disclosure-2017-2017-6.

7. "A T-BONE IN A KENNEL"

100   clicking away while Trump: "Are We Having Fun Yet, Marla?" by Wayne Grover, *National Enquirer,* July 20, 1993.

100   Trump and Maples showed: Interview, Wayne Grover.

101   "Watching our baby's birth": "Donald's Baby" by Wayne Grover, *National Enquirer,* November 2, 1993.

101   The editors avoided: *Palm Beach Daily News,* October 14, 1993.

101   "When I look at Trump Plaza": *Palm Beach Daily News,* November 14, 1993.

102   "**Marla Maples:** Miss America looks": *Palm Beach Daily News,* November 7, 1993.

103   "Larry, do you really": Interview, Wayne Grover.

103   "I was bored when she": O'Brien, *TrumpNation,* p. 7.

103   "I give this marriage": Interviews.

103   placed a Maples's life-size cardboard: O'Brien, *TrumpNation,* p. 203.

104   "What's going on?": *Palm Beach Daily News,* December 11, 1994.

104 "the town government is in": *Palm Beach Daily News*, December 4, 1994.

104 "There's a lot of resistance": *Palm Beach Post*, November 28, 1994.

104 bringing in the sorts of people: *Palm Beach Daily News*, December 1, 1994.

104 laws of the island: *Palm Beach Daily News*, December 6, 1994.

105 "the notorious New York developer": *Palm Beach Post*, November 28, 1994.

105 flew a Mustang fighter: *Palm Beach Daily News*, January 2, 2005.

105 Rumbough believed that: Interview, Stanley Rumbough.

105 "that by your actions, words": *Palm Beach Daily News*, December 22, 1994.

105 he hosted a fund-raiser: *Palm Beach Daily News*, February 14, 1994.

106 "It was a challenge to work": Interview, Wes Blackman.

106 He came over to Rampell's house: Interviews.

107 "I lost 25 pounds": "Trump loses 25 lbs. & wins $200,000 bet" by Wayne Grover, *National Enquirer*, December 10, 1996.

107 He wanted to expand: Interview, Paul Rampell.

108 "You know, there's some other properties": Interview, Paul Rampell.

108 two hundred acres owned by the Palm Beach: *Palm Beach Post*, January 12, 1994.

108 "This might work": Interview, Paul Rampell.

108 would lease the land: *Palm Beach Post*, May 28, 1994.

108 reconfigured to serve seventy-five dinner guests: *Palm Beach Post*, November 28, 1994.

108 removing the unread: *New York Times*, March 15, 2016.

108 the unwanted furniture: Interview, Tony Senecal.

108 only around 4 percent: *Palm Beach Daily News*, March 31, 1995.

109 "If I'd known": Interview, Tony Senecal.

109 "the Streisand factor": *Palm Beach Daily News*, March 31, 1995.

109 minor collectibles sold for a total: *Palm Beach Daily News*, July 16, 1995.

109 Christmas lights with broken bulbs: *Palm Beach Daily News*, April 19, 1995.

109 "CHARLES, DIANA JOIN MAR-A-LAGO CLUB": *Palm Beach Daily News*, December 26, 1994.

110 "'Liar, liar, pants on fire'": *Palm Beach Daily News*, December 30, 1994.

110 membership director misunderstood: *Palm Beach Post*, January 8, 1995.

111 Gloria Swanson in *Sunset Boulevard*: *New York Times Magazine*, March 12, 1995.

111 "I can state with great": *New York Times*, April 23, 1995.

8. THE PROMISES OF LIFE

112 twenty workers spent six months: *Palm Beach Daily News*, December 11, 1995.

112 brought in seventy-two thousand watts of additional: Ibid.

112 "People can't believe": Ibid.

113 most of the first one hundred: Interview.

113 "I had half a dozen clients": Interview, Richard Rampell.

113 "Half of his body was out": Interview.

113 where professional dancers dressed as flappers: *The Mar-a-Lago Club: The Jewel of Palm Beach* (1996).

114 Those who could not squeeze in: *Palm Beach Post,* December 10, 1995.

114 "It was a scene out of *The Great Gatsby*": *Palm Beach Daily News,* December 11, 1995.

114 "I'm very pleased that the club": Ibid.

115 "I don't want to go back there": Interview, Celia Lipton Farris.

115 Robert Montgomery Jr., had earned $206 million: *New York Times,* August 8, 2008.

115 "It's quite simple. If you've got the dough": *The Mar-a-Lago Club: The Jewel of Palm Beach.*

115 "seemingly has done more": Ibid.

116 "Donald and I are cut out of the same cloth": Ibid.

116 "In championships, he's a chronic cheater": Interview.

116 "Those early years, it was": Interview.

117 Joseph Visconti paid twenty-five thousand dollars: *Palm Beach Post,* December 9, 1995.

117 "Obviously, he needs money": Ibid.

117 "false and defamatory statements": *Palm Beach Daily News,* December 29, 1995.

117 Visconti caved: *Palm Beach Daily News,* February 29, 1996.

118 he brought members: Interview.

118 "whether Florida's Native Americans": *Palm Beach Daily News,* March 24, 1996.

118 "Every time we flew to Palm Beach": Interview, Mike Donovan.

119 "This doesn't pass the smell test": *The New York Times,* October 2, 2018.

119 "I felt that's what": http://people.com/tv/marla-maples-opens-up-about-life-after-split-from-donald-trump/.

119 "Look," Grover said, "we've got this story": Interview, Wayne Grover.

120 "SHOCK FOR TRUMP! MARLA": "Marla Caught With Hunk," no byline, *National Enquirer,* May 7, 1996.

121 "Along the lines of Elvis": *New York Daily News,* April 27, 1996.

121 "Any man would be shocked": "Trump & Marla Talk About That Beach Scandal," by Larry Haley, *National Enquirer,* May 14, 1996.

121 Leone Jr. brought him food: Interview, Nick Leone.

121 "MY SECRET AFFAIR WITH MARLA": *Palm Beach Daily News,* November 5, 1997, and *New Jersey Courier-News,* November 3, 1997.

121 died of a drug overdose: www.insideedition.com/headlines/16130-trump-body-guard-once-accused-of-having-affair-with-marla-maples-never-got-over-the-scandal.

122 "discriminatory, unfair": *Palm Beach Daily News,* May 11, 1996.

122 "We've always felt": *Palm Beach Daily News*, May 11, 1996.

123 "TRUMP RIPS PALM BEACH JEW-HATERS": *Palm Beach Daily News*, September 21, 1996.

123 "Sending out *Gentleman's Agreement*": Interview, Robert Moore.

123 "crude effort to interject anti-Semitism": *Palm Beach Daily News*, September 21, 1996.

123 "We proudly have Jewish members": *Palm Beach Daily News*, September 18, 1996.

123 CEO of a major corporation: *Palm Beach Daily News*, January 22, 1995.

124 offering him a free Mar-a-Lago membership: Interview.

124 a lease on 214 acres of scrubland: *Palm Beach Post*, September 4, 1996.

124 "THERE IS NO DISCRIMINATION": *Palm Beach Daily News*, September 18, 1996.

124 "I'm very proud of what's": *Palm Beach Daily News*, September 21, 1996.

124 "non-discriminatory fashion": Minutes of Palm Beach Town Council, September 16, 1996.

125 "You forgot scratch golfer": *Palm Beach Daily News*, September 21, 1996.

125 156 letters received in Town Hall: *Palm Beach Daily News*, October 10, 1996.

125 they should step down: *Palm Beach Daily News*, November 5, 1996.

126 "To listen to the trash": *Palm Beach Daily News*, December 21, 1996.

126 "In our view, raising the": *Palm Beach Daily News*, October 6, 1996.

126 "All they [ADL] would have to do": Ibid.

126 "Abe, it's anti-Semitism": *Jerusalem Post*, September 19, 2016.

9. THE CONTEST

127 Oprah Winfrey staged: *Palm Beach Post*, April 6, 2008.

128 "Donald Trump will be giving": *Palm Beach Daily News*, November 28, 1996.

128 "I love getting even": *Charlie Rose*, November 6, 1992.

128 "Let's make a deal": http://www.palmbeachdailynews.com/lifestyles/before-twitter
-name-calling-letter-from-donald-trump/KaGSV40cQnefESyXhe5CuN/.

128 Leone was the overwhelming: Interview, Nick Leone.

129 "I'm sorry to see you go": Ibid.

129 "Trump's ego is everything": Ibid.

129 When Trump gave Lembcke: Interview.

130 "I am no cow or something like that": *Palm Beach Post*, February 16, 1997.

130 "After a long relationship and": *New York Times*, May 3, 1997.

130 their prenuptial agreement: *Orlando Sentinel*, May 16, 1997.

131 two and a half billion people worldwide: *Tampa Bay Times*, May 18, 1997.

131 Miss Utah Temple Taggart recalls Trump: *New York Times*, May 14, 2016.

131 "They were like zombies": Interview.

132 "Wait until you see my date": Interview.

132 six-foot-tall Victoria Silvstedt: *Palm Beach Daily News*, November 23, 1997.

132   Playmate of the Year: *Philadelphia Inquirer,* February 20, 1997.

132   "a smooth, soft outer layer of skin": *St. Louis Post-Dispatch,* December 13, 2001.

132   he threw Silvstedt: *Palm Beach Daily News,* November 23, 1997, and Interview.

132   "would constantly criticize me": Trump with Bohner, *Trump: The Art of the Come-back,* p. 64.

133   Rumbough wanted to get: Interview, Stanley Rumbough.

133   "How lovely": *Palm Beach Daily News,* November 9, 1997.

133   "who used himself mainly": Philip Roth, *American Pastoral* (1997), p. 29.

133   "What are you guys doing?": Interview.

133   Mar-a-Lago's Super Bowl party in January 1998: My sources are Mar-a-Lago members who were present. Their best recollection is that this took place in 1998, but there is no documentation.

134   "Give me your apron": Interview.

134   homes had been torn down: *Palm Beach Post,* January 31, 2014.

136   "I don't know if it's a good": Interview, Tony Senecal.

136   He set up a ten-thousand-square foot: *Palm Beach Daily News,* October 24, 2004.

136   violating the rule eleven times: *Palm Beach Post,* June 10, 1999.

136   Mar-a-Lago's director of projects wrote a letter: Wes Blackman to Robert Sterling, April 3, 1999, Palm Beach town archives.

137   "After you asked to come": Donald J. Trump to Alyne Massey, April 8, 1999, Palm Beach town archives.

137   Trump had sued Palm Beach: *Palm Beach Daily News,* December 21, 1996.

137   town council gave him almost: *Palm Beach Post,* October 14, 1999.

138   "If I were to write a newspaper": *Palm Beach Daily News,* October 15, 1999.

138   celebrating the beginning: *Sun Sentinel,* January 1, 2000.

138   Thirty pounds of caviar: *Sun Sentinel,* January 1, 2000.

139   "Melania was quiet": Interview.

139   set up their satellite trucks: *Palm Beach Post,* January 2, 2000.

140   royal palms for only three hundred dollars: *Palm Beach Post,* January 5, 2000.

140   at a cost of three million dollars: Ibid.

140   Trump bought him a set: Interview, Richard Haynes.

140   just broken up with Melania: *Palm Beach Post,* January 12, 2000.

140   Trump fired Fink: *Palm Beach Post,* January 14, 2000.

141   instituted a mock campaign: *Palm Beach Post,* February 27, 1998.

141   "3-foot-long rubber item": *Palm Beach Post,* May 20, 1998.

141   One of his favorites: *Palm Beach Post,* May 2, 1999.

141   "The green fees for one round": *Palm Beach Post,* January 8, 2000.

141   "Perhaps Mr. Cerabino has problems": *Palm Beach Post,* January 13, 2000.

141   "Can I join you guys for dessert?": Interview, Frank Cerabino.

10. A PROPER PRESIDENT

143   "One man could turn": Michael Kranish and Marc Fisher, *Trump Revealed* (2016), p. 257.

144   "Let's not let our great": Kranish and Fisher, *Trump Revealed*, p. 259.

144   "He's going to have": *Palm Beach Daily News*, November 12, 1999.

144   "It is nonsensical for someone": *Palm Beach Daily News*, October 10, 1999.

144   "If you don't win, what is the point?": *National Post*, January 15, 2000.

144   spotted in the VIP room: *Sun Sentinel*, January 19, 2000.

145   been indicted for murder and robbery: *Miami Herald*, December 4, 1999.

145   "The Reform Party is a complete mess": *Chicago Tribune*, February 14, 2000.

145   primaries in California and Michigan: Kranish and Fisher, *Trump Revealed*, p. 271.

146   That evening Trump marched into the kitchen: Interview, Bernard Goupy.

146   "swearing like a truck driver": *Sun Sentinel*, February 11, 2004.

147   "Trump tips well if someone": Interview.

148   "You have been abusing numerous": *Palm Beach Daily News*, February 5, 2010.

148   held on to his: *Sun Sentinel*, October 30, 2012.

149   Rybolovlev watched the 1987: Russian *Forbes*, May 3, 2008.

149   Rybolovlev's attorneys made: Ibid., and research materials of the British journalist Mark Hollingsworth.

149   sold for a total of $71.34 million: *Palm Beach Daily News*, October 6, 2017.

149   about having to spend twenty million dollars: *Sun Sentinel*, October 3, 2006.

150   brought tour groups: Reuters.com, March 17, 2017.

150   "a cultural attaché": Elena Baronoff's LinkedIn profile.

150   $98.4 million dollars buying: Reuters.com, March 17, 2017.

151   Anatoly Golubchik and Michael Sall: *USA Today*, March 28, 2017.

151   "The Russian Hand of Donald Trump": https://twitter.com/riotwomennn/status /911704785405046784

151   Pecker joined Mar-a-Lago: "The *National Enquirer*'s Fervor for Trump" by Jeffrey Toobin, *The New Yorker*, July 3, 2017.

152   "the Bath & Tennis Club's deplorable truck dock loading area": *Palm Beach Daily News*, January 21, 2002.

152   "You should air-condition the kitchen": *Palm Beach Daily News*, October 10, 2002.

152   B&T agreed to put up hedges: *Palm Beach Daily News*, December 12, 2002.

11. THE APPRENTICE

153   "He knows what to say": *Palm Beach Daily News*, January 10, 2004.

154   "It wasn't easy being his child": Interview, Mike Donovan.

154   "From what I've seen": Donald Trump with Charles Leerhsen, *Trump: Surviving at the Top* (1990), p. 24.

155 Top chef Jean-Georges Vongerichten: *New York Times,* January 13, 2005.

155 Rev. Leo Frade, the bishop of Southeast Florida: *Palm Beach Post,* January 26, 2005.

155 "The wedding may come": *Palm Beach Post,* January 6, 2005.

156 members of the audience applauded: *Sun-Sentinel,* January 22, 2005.

156 a chauffeured Rolls-Royce: Pat O'Brien, *I'll Be Back After This* (2016), p. 272.

157 candelabras wreathed in white roses: *Palm Beach Daily News,* January 24, 2005.

157 The newlyweds entered the ballroom: *Palm Beach Post,* January 24, 2005.

157 O'Brien got so loudly drunk: O'Brien, *I'll Be Back After This,* p. 273.

157 had fought as a mechanic: Interviews, Ronald Jones and Don Mendyk.

158 copies of antiques: *Palm Beach Post,* June 4, 2006.

158 that came to $33,997: *Palm Beach Post,* February 18, 2005.

158 "When Mr. Trump came to buy": *Palm Beach Post,* January 26, 2005.

158 "You want a story": *Palm Beach Post,* January 28, 2005.

159 "stiffed in the past": New York *Daily News,* February 2, 2005.

159 "It would not surprise me": Interview, Don Mendyk.

159 served him with papers: "Here's How Trump (Allegedly) Stiffed an 82-Year-Old Immigrant over an Unpaid Bill" by Stephanie Mencimer, *Mother Jones,* June 10, 2016.

159 filing his own suit: *Palm Beach Post,* March 11, 2005.

159 "much less than we sought": Interview, Ronald Jones.

160 "The Red Cross said": Interview, Simon Fireman.

161 had risen from 65,000 to 430,000: *Wall Street Journal,* May 20, 2005.

161 Sydell Miller, an early Mar-a-Lago member: *The Mar-a-Lago Club Official Club Newsletter,* 2016.

161 building an 84,626-square-foot structure: Palm Beach County Property Records.

161 he demolished Four Winds: *Wall Street Journal,* May 20, 2005.

161 "Palm Beach to me": "Palm Beach" by Bob Colacello, *Vanity Fair,* February 2004, p. 137.

162 just happened to take place at the Breakers: *Palm Beach Post,* January 19, 2005.

162 "We have twenty-six ambassadors": *Palm Beach Daily News,* January 31, 2005.

162 "People here are worried": *Wall Street Journal,* May 20, 2005.

162 "SIMON FIREMAN: INNOVATOR, LEADER, HUMANITARIAN": Ibid.

163 also sold them: Interview, Chris Ruddy.

163 "Yes, these people give money": Interview, Shannon Donnelly.

163 "I took the Palm Beach County Red": Ibid.

163 "The marines were there": *The Howard Stern Show,* July 16, 2008.

164 Only Trump and one other man jumped: The author was the other person.

164 "I thought he died": *The Howard Stern Show,* July 16, 2008.

164 "There's a lesson in timing here": *Palm Beach Daily News,* February 1, 2006.

165   he decided not to pay: *Palm Beach Post*, January 17, 2007.

165   "There's nothing in writing": Interview, Simon Fireman.

165   "Bring a pretty girl": Interviews, Daryl and Ken Davidoff.

166   "You know, Mr. Trump, the money"; Interview, Daryl Davidoff.

166   Her lawyer called: Interview, Ken Davidoff.

167   "it surely disturbs the view": *Palm Beach Daily News*, October 22, 2006.

167   four times the maximum: *Palm Beach Post*, October 6, 2006.

167   "He should know": *Palm Beach Daily News*, December 24, 2006.

168   "Most U.S. cities would be ashamed": *Palm Beach Daily News*, December 24, 2006.

168   twenty instances where flags violated: *Palm Beach Post*, January 19, 2007.

168   "I think the returning wounded": *Palm Beach Daily News*, January 8, 2007.

168   imposing a $1,250-a-day penalty: *Palm Beach Daily News*, January 19, 2007.

168   Trump's flagpole could be: *Palm Beach Daily News*, April 22, 2007.

168   Tax records show that little: *Washington Post*, September 20, 2016.

169   contributed $4,055,000 to be given: The Donald J. Trump Foundation, Form 990-PF, Return of Private Foundation, 2007.

169   "The most important thing is that": The author was present and recorded the talk.

12. TRUMPED AGAIN

171   against his stern advice: *The Howard Stern Show*, January 13, 1997.

171   Ivana knew he was really: Ivana Trump, *Raising Trump*, p. 237.

171   "I'd rather be a babysitter": Ivana Trump, *Raising Trump*, pp. 234–235.

172   waived the twenty thousand dollars he would: Ivana Trump, *Raising Trump*, p. 236.

172   Getty to pay her $250,000: *Sunday Independent* (Dublin), March 30, 2008.

172   "She's got some mileage on her": *Palm Beach Daily News*, April 16, 2008.

172   "And, Rossano, we are in the": *Palm Beach Post*, April 16, 2008.

172   Two months after the wedding: Ivana Trump, *Raising Trump*, p. 238.

173   setting a spigot of water: Interview, and Mark Bowden, "The Art of the Deal," *Playboy*, May 1997.

173   "a major lawsuit against you": *Palm Beach Daily News*, June 28, 2009.

173   "Over the years we have had": Ibid.

173   no choice but to sue: Murray Fox v. Mar-a-Lago Club in the Circuit Court in Palm Beach County, Florida. Action dismissed with prejudice, August 3, 2010.

173   "continued to issue new memberships": *Palm Beach Daily News*, June 28, 2009.

174   "Nobody wants to play tennis": Interview.

174   "Didn't your lawyer object?": Interview.

174   "Murray's had two heart attacks": Interview.

175   "new information": *Palm Beach Daily News*, May 25, 2011.

175   fled the island: *Palm Beach Daily News*, April 25, 2012.

176   crystal and fine silver for $7.37 an hour: *Palm Beach Post*, December 23, 2007.

176   serving a twenty-year sentence: *Palm Beach Post*, February 21, 2008.

177   "Paul took me under his wing": Interview, Melissa Legare.

177   "This suit will uncover": *Palm Beach Post*, February 21, 2008.

177   those with criminal records: *Melissa Legare, Plaintiff, vs. The Everglades Club Inc., Defendant* in the Circuit Court of Palm Beach County, February 20, 2000.

177   "In my opinion, there will be": *Palm Beach Daily News*, December 21, 2008.

178   Trump received the Palm Tree Award: *Palm Beach Daily News*, January 17, 2010.

178   as would be reported in September 2016: *Washington Post*, September 10, 2016.

179   a magnificent $200,000 contribution: https://projects.propublica.org/nonprofits /organizations/133404773.

179   Of the $706,000 paid out: *Palm Beach Post*, July 6, 2018.

179   as much as $150,000: *Boston Globe*, September 26, 2016.

179   "You can always tell": *New York Times*, January 1, 2017.

179   "It's a slice of a billionaire's": Interview, Ronni Fingold.

180   "Which one of you is Thom Smith?": Interview, Thom Smith.

181   "He comes from Martin": Interview, Moira Fiore.

181   In January 2015, Trump sued: *Palm Beach Daily News*, January 10, 2015.

181   kept mentioning one hundred thousand dollars: *Mar-a-Lago Club, L.L.C., vs. Palm Beach County, Florida*, March 2, 2016, p. 13.

182   a record $29.8 million: http://www.businessinsider.com/how-much-does-trump -make-on-maralago-financial-disclosure-2017-2017-6.

182   "He'd probably run the country": *Palm Beach Post*, March 27, 2011.

182   tied with former: *Albuquerque Journal*, April 16, 2011.

183   "If he wasn't born": https://www.cnn.com/2016/09/09/politics/donald-trump -birther/index.html.

183   turning his back on the liberal: Joshua Green, *Devil's Bargain: Steve Bannon, Donald Trump, and the Nationalist Uprising* (2017), ebook.

185   "I thought Obama was the Manchurian": Interview.

186   "This was one of the first": Interview, Chris Ruddy.

186   "Yes, Mr. Trump": Ibid.

186   "show business over substance": *Palm Beach Daily News*, December 14, 2011.

187   "You don't know what the fuck": Interview, Chris Ruddy.

187   proclaimed that he was leaving: *The Rachel Maddow Show*, December 27, 2011, and *Seattle Post-Intelligencer*, December 23, 2011.

188   he would stay in at least long enough: Interview.

189   who had made his fortune: Discussion, Bob Kramer.

13. THE CANDIDATE

190   according to court documents: *The United States of America v. Michael Cohen*. This charging document does not mention Donald Trump and David Pecker by name, but it is obvious that is who are the subjects; https://www.documentcloud.org /documents/4779697-Michael-Cohen-Charging-Documents.html.

191   disliked by 70 percent of Americans: *New York Times*, June 15, 2015.

192   media mogul Rupert Murdoch: Interview and "Rupert Murdoch Wants to Stop Donald Trump, But First He's Got to Rein in Roger Ailes" by Gabriel Sherman, *New York*, July 22, 2015.

192   Fox News used the crucial: Interview and "Donald Trump's Newest Enemy: Fox News" by Gabriel Sherman, *New York*, August 7, 2015.

193   Barron was usually shy: *New York Post*, December 26, 2015, and interview.

194   "You're going to be able": Interview, Father Hugh Duffy.

195   only five residents had contributed: *Sun Sentinel*, March 27, 2016.

195   "We do not need reality TV": https://www.politico.com/blogs/2016-gop-primary -live-updates-and-results/2016/02/chris-christie-endorsement-donald-trump -shouldnt-be-president-219864.

196   his retired butler Senecal: *Irish Times*, March 19, 2016.

196   Trump walked outside: The author was present.

196   what he called "garbage": *Palm Beach Post*, March 20, 2016.

198   "dragging that ball-less dick head": "On Facebook, Trump's Longtime Butler Calls for Obama to Be Killed," by David Corn, *Mother Jones*, May 12, 2016.

199   "Maybe he gets hit by a truck": *Washington Post*, July 24, 2018. The author has shortened the transcript.

199   "One of the worst things [Trump] said": *New York Times*, September 27, 2016.

200   ten women to come forward: New York *Daily News*, October 15, 2016.

200   Cathy Heller recalled an incident: *Guardian*, October 13, 2016.

200   "Melania followed him": Interview, Mindy McGillivray, and *Palm Beach Post*, October 13, 2016.

201   "Donald just grabbed my ass": Interviews, Mindy McGillivray and Ken Davidoff.

201   "You know we're going": Physically Attacked by Donald Trump—a PEOPLE Writer's Own Harrowing Story" by Natasha Stoynoff, *People*, October 12, 2016.

201   "like many women, I was ashamed": Ibid.

202   left her apartment: *Palm Beach Post*, October 14, 2016.

202   "our superman Trump": *Palm Beach Daily News*, October 29, 2016.

202   "Trump is, in his way": http://rackjite.com/daily-show-desi-lydic-makes-a-fool-of -trumpette-toni-holt-kramer-wink-martindale/.

203   more than 250 members: *Palm Beach Daily News*, November 9, 2016.

203   "I'm surprised you won": Interview, Chris Ruddy.

204   were 150 Secret Service personnel: *NBC Nightly News,* November 23, 2016.

204   coast guard boats monitoring: TCA Regional News, November 24, 2016.

204   "It is my prayer that": AFT International, November 23, 2016.

205   claiming that Peerenboom: *Hollywood Reporter,* June 16, 2017.

205    $275,000 and $450,000: Palm Beach Town Application for Permit to Solicit Funds for Charitable Purposes for 2010, 2011, and 2012.

205   two fifty-foot-long Lois Pope Red Star Rescue vehicles: PR Newswire, May 23, 2015.

206   "I want to set an example": *Palm Beach Daily News,* May 31, 2015.

206   "How does flying or busing": *Sun Sentinel,* June 3, 2015.

206   "big smile came over": *Washington Post,* December 6, 2016.

14. THE SUN KING

208   "corporate lobbyists for Carlos Slim": *Roll Call,* October 16, 2016.

208   "great guy": *Independent,* December 22, 2016.

208   "just a block from the White House": *Washington Post,* December 22, 2016.

208   gold-flecked sofa beneath a glittery chandelier: *New York Times,* January 2, 2017, and interviews.

209   switched seamlessly to the national anthem: *Palm Beach Post,* December 27, 2016.

209   Later that evening: *Washington Post,* December 25, 2016.

209   "Hear, hear!" some shouted: *Palm Beach Daily News,* December 26, 2016.

210   thirty-four Secret Service officers: *Palm Beach Daily News,* November 27, 2016.

210   "Happy New Year to all, including": http://www.trumptwitterarchive.com/archive, December 31, 2016.

210   "It was dishonest media": *Boston Herald,* January 2, 2017.

211   about 920 Secret Service personnel: https://www.nbcnews.com/news/us-news/cost -protecting-jet-setting-president-elect-trump-yuge-n687336, November 23, 2016.

213   entering the plane: White House pool coverage, http://www.presidency.ucsb.edu /report.php?pid=630, February 10, 2017.

213   Christie sensed the fine hand: *Politico,* November 17, 2017.

213   Christie managed to leave: Interview.

214   one longtime Mar-a-Lago member: *New York Times,* February 18, 2017.

214   "I thought you were going": *New York Times,* February 19, 2017.

214   included club member Robert Kraft, the owner: *New York Times,* February 1, 2017.

214   "Mr. President": Interview, Nicholas Papanicolaou.

215   Bannon had stood still: *Washington Post,* February 13, 2017.

215   who said his name was Rick: *Palm Beach Daily News,* February 13, 2017.

215   for the season on H-2B visas: *Palm Beach Daily News,* July 23, 2017.

216   "$11.88/hr min, no tips": *Palm Beach Post,* July 30, 2017.

216   But the tips were added: Interviews.

216   A laptop was opened: *Washington Post,* February 13, 2017, and interviews.

216   Michael Flynn and chief strategist Stephen Bannon: https://www.cnn.com/2017/02
      /12/politics/trump-shinzo-abe-mar-a-lago-north-korea/index.html, February 12,
      2017.

216   "HOLY MOLY!!!" DeAgazio posted later: *Washington Post,* February 13, 2017.

217   What was the big deal: Interview, Jay Weitzman.

217   contributed one hundred thousand dollars to Super PACs: *New York,* February 13,
      2017.

217   The bride's father, Bob Falk: https://www.tennessean.com/story/news/2017/02/13
      /trump-crashes-nashville-socialites-wedding-mar—lago/97855650/, February 13,
      2017.

217   "I saw them out on the lawn": https://www.cnn.com/2017/02/13/politics/donald
      -trump-north-korea-wedding-reception/index.html.

217   "They've been members of this": Ibid.

218   LaBelle leading the fifty-member Abyssinian Baptist: *Washington Post,* February 18,
      2017, and http://www.slate.com/articles/business/moneybox/2007/06/the_golden
      _ass.html.

218   Ivanka Trump, Jared Kushner, Donatella Versace: *New York Post,* February 14,
      2017.

218   "$7 million to $9 million": *New York Times,* February 15, 2017.

219   pay a 15 percent personal income tax rate: *Daily Beast,* August 17, 2010.

219   "It's like when Hitler": http://www.newsweek.com/schwarzman-its-war-between
      -obama-wall-st-71317.

219   the leader of his Strategic and Policy Forum of business leaders: Associated Press,
      Financial News, February 2, 2017.

220   *The Sound of Mucus*: https://www.cnn.com/2017/02/13/politics/donald-trump
      -north-korea-wedding-reception/index.html.

220   "seen it like 75 times": *Palm Beach Daily News,* February 12, 2017.

220   Park was not right: Interview.

15. GAMES OF CHAOS

221   "I think there's a lot of": https://www.cnn.com/2017/02/12/politics/trump
      -christopher-ruddy-reince-priebus-cnntv/index.html, February 12, 2017.

221   "keep an open mind": *New York Times,* February 12, 2017.

221   "I like conflict": https://www.realclearpolitics.com/video/2018/03/06/trump
      _everybody_wants_to_work_in_the_white_house.html.

222   "a bomb thrower, not a political": Interview, Chris Ruddy.

222   "You know, we always say": Interviews.

223   "I have control of Steve": Interview.

225   "She wants her husband to be on the Forbes 400": *Forbes,* December 12, 2017.

225   worth seven hundred million dollars or maybe even: Ibid.

225   forming International Coal Group Inc.: "12 Coal Miners Died on This Man's Watch in 2006. Now Trump Wants to Make Him Commerce Secretary" by Zoë Carpenter, *The Nation,* November 15, 2016.

225   He and his associates did little: http://abcnews.go.com/Primetime/story?id =1872255&page=1.

225   partied almost every night in Palm Beach: *New York Daily News,* January 26, 2006.

225   "lost to the Irish people": "European Parliament Report Accuses Wilbur Ross of Insider Trading" by Hannah Levintova, *Mother Jones,* December 12, 2017.

226   Department of Defense spent $58,875.69: https://www.sparrowmedia.net/2018/03 /foia-litigation-reveals-department-of-defense-spent-138093-at-mar-a-lago-and -trump-businesses/.

226   Ruddy tweeted a photo: https://www.townandcountrymag.com/society/politics /news/a9923/doanld-trump-mar-a-lago/.

226   They were joined for dessert: TCA Regional News, March 19, 2017.

227   "They're waiting there for him": Interview.

227   Trump brought with him: In-town White House pool report #5, http://www .presidency.ucsb.edu/report.php?pid=932, April 6, 2017.

228   "the most beautiful piece of chocolate": *Washington Post,* April 12, 2017.

228   "Mr. President, let me explain something": Ibid.

230   a forty-five-page prenuptial: Agreement between William J. Koch and Angela B. Gauntt, November 22, 1996, part of *Koch v. Koch,* Palm Beach County.

230   hosted a fund-raiser for Trump: "Not All the Koch Brothers Have Sworn Off Donald Trump" by Russ Choma, *Mother Jones,* August 3, 2016.

230   picking between Trump and Clinton: *Politico,* April 9, 2107.

230   kicked him off: https://www.politico.com/story/2016/12/trump-biographer-golf -course-233092.

230   "The Koch brothers came": Interview.

231   "I think there is blame on both sides": *Washington Post,* August 16, 2017.

231   the forum was terminating: *New York Times,* August 16, 2017, and *Wall Street Journal,* August 17, 2017.

232   "In Palm Beach, you're only": Interview.

233   The evening began with selections: *Sun Sentinel,* December 14, 2017.

233   "I don't think she cared": Interview.

233   "The darkest places in hell are reserved": *Washington Post,* August 17, 2017.

233   chamber of commerce immediately apologized: *Palm Beach Daily News,* August 24, 2017.

233   "It's just not the same place": Interview, Laurel Baker.

233   in November 2016, a wealthy couple: Town of Palm Beach Police Department Report, interviews, and http://www.gossipextra.com/2017/02/16/don-malasky-palm-beach-burglary-jewelry-stolen-6841-70811,

234   One day Paul Trupia: Interviews.

234   "Now they can find our addresses": Interview.

235   "the Zelig of the Trump administration": "Newsmax and the Rise of Trump" by Rosie Gray, *Atlantic*, March 10, 2017.

235   "was bored by vacation and wanted": *New York Times*, December 29, 2017.

236   "But there is tremendous collusion": *New York Times*, December 28, 2017.

236   "All around the property": Interview.

236   "All kinds of people": Interview.

16. "THE PRESIDENT!!! THE GREAT PRESIDENT!!!"

238   "Why are we having": *Washington Post*, January 12, 2018.

240   "record numbers of illegal aliens": The author was present at the event and recorded much of it.

241   Sixty people sat in the small ballroom: Interview, Torrance Harder.

241   "Somebody needs to take": *Palm Beach Post*, August 25, 2017.

241   That evening about a third: Interview.

242   "As soon as we announced": Interview, Steven Alembik.

242   Perlmutter brought in another Mar-a-Lago: *New York Times*, August 10, 2018.

242   "Everyone has to go down": "The Shadow Rulers of the VA" by Issac Arnsdorf, ProPublica, August 7, 2018.

243   "Many of those who worked": "New Details About Wilbur Ross' Business Point to Pattern of Grifting" by Dan Alexander, *Forbes*, August 7, 2018.

244   "Are you okay?": Video of conversation courtesy of Samantha Fuentes.

244   "When I compare": Interview, Samantha Fuentes.

245   President Trump tweeted twenty times: http://www.trumptwitterarchive.com/archive.

245   There were the ubiquitous Bentleys: *Town & Country*, April 24, 1018.

245   "I always said that": *New York Times*, March 1, 2018.

246   "He had just come off": Interview, Chris Ruddy.

246   Someone had placed seventeen: "More than a Million March for Gun Control including in Trump's Backyard" by Ilene Prusher, *The Forward*, March 25, 2018.

248   Errol Morris in 2002: https://www.buzzfeed.com/alisonwillmore/how-donald-trump-rewrote-citizen-kane?utm_term=.pywOA0mb2#.xulvLgEn8.

248   "He had the wealth, but": https://www.youtube.com/watch?v=aeQOJZ-QzBk.

250   only joined a few months earlier: https://patch.com/florida/west-palm-beach/don
      -king-joined-trump-mar-lago-over-holiday-daughter.

250   served almost four years: *New York Times*, January 5, 1983.

250   let fly with the n-word: https://www.cnn.com/videos/politics/2016/09/21/don
      -king-n-word-trump-church.cnn.

251   King followed behind: The author was present.

Bibliography

Barrett, Wayne. *Trump: The Greatest Show on Earth*. New York: Regan Arts Reprint, 1992.

Boorstin, Daniel Joseph, and Douglas Rushkoff. *The Image: A Guide to Pseudo-Events in America*. New York: Vintage, 2012.

Chandler, David Leon, and Mary Voelz Chandler. *The Binghams of Louisville: The Dark History Behind One of America's Great Fortunes*. New York: Random House, 1989.

Curl, Donald W. *Palm Beach County: An Illustrated History*. Northridge, C.A.: Windsor Publications, 1987.

D'Antonio, Michael. *The Truth About Trump*. New York: St. Martin's Press, 2016.

Devine, Olympia. *Mar-a-Lago: Ocean to Lake*. Palm Beach: Golden Lion Publishing, 2016.

Fitzgerald, F. Scott. *The Great Gatsby*. New York: Scribner, 2004.

Green, Joshua. *Devil's Bargain: Steve Bannon, Donald Trump, and the Storming of the Presidency*. New York: Penguin Press, 2017.

Hays, Charlotte. *The Fortune Hunters*. New York: St. Martin's Press, 2007.

Johnston, David Cay. *The Making of Donald Trump*. Brooklyn: Melville House, 2016.

Kranish, Michael, and Marc Fisher. *Trump Revealed: The Definitive Biography of the 45th President*. New York: Scribner, 2016.

Leamer, Laurence. *Madness Under the Royal Palms: Love and Death Behind the Gates of Palm Beach*. New York: Hyperion, 2009.

Lewandowski, Corey R., and David N. Bossie. *Let Trump Be Trump: The Inside Story of His Rise to the Presidency*. New York: Center Street, 2017.

Mayhew, Augustus. *Palm Beach: A Greater Grandeur*. New York: East Side Press, 2016.

McGoun, William W. *Southeast Florida Pioneers: The Palm and Treasure Coasts*. Sarasota: Pineapple Press, 1998.

O'Brien, Pat. *I'll Be Back Right After This: My Memoir*. New York: St. Martin's Press, 2015.

O'Brien, Timothy L. *TrumpNation: The Art of Being the Donald*. New York: Grand Central Publishing, 2005.

O'Donnell, John R., with James Rutherford. *Trumped! The Inside Story of the Real Donald Trump—His Cunning Rise and Spectacular Fall*. New York: Crossroad Press, 2017.

Patterson, James, John Connolly, and Tim Malloy. *Filthy Rich: The Billionaire's Scandal—The Shocking True Story of Jeffrey Epstein*. New York: Grand Central Publishing, 2017.

Raviv, Dan. *Comic Wars: How Two Tycoons Battled over the Marvel Comics Empire—and Both Lost*. New York: Broadway Books, 2002.

Rubin, Nancy, *American Empress: The Life and Times of Marjorie Merriweather Post*. New York: Villard Books, 1995.

Ruddy, Christopher. *The Strange Death of Vincent Foster: An Investigation*. New York: Free Press, 1997.

Singer, Mark. *Trump and Me*. New York: Tim Duggan Books, 2016.

Smith, Liz. *Natural Blonde: A Memoir*. New York: Hachette Books, 2000.

Tifft, Susan E., and Alex S. Jones, *The Patriarch: The Rise and Fall of the Bingham Dynasty*. New York: Summit Books, 1991.

Trump, Donald, and Kate Bohner. *Trump: The Art of the Comeback*. New York: Times Books, 1997.

———, and Charles Leerhsen. *Trump: Surviving at the Top*. New York: Random House, 1990.

———, and Tony Schwartz. *Trump: The Art of the Deal*. New York: Ballantine Books, 1987.

Trump, Ivana. *For Love Alone*. New York: Pocket Books, 1992.

———. *Raising Trump: Family Values from America's First Mother*. New York: Gallery Books, 2018.

Von Hoffman, Nicholas. *Citizen Cohn*. New York: Doubleday. 1988.

Index